AFFECT AND EMOTION
A NEW SOCIAL SCIENCE UNDERSTANDING

MARGARET WETHERELL

Los Angeles | London | New Delhi
Singapore | Washington DC

First published 2012

Reprinted 2014

SAGE Publications Ltd
1 Oliver's Yard
55 City Road
London EC1Y 1SP

SAGE Publications Inc.
2455 Teller Road
Thousand Oaks, California 91320

SAGE Publications India Pvt Ltd
B 1/I 1 Mohan Cooperative Industrial Area
Mathura Road
New Delhi 110 044

SAGE Publications Asia-Pacific Pte Ltd
3 Church Street
#10-04 Samsung Hub
Singapore 049483

Library of Congress Control Number: 2011937032

British Library Cataloguing in Publication data

A catalogue record for this book is available from the British Library

ISBN 978-0-85702-856-3
ISBN 978-0-85702-857-0 (pbk)

Typeset by C&M Digitals (P) Ltd, Chennai, India
Printed and bound by CPI Group (UK) Ltd, Croydon, CR0 4YY
Printed on paper from sustainable resources

MIX
Paper from
responsible sources
FSC
www.fsc.org   FSC® C013604

For Pete

Contents

Acknowledgements

The research for this book was funded by a one-year Economic and Social Research Council Director's Fellowship (RES 065-27-0007). I am grateful to the ESRC for their support, enabling the extension of our collective work on the ESRC Identities and Social Action Programme into this new territory, and to the Open University for the award of study leave around the fellowship. Most of the thinking and writing was conducted while I was a visiting scholar in the Psychology Department at the University of Auckland. My colleagues there, Nicola Gavey, Ginny Braun and Niki Harré, were brilliantly facilitating. Nicola, too, set up one of the nicest reading groups I have ever belonged to, with Peter Adams and Richard DeGrandpre, resulting in many stimulating conversations as we rambled our way through each other's writing with lots of wine. I owe a particular debt to the Sage editorial team – Michael Carmichael and Sophie Hine. Michael and I have worked on many projects now and I have immense admiration for his style and skills. My NZ friends and family – Diana Ward, Tim McCreanor, Louise Webster, Alison Jones, John and Diane Wetherell and Dave Wetherell – were incredibly hospitable and responsible for so many good times, along with Sam Wetherell who choreographed a stream of entertaining Skype distractions from Boston.

In the UK there are two people whose detailed comments and discussion substantially improved my argument – Jean McAvoy, whose own emerging work will set this field alight, and Johanna Motzkau, who saved me from too many clumsy generalisations about Deleuze (any remaining infelicities are my own). Johanna's own thinking on the psychosocial is razor sharp and inspirational. I am particularly grateful also to Rachel Thomson, John Clarke, Janet Newman, Pete Williams, Ian Burkitt, Kevin Durrheim, Janet Maybin and Stephanie Taylor for their critical reading and for the kind of lovely comment that keeps the solitary writer feeling that they might be doing something worthwhile. This book is the product of debates over many years now about the psychosocial. I know they don't agree with me, but I owe so much to Wendy Hollway, Gail Lewis, Peter Redman, Ann Phoenix, Stephen Frosh and Kath Woodward. Peter, in fact, spotted before I did how obsessed I was with 'pattern'.

This book is in memory of my mother, Sybil Wetherell (1926–2011), and dedicated to my wonderfully supportive partner, Pete Williams.

ONE

Introducing affect: Lines of argument

Affect (1)

vb [...] (tr)

1. to act upon or influence, esp in an adverse way *damp affected the spark plugs*
2. to move or disturb emotionally or mentally *her death affected him greatly*
3. (Medicine) (of pain, disease, etc.) to attack

n [...]

(Psychology) *Psychol* the emotion associated with an idea or set of ideas. See also <u>affection</u>

[from Latin *affectus*, past participle of *afficere* to act upon, from *ad–* to + *facere* to do]

Affect (2)

vb (mainly tr)

1. to put on an appearance or show of; make a pretence of *to affect ignorance*
2. to imitate or assume, esp pretentiously *to affect an accent*
3. to have or use by preference *she always affects funereal clothing*
4. to adopt the character, manner, etc., of *he was always affecting the politician*
5. (Life Sciences & Allied Applications / Biology) (of plants or animals) to live or grow in *penguins affect an Arctic climate*
6. to incline naturally or habitually towards *falling drops of liquid affect roundness*

[from Latin *affectare* to strive after, pretend to have; related to *afficere* to AFFECT (1)]

(*Collins English Dictionary*, Sixth Edition, 2003)

In recent years there has been a huge surge of interest across the social sciences in the study of affect. What is 'affect', though? For a psychologist or neuroscientist, this is pretty much straightforward. Affective scientists (as they are now called) investigate emotional states and the distinctive perturbations they cause in the body and mind. Sometimes 'affect' includes every aspect of emotion and sometimes it refers just to physical disturbance and bodily activity (blushes, sobs, snarls, guffaws, levels of arousal and associated patterns of neural activity), as opposed to 'feelings' or more elaborated subjective experiences.

So far, so conventional – but the term 'affect' could also key into much more general modes of influence, movement and change. We could talk, for instance, about 'being affected' by an event, even if it is not quite clear what the impact is. Affect in this sense need not be confined to humans or even animate life – the sun affects the moon, a magnet affects iron filings, and the movement of waves affects the shape of the coastline. *Damp affects spark plugs* as the Collins Dictionary prosaically puts it. Affect now means something like a force or an active relation. The term loses its moorings in studies of human emotion and expands to signify disturbance and influence in their most global senses. Thus, for Felicity Coleman (2005, p. 11), 'affection is the intensity of colour in a sunset on a dry and cold autumn evening [...] affect is that audible, visual and tactile transformation produced in reaction to a certain situation, event or thing'. While, for Kathleen Stewart (2007, p. 1), affect is evident when '*something* throws itself together in a moment as an event and a sensation; a something both animated and inhabitable' (emphasis in the original).

We have, then, two alternative connotations – a familiar psychologised notion focused on 'the emotions' as these are usually understood, and also a 'wilder' more encompassing concept highlighting difference, process and force in more general terms. With these two contrasting meanings in play, what Clough and Halley (2007) describe as the new 'turn to affect' in social research could become quite a complex act. It could become very confusing.

For many social researchers, the new interest in affect is principally topic-based. It is about infusing social analysis with what could be called psychosocial 'texture'. The turn to affect is mainly a stimulus to expand the scope of social investigation. It leads to a focus on embodiment, to attempts to understand how people are moved, and what attracts them, to an emphasis on repetitions, pains and pleasures, feelings and memories. How do social formations grab people? How do roller coasters of contempt, patriotism, hate and euphoria power public scenes? The advantage of affect is that it brings the dramatic and the everyday back into social analysis. It draws attention to moments of resentment, kindness, grumpiness, ennui and feeling good, to the extremities of distress that can result from ill use, and to the intensities of ecstasy. Interest in affect opens up new thinking about nebulous and subtle emotions like *schadenfreude*, or mixed and ambivalent phenomena such as reluctant optimism, intense indifference, or enjoyable melancholy.

For others, however, the turn to affect involves more than adding emotion to the inventory of social research topics. It signifies a more extensive ontological and epistemological upheaval, marking a moment of paradigm change. An interest in affect badges a particular theoretical attitude or standpoint supported particularly by the philosophy of Gilles Deleuze, but also the philosophies of Baruch Spinoza, Alfred North Whitehead and Henri Bergson. In the hands of these proponents, the turn to affect becomes a decisive shift away from the current conventions of critical theory, away from research based on discourse and disembodied talk and texts, towards more vitalist, 'post human' and process-based perspectives. (Recent Special Issues of journals exploring this broad theme include Adkins and Lury, 2009; Ahmed, 2007/2008; Blackman and Cromby, 2007; Blackman and Venn, 2010; Davidson et al., 2008; and Fraser et al., 2005.) This focus on affect – generalised as the process of making a difference – slides over distinctions between human and non-human, animate and inanimate. Advocates are often intensely critical of previous research on discourse. Attention is thrown onto becoming, potential and the virtual (e.g. Massumi, 1996) in preference to the already formed objects that are the usual fare of social science (institutions, identities, economies, social classes, etc.).

A Way In

This book is driven by a desire to develop a pragmatic way of thinking about affect and emotion as a basis for social research, especially new empirical research. I will be arguing that neither of the two connotations of affect already in play, and the ways in which these have been taken up in social research, provides quite the right foundations. Conventional psychological research on emotions is too narrow and restrictive to support all the things social research could do in this area. Ordinary 'basic emotion' terms used by psychobiologists (sadness, anger, fear, surprise, disgust and happiness) do not adequately describe the range and variety of affective performances, affective scenes and affective events. But, although I will borrow fairly substantially from this general line of thinking, some dominant approaches applying Deleuzian inspired concepts of affect understood as force don't always work well either.

The conceptualising of affect as influence, intensity and impact is part of a broader philosophical project (see Patton, 2000, on Deleuze's notion of the aims of philosophy and the function of concepts). Translating this into the registers of social research requires care. Formulating a philosophy of force, becoming, potential, encounter and difference is a different enterprise from working out the most useful approaches for investigating specific affective phenomena and their consequences, such as the forms of liberal well-meaningness that infuse some white citizens' relations with indigenous people in settler societies, for instance, or the prevalence of feelings of victimhood in niches of contemporary political life, or understanding why emotions of 'righteous indignation' might maintain a status quo rather than undermine it. I will be arguing in Chapter 3 that, although Deleuzian concepts are valuable for thinking about process, some applications of

Deleuze and related philosophical traditions (e.g. Clough, 2008a; Massumi, 1996; Thrift, 2008a) have been radically unhelpful in their assertions about the functioning of affect, and in their disdain for previous work.

These various complications mean that the turn to affect in social research currently struggles to deliver a way of working that is consistently productive and generative. To decipher why this is so, and what might work better, I conducted a reading marathon across psychology and neuroscience, critical and social psychology, cultural studies, and the sociology of emotion, seeking to understand what was around, and what was available. Why does the new field of affect take the shape it does, and how might it be twisted and distorted by the past it reacts against?

I found myself drawn to some of the other connotations for affect the dictionary throws up, such as performance and pretence (*affecting the persona of the politician, affecting an accent*) and habit and character (*affecting roundness, affecting an Arctic climate*). I kept coming back to pattern and order, since these are comforting and familiar standbys in empirical research. I became interested in how the affective textures and activities of everyday life are shaped. A central aim was to develop a way of thinking and a line of argument that might flow from psychobiology through to social analysis. It took quite a bit of detective work to understand the blocks preventing this, leading to cul-de-sacs. Some of these initially seemed so serious as to scupper the whole enterprise, but with some navigating it did seem possible to put together integrated readings of the somatic, discursive, situated, historical, social, psychological and cultural bases of affective activity.

I settle in this account on the concept of *affective practice* as the most promising way forward. Practice has old and familiar connotations in the social sciences, and these are useful and still extremely valuable. But, practice is also capacious enough to extend to some of the new thinking available about activity, flow, assemblage and relationality and to follow translations of aspects of Deleuzian and other philosophical projects into social research. Practice conjures forms of order but recognises their 'could be otherwise' qualities (Edwards, 1997). Affective practice focuses on the emotional as it appears in social life and tries to follow what participants do. It finds shifting, flexible and often over-determined figurations rather than simple lines of causation, character types and neat emotion categories.

Despite the advantages of toppling sovereign human subjectivity, and expanding the range of social agents to include animate life and material objects, I have to confess that I am not really interested in non-human affect in this book. Research on affect in cultural studies (e.g. Thrift, 2008a) is often obfuscating when it elides together affect as topic (the study of emotion) with affect defined as becoming and intensity so that sunsets, iron filings, talking parrots, financial meltdowns, earthquakes, sobbing Englishmen, angry Libyans, etc., are studied under the same rubric. By affect, I will mean *embodied meaning-making*. Mostly, this will be something that could be understood as *human emotion*.

This first chapter introduces the field and the lines of argument I will be developing throughout the book. First, though, I want to look at three brief examples, sketching affect in action, presented with minimal commentary. These illustrate the kind of phenomena I think the study of affect should pick out, why affect is interesting and important for social research, and why it is so incredibly difficult.

Frenzied bodies

14 July 1518 – Somewhere amid the narrow lanes, the congested wharves, the stables, workshops, forges and fairs of the medieval city of Strasbourg, Frau Troffea stepped outside and began to dance. So far as we can tell no music was playing and she showed no signs of joy as her skirts flew up around her rapidly moving legs. To the consternation of her husband, she went on dancing throughout the day. And, as the shadows lengthened and the sun set behind the city's half-timbered houses, it became clear that Frau Troffea simply could not stop. Only after many hours of crazed motion did she collapse from exhaustion. Bathed in sweat and with muscles twitching, she finally sank into a brief restorative sleep. Then, a few hours later, she resumed her solitary jig. Through much of the following day she went on, fatigue rendering her movements increasingly violent and erratic. (Waller, 2008, pp. 1–2)

In his book, *A Time to Dance and a Time to Die*, historian John Waller re-constructs Frau Troffea's frenzied jig as the first manifestation of the dancing plague that would spread through Strasbourg in 1518. The epidemic travelled rapidly and lasted throughout the summer. It was spooky, eerie and extreme in its effect. At its peak, hundreds of people succumbed, with perhaps as many as 15 dying each day. Waller states that similar plagues had occurred for several centuries previously (equivalent events had been recorded from 1017), but this late 16th century example seems to have been the second largest of Europe's dancing epidemics and is the best documented.

Waller describes how among the various possibilities for explaining what was going on, contemporary observers settled on the view that Frau Troffea, and those who followed her, were suffering from a visitation from St Vitus, who was punishing the people of Strasbourg. Frau Troffea's fellow citizens apparently briefly considered the possibility that she was rebelling against her husband, showing him up with an insubordinate display, or had been taken over by Satan or a demon. But, after much discussion, and as the plague spread, they concluded that this was a heavenly omen. Perhaps this interpretation was favoured because something practical could then be done. Sufferers were taken by cart to Saverne, to a grotto and chapel dedicated to St Vitus, to appease the Saint and to recover.

Over 500 years later, historians make sense of this event through very different theoretical apparatuses. For Waller, it becomes an example of mass suggestion understandable in the context of the times. He argues that Strasbourg's dancing plague was not so extraordinary viewed in the light of the contemporary 'environment of belief' and in light of the misery of the ordinary population in 1518. The dancing plague was preceded by severe famine, waves of sickness and disease, and unusual extreme cold. Waller describes the great anguish, distress and foreboding of the population, their loss of faith in the goodness of the clergy and their landlords, resulting in pervasive feelings of abandonment and uncertainty. While they were suffering, their priests and landlords were well off. They had the spare capital to stockpile grain and other essential commodities and were selling them at hugely inflated prices.

Waller points out the investment of the citizens of Strasbourg in the idea of the supernatural. Everyday events were explicable in terms of the battle between God and the Devil, rendering people permeable to demons and spirits. He argues that Frau Troffea's actions, the dancing plague she set off, and the trance-like state the dancers seemed to enter, were a kind of hysterical manifestation. The epidemic was an over-determined symptom of the times. It was an act of muted rebellion expressing a huge dissatisfaction. This distress, Waller suggests, could be performed and assuaged only by turning suffering and anguish self-destructively against one's own body in forms of dance which in better times had been familiar ways of escape and pleasure.

It is not my intention with this illustration to set up the citizens of 16th century Strasbourg as poor benighted fools, although, inevitably, the dancing plague is a spectacle and the reader does become a judge and voyeur. I cite this example because in this case affect emerged as something enigmatic and difficult to interpret. The push of the body seemed particularly strong and intensely located in a nexus of relations. This did not appear, however, to be an example of emotion in any conventional sense – Frau Troffea's actions do not seem to fit any list of standard emotions in a psychology textbook. Yet something was felt. Bodies became organised and a situation was formulated, evaluated, negotiated and, crucially, communicated. It demonstrates why social researchers might want to expand the connotation of affect beyond the familiar emotion palettes.

Melancholic communities

At the end of the day, if you're coming over from another country, you've got to understand how our country works, do you know what I mean, so you know, you should respect and understand what our law ... you know what is acceptable and what is unacceptable. You can't come into another country and get everything handed to you on a plate. I'm sorry, I just don't agree with that.

There was a case about an Indian family staying in a hotel and they just kept paying for them. And I said to them, if I was black or wore a sari and had half a dozen kids, I said, you'd put me in a place right now. They said, that's not very nice, Mrs Butler. I said, 'no it isn't', but that happens to be true ... And I'm not prejudiced, but we should come first, we are British, we are born here.

... going up to Liverpool on a stag weekend that he's organised because he is a passionate Everton fan, he's a second generation Asian, but you just wouldn't know it because he is a Scouser, and he waves the flag for England for the cricket ... That's my kind of immigrant. If everybody was like that, there would be no problem, you know but they aren't. They want to have, they want to import somehow too much ...

... some census that they're doing and it had every nationality, every denominal (sic) mixture, anything that you could possibly think of except English.

And I just think, the Scots can be Scottish, the Welsh, you know, they're Welsh, but we have to be British. … I had never bothered about it before, but I am bothering about it now.

(Extracts from Clarke et al., 2009, pp. 141–9)

These extracts come from interviews with white English citizens living in middle-class residential areas and working-class estates in Plymouth and Bristol in the South West of the UK. They were interviewed twice between January 2005 and May 2006 in a study conducted by Clarke, Garner and Gilmour, covering a range of topics including home and community, Britishness, immigration, the European Union and welfare policies. Clarke et al.'s work on this material (e.g. Clarke and Garner, 2009) has contributed to whiteness studies (Garner, 2007), and they have developed psychosocial analyses of how public identities and affiliations are mediated through personal histories (Clarke, 2009).

There is a kind of consistency here, not just in the type of arguments presented about 'proper behaviour' and 'fitting in' (what Clarke et al., 2009, call the 'when in Rome' trope repeated over and over) but also in the apparent feelings. Frau Troffea's affect was performed intensely and primarily physically, while in this example there seem to be more obvious kinds of 'affective–discursive loops' operating. The rhetoric and narratives of unfairness, loss and infringement create and intensify the emotion. Bile rises and this then reinforces the rhetorical and narrative trajectory. It goes round and round.

Because I disagree with the views expressed (and enjoy the privilege of safe distance), I can see it as like lifting the lid to reveal the squabbling siblings in family disputes arguing over who has got more than their fair share and who should rightfully come first. It might be funny if it wasn't so grave. Global political issues, multicultural futures, colonial history, immigration and national identity are being discussed. Yet what is fascinating is how we refract those conjunctions through domestic, ordinary, and wearing affective routines – through the well-worn and intimate practice of 'taking umbrage' and 'righteous indignation', intertwining with other practices such as the more poignant figurations that go with the sense of 'missing out', being a victim, and the discomfort of not having 'natural' claims recognised. Affect can be uncanny and extreme but it can also be ordinary (Stewart, 2007). Through this ordinary affect, people engage with the momentous and the global political.

In an insightful analysis of the UK situation, Paul Gilroy (2004) argues that much of white Britain is suffering from 'post-imperial melancholia'. He suggests there has been a failure to mourn the loss of imperial prestige and find new national narratives to refurbish now unconvincing and dated imaginings of plucky and stoical Britons winning World Wars and maps covered in pink territories. Britain is 'melancholic', for Gilroy, because it has not moved on as Freud suggested those grieving must do, and the country seems unable to refashion the nation for new actualities. Nostalgia and football chants such as 'two world wars and one world cup' fail to sustain. In a bizarre twist, some members of a nation that acted as the colonial oppressor have come to understand themselves as the victims, claiming unfairness, infringement and lamenting in particular the loss of English identity.

Becoming the victim, as Gilroy notes, is currently a culturally precious and exalted position for which many compete (see also Berlant, 1997). As the extracts above indicate, it often depends on practical affective work to establish entitlement and rightful status, a sense of self as good and fair but abused, and an affective subject position as a warm, hospitable and powerful host whose generosity and largesse is extended to others who turn out to be ungrateful wretches. White British citizens are encouraged in these affective positions by some of their politicians. Former British Prime Minister Tony Blair had this to say in a speech on extremism and 'the duty to integrate' given in December 2006 towards the end of his premiership:

> [extremism] has thrown into sharp relief, the nature of what we have called, with approval, 'multicultural Britain'. We like our diversity. But how do we react when that 'difference' leads to separation and alienation from the values that define what we hold in common? For the first time in a generation there is an unease, an anxiety, even at points a resentment that our very openness, our willingness to welcome difference, our pride in being home to many cultures, is being used against us; abused, indeed, in order to harm us.
>
> I always thought after 7/7 [the London terrorist bomb attacks] our first reaction would be very British: we stick together; but that our second reaction, in time, would also be very British: we're not going to be taken for a ride.

Blair is attempting here to construct, define and appeal to what Barbara Rosenwein (2006) calls an 'emotional community'. He seems very confident that he knows who his 'we' and 'us' are and what they might feel. And, interestingly, this act of constructive mobilisation is liable to invoke 'as if' replays of affect among those who can identify and position themselves as included. Pride can swell at 'our' great qualities. There is comfort in being part of a 'we' who stick together, but there is also anxiety rising at the possibility of being taken as a mug.

Bumping bodies

The final example comes from Maggie Turp (2001, p. 147–53) and is a case study from her psychotherapy practice. Her account of the client she calls 'Richard' is a moving one. Here are some of the basic details she sets up:

> Richard was a man who came to see me at the age of 28, suffering from painful feelings of isolation and describing himself as depressed and beset by feelings of hopelessness. ...
>
> A few sessions into our work together, Richard began to speak, with considerable embarrassment, about his behaviour in London underground stations. He told me very hesitantly that on every journey, he engineered a number of 'gentle bumps', small collisions with other passengers. These incidents took place in corridors and hallways that he traversed when changing trains on his journey to and from work.

I said that I could see it was difficult for him to speak about these matters, but that I thought they were important and that I would like to know more. Richard told me that his strategy was to almost avoid the person coming towards him, then at the last moment to make a very slight adjustment of direction and posture so that physical contact was made. It was important to him that the collision passed more or less unacknowledged. A 'successful bump' caused no pain to either party, and was not sufficiently significant to warrant an apology. Richard tried to manage six to ten such bumps on each journey. I asked Richard what he made of the situation he was describing, but he clearly had no idea what motivated his behaviour. (Turp, 2001, p. 147)

Turp describes in this case study what she calls, in a useful phrase, the 'body story line' Richard has put together. She argues that this pattern, presented as a symptom, is over-determined. It is a way of dealing with profound physical isolation and loneliness and of seeking some comfort. It is a method of controlling amounts of physical contact in ways that are manageable for Richard and on his own terms. It is deeply gendered also. And, later in the therapy, the 'gentle bumps' take on a hostile tinge as Richard comes to recognise what Turp describes as the impoverished and thin nature of his childhood and the lack of warmth received from his mother.

Richard's therapy with Maggie Turp becomes a form of affective re-training as he gradually disentangles his old practice. He comes to know it, formulate it and understand it as a particular kind of affective stand-in. He comes to inhabit what Despret (2004a, p. 209) describes as the moment of hesitation in emotion when it is possible to launch body and mind on new alternative trajectories and choose other forms of becoming. In this moment, body/mind is unlabelled potential – unscripted and undifferentiated. The old scripts, figurations, positions and narratives are always available waiting in the wings, but Turp's story has a good outcome. Richard is successful in his refiguring and develops new ways of being in relation with others.

The Challenge of Affect

The three examples just considered indicate how dominating bodies and feeling states often are – whether in the extremity of frenzy, the self-pity of melancholy, or the tacit life of underground encounters. They begin to suggest why new work on affect wants to introduce the energetic, the physical, and the sensual back into the social sciences, and why it might be important to do so. 'Rather than have to think, always and endlessly, what else there could be, we sometimes seem to connect with a layer in our existence that simply wants the things of the world close to our skins' (Gumbrecht, 2004, p. 106, cited in Thrift, 2008a, p. 5).

There is a lot to be gained. Advocates argue that we can better understand the panicky rhythms of current politics and recurring waves of appeal to terror and security (Burkitt, 2005; Clough, 2008a; Massumi, 2005). Affect is central to new forms of emotional labour and to responses to the precariousness of neo-liberal workplaces (Gill and Pratt, 2008; Hardt, 1999; Negri, 1999). In the field of identity studies, researchers are increasingly turning to analyses of feeling practices to better understand people's allegiances and investments, and the activities of categorising, narrating, othering, differentiating and positioning (see the chapters in Wetherell and Talpade Mohanty, 2010). Many have argued that affect is the key to building a halfway decent account of the unpredictable psychosocial actor, the ways in which she or he is suffused with feeling (Cromby, 2007a), and unconsciously connected (Baraitser and Frosh, 2007; Campbell, 2007).

Above all else, it is clear that coming to terms with affect implies coming to terms with the body. Social researchers are nervously dusting off their psychological knowledge and recalling scraps of biology, reading neuroscience texts and seizing on promising bits of popular science and psychoanalysis. How can the relays and ricochets of the human body be grasped, and the visceral put in touch with the social? It is an anxious business because the bridges between biology and social science, and between psychology (the main site of research on embodied affect) and the rest of the social sciences, are so fragile and shaky. It is also disquieting because most of us in social research want to approach this territory critically. We don't buy the realist and objectivist presumptions and the claims that with every investigation the biological sciences are moving closer and closer to discovering the truth. Psychology and biology are interesting as counter-narratives, formulating sometimes unfamiliar and generative 'ontoverses'. But there is so little time to think about it, enormous pressure to publish, and we can only get so far debating familiar meta-theory, epistemology and the philosophy.

Scholars have adopted a number of knowledge strategies. There is endless exhortation to pay attention to the physical and the visceral. But most of the actual attempts to do so have been half-hearted. Those who try to engage with research in the affective sciences often struggle to understand the significance, limits and implications of the striking findings attracting their attention. A number are candid that there is an immense amount of relevant material out there but they haven't yet come to terms with it (e.g. Thrift, 2004, p. 59). Some dismiss this work as 'positivistic', although others, such as the historian William Reddy (2001), take pains to sort out non-positivistic ways of thinking about recent developments in cognitive psychology and neuroscience. Reddy recognises the epistemological limitations but moves ahead anyway. A number of scholars (e.g. Brennan, 2004; Massumi, 1996) cherry-pick existing work on affect and the body in a relatively shameless way, rooting out a few interesting-looking studies from *Scientific American* or from circumscribed areas such as studies on pheromones. As Chapters 3 and 7 in particular will try to show, a few spectacular theoretical edifices have been built on pretty shaky neuroscientific ground.

Some in cultural studies have followed a familiar 'find one great theorist of the past' strategy. The philosopher/psychologist William James, writing in the late 19th century, often fills the bill. Ranging further afield, Eve Kofosky Sedgwick and Adam Frank (1995) 'rediscovered' the works of Yale psychologist Silvan Tomkins, from the 1960s, editing a collection of his writings (cf. also Probyn, 2004a, 2005; Frank, 2007; McIlwain, 2007). It is easy to see the appeal of Tomkins and why Sedgwick and Probyn say that they 'fell for' him. His writing was quirky, humane and phenomenologically acute. Re-discovery was a lovely thing to happen, but it does feel rather random. Why not take up Magda Arnold who also produced an opus on affect in the 1960s? Arnold was one of the few established women researchers in mid-20th century psychology. Her work on emotional appraisal (Arnold and Glasson, 1954) is much more congenial to cultural investigation in so very many ways. Whatever the routes, the writings of William James, Silvan Tomkins and Magda Arnold need to be set, however, in the context of recent psychobiological research.

One of my goals in writing this book is to try to be a bit more systematic and review more thoroughly the key threads of existing knowledge around affect and emotion. My aim is to build the basis for an inter-disciplinary account of affect (thereby setting myself up for a fall for sure). I come to this from the standpoint of social psychology, and that feels like an advantage. Social psychologists are more used to treading the shaky bridge between conventional psychology and the social sciences. We can offer a more confident and critical approach to psychobiology, and yet we also read sociology, social theory and cultural studies. We know some of the fault-lines in psychobiology, just as we can often tell when political science and cultural studies are winging it in their appeals to the psychological.

The new emphasis on affect leaves social science somewhat rudderless – the old conceptual tools and knowledge technologies no longer seem trustworthy. Yet affect presents a huge theoretical and practical challenge. How can we engage with phenomena that can be read simultaneously as somatic, neural, subjective, historical, social and personal? What are the best ways to move forward?

Lines of Argument

As I noted earlier, like other social psychologists before me (e.g. Brown and Stenner, 2009; Burkitt, 2002; Walkerdine, 2009), I will be suggesting that the familiar social science concept of *practice* offers the best, bare bones, synthesising rubric for research on affect. It offers the most effective, accurate and productive account of affect's pattern and logic. I'll explain that claim shortly. First, I want to describe three lines of approach that need to be at the heart of new work on affect. I see these as conceptual and empirical routes into the central features of affect for social research, picking out the things needing to be explained and summing up the best ways in. Then, in the following section, I want to identify three lines of approach I will be arguing constitute wrong turns. Some of these are historical and some are current. These are the moves I think block and impede social research on affect and stand in the way of adequate accounts. Claims sketched here are developed across the book as a whole.

Affect as flowing activity

Affect is always 'turned on' and 'simmering', moving along, since social action is continually embodied. But, affect also comes in and out of focus. The ongoing flow of affective activity can take shape as a particular kind of affective performance, episode or occasion, as in, for instance, a child's tantrum, a self-aggrandising narrative, or a bounded experience of joy. Affective practices unfurl, become organised, and effloresce with particular rhythms. Understanding the chronological patterning of these figurations, along with their sequencing and 'parsing', is crucial. Something like self-pity, for instance, can flare up, rise to a crescendo and diminish in pace with the changing medley of 'interpretative repertoires' being articulated. (Interpretative repertoires are threads of sense-making that work through familiar tropes, metaphors and formulations – Wetherell and Potter, 1988.) Self-pity can vanish and then re-appear half an hour later.

Figurations of affect have different durations. Affective phenomena distinguished by the most intense bodily pushes (such as a panic attack) usually occur in bursts or relatively short episodes, simply because bodily manifestations of strong affect tend to decay quite quickly and the body moves on quite rapidly. Even Frau Troffea and the dancing afflicted seem to have wound down eventually. Other types of affective practice can involve a semi-continuous set of background feelings which are more long-lasting, moving in and out of focus as a steady shifting accompaniment to one's days, perhaps shifting now and then into more intense phases dominated by the body. An affective practice can be made up of cycles of recurrence of affective activities over days, weeks and months, like the Christian year, or the cycle of 'work on the self' as good intentions lead to determined resolutions, to failures, to guilt, to the berating of self, to giving up, to self-indulgence, to good intentions, etc. Cycles of affective practice might persist for a short period or they may last, and be reworked, over many hundreds of years. Like the dancing plagues, an affective practice may endure as a potential figuration for several centuries, as a latent if rare response, before becoming almost unimaginable to later populations.

This dynamic and mobile character of affect has come into focus through the relational and process ontologies and methodologies characteristic of new directions in social theory found, for example, in Actor Network Theory (Latour, 2005; Law, 1994; Law and Hassard, 1999; Law and Mol, 2006), feminist technoscience (Haraway, 2004), in cultural geography (Massey, 2005; Thrift, 2008a), in Deleuzian scholarship (Deleuze 1988, 1994) and in recent revivals of Whitehead's metaphysics (Stengers, 1997; Stenner, 2008, see Brown and Stenner, 2009, for a lucid overview of Deleuze and Whitehead). This work emphasises the interconnected nature of social life and provides ways to think about these relations. Haraway, for example, describes her 'pulling on the threads' approach (2004, p. 338). She works with 'figures' – genes, races, cyborgs, coyotes, seeds – and treats these like balls of yarn or knots where her task is to pull out the dense connections that produce these patterns. Pursuing the figure of the foetus, for example, she finds herself discussing corporate investment strategies, and then migration patterns in north-eastern Brazil, and then why little girls perform caesarean sections on their dolls ...

Affective practices can be knotted and entangled in the same kinds of ways with wide ranges of potential connections. Flows of affect can mesh, for example, with the manufactured flows of images on television screens (Wood, 2009) and with the imaginaries streaming through darkened cinemas (Connolly, 2002). They can unfurl in step with the animation, technology and potentialities of the video game (Walkerdine, 2007). Affective flows can become articulated with large-scale social changes such as patterns of modernisation, rural–urban shifts, equality movements and the logics of capitalism. Harriet Nielsen and Monica Rudberg compared, for instance, stories of adolescence from three Norwegian generations of women (daughters, mothers and grandmothers spanning the period from 1910 to 1990). They documented how the modest stoicism of emotional 'coping' and 'enduring' evident among the grandmothers gave way to hyper-reflexive exploration of the significance and meaning of one's feelings among the urbanised modern mothers, and then to ironic play with confessional genres among the postmodern daughters (Nielsen, 2003; Nielsen and Rudberg, 2000). Similarly, in a banal but profound way, the body story line developed by 'Richard' (Maggie Turp's patient) was enacted through his colliding intersections with flows of commuters moving through the city, while the spaces of the underground became his affective theatre.

Analyses of affective practices, in other words, will take as their subject how these practices are situated and connected, whether that articulation and intermeshing is careful, repetitive and predictable or contingently thrown together in the moment with what else is to hand. Affective practice is continually dynamic with the potential to move in multiple and divergent directions. Accounts of affect will need to wrestle with this mobility. But, does that mean, then, that a flow of affect is entirely indeterminate?

Pattern – grooves, habits, machines, assemblages

I will be arguing that affect does display strong pushes for pattern as well as signalling trouble and disturbance in existing patterns. Many recent commentators would disagree with this emphasis. From their perspective, the disruptive force of affect seems its most impressive and important feature. The philosopher Alphonse Lingis (2000), for instance, argues that emotions are 'dangerous'. Following a long philosophical tradition, he regards emotions as like colours and energies. Emotions resemble, he suggests, gusts of wind, the movements of molecules, the power of the lion, and the shivering of the sea. Similarly, but less viscerally and poetically, Martha Nussbaum (2001) defines emotions as 'upheavals of thought', while Sianne Ngai (2005) argues that emotions can be seen as 'unusually knotted or condensed interpretations of predicaments' (p. 3, following Terada, 2001). It is affect's dramatic and turbulent qualities, along with the random, the chaotic and the spontaneous, which have marked it out as special for many.

This is misleading. Affect is about sense as well as sensibility. It is practical, communicative and organised. In affective practice, bits of the body (e.g. facial muscles, thalamic-amygdala pathways in the brain, heart rate, regions of the prefrontal cortex, sweat glands, etc.) get patterned together with feelings and thoughts, interaction patterns and relationships, narratives and interpretative repertoires, social relations, personal histories, and ways of life. These components and modalities, each with their own logic and trajectories, are assembled together in interacting and recursive, or back and forth, practical methods. Pattern layers on pattern, forming and re-forming. Somatic, neural, phenomenological, discursive, relational, cultural, economic, developmental, and historical patterns interrupt, cancel, contradict, modulate, build and interweave with each other. Some affective practices might involve only a couple of contributing patterns, and some of these might decompose quickly. Other affective practices, in contrast, might be very densely knotted in with connected social practices where the degree of knitting reinforces the affect and can make it resistant and durable, sometimes unbearably so. Different elements in an affective pattern can vary in their intensity and in their dominance in the whole. In a panic attack, for example, the push of the body and the power of a figuration of a situation as threatening are extreme and unusually resistant to any other ordering forces.

Interweaving patterns often form affective ruts. The first instance of frenzied dancing in 1518 Strasbourg, although it had precursors, must have been quite eerie and strange. But, thereafter, a groove was cut in the social psychological life of the community. The dancing plague attributed to St Vitus created channels through which meanings and body/brain responses flowed for a few months. Among all the very many things that bodies and brains can do, and among all the jostling possibilities for interpreting, representing and making sense, some became recruited, selected and articulated together. Similarly, for melancholic communities and the body story lines of personal history, some affective practices clearly stabilise, solidify and become habit.

The interrelated patterning of affective practice can be held inter-subjectively across a few or many participants. It can thread across a scene, a site or an institution and is spatialised, too, in complex ways. Intriguingly, an affective practice can be 'held' in a particular place. Further solidification comes into view when we consider the affective practices of entire social categories and historical periods. We begin to discern what Raymond Williams (1977) called 'structures of feeling', although 'structure' is not the right term for the complex coalescences Williams was trying to evoke. Swirling and dissolving emotion, he suggested, precipitates in social formations, becoming distinct ways of doing things, familiar figurations repeated often *ad nauseam*. We begin to see how particular kinds of emotional subjects and citizens are repetitively materialised (see Ahmed, 2004a).

In effect, you could say that over time 'affective machines' emerge in social and personal life. I am using the term machine here, at first at least, metaphorically in the novelist Iris Murdoch's sense rather than going straight to Deleuze and Guattari's (1977) concept, although the latter is probably more familiar to social researchers. In a series of novels written in the 1960s and early 1970s Murdoch talked about her characters as enslaved by machines. What she meant was a conventional socio-emotional pattern of feelings, thoughts, positions and desires that had a kind of inexorable and often damaging logic. Murdoch's most frequent reference was to the machine of romantic infatuation (cf. her novels *The Black Prince* and *The Sacred and Profane Love Machine*). Once this possibility appeared on the horizon, her characters became tied into a predictable range of daydreams, idealisations, mistakes, narcissisms and despairs unfolding with an already outlined and familiar pace and shape. Other machines in her novels were the machine of guilt, confession, penitence and redemption, and the machine of masochistic self-exclusion. Affective machines draw people like magnets, 'herding us along like brutes', and in her novels require a supreme act of reformulation and self re-making or the dramatic intervention of others to be broken (e.g. Murdoch, 1967 [1964], p. 167).

Deleuze and Guattari's philosophical concept of 'desiring machines' has some similar resonances. Here, the notion of machine is also in part shorthand for the organisation of activity and desire into social psychological pattern ('paranoiac machines, miraculating machines, and celibate machines', 1977, p. 38). Deleuze and Guattari were interested in how forms of order create breaks and cuts in flows of action, making connections between different patterns, and come to constitute flows in the first place. A desiring machine could thus be a positive or a negative form of order, or both, depending on the oppressive or creative consequences. As Brown and Stenner (2009, p. 192) describe, it was superseded in Deleuze and Guattari's later work by the term 'assemblage' (sometimes proposed as 'machinic assemblages', e.g. Tamboukou, 2008a):

> In *A Thousand Plateaus*, Deleuze and Guattari substitute the word *agencement*, usually translated as *assemblage*. Whilst the term machine carries with it unfortunate resonances of functionalism and boundedness, assemblage has the various meanings of 'arrangement', 'laying out' or 'putting together' (see Wise, 2005, p. 77). It also connotes the process activity of arranging things together. An assemblage of desire is then, like Foucault's apparatus, a heterogeneous arrangement of elements that are contingently laid out together. (Brown and Stenner, 2009, p. 192)

I agree with Brown and Stenner that the connotations don't work – machine is evocative but not quite right. Machines, mechanical processes and mechanisms suggest something automatic, industrial, causal and determined, which is why some writers in the late 18th and early 19th centuries such as Thomas Carlyle and Matthew Arnold (Williams, 1958) were so wary of them. The English translation of *agencement* as 'assemblage' is a bit static also. It misses the agency and the 'could be otherwise'. Uses of 'assemblage' in archaeology, for instance, assume that once elements accumulate, their relation and the information they convey is fixed, while *agencement* in French implies something much more active, such as the making of a tool or a kit bag of possibilities. In general, the kind of patterning I am trying to highlight is best captured by more active terms such as 'composing', 'figuring', 'entangling', 'mobilising' and 'recruiting'. Something, in other words, that comes into shape and continues to change and refigure as it flows on. Bruno Latour (2004) and Vinciane Despret (2004a, 2004b) talk usefully in this vein about the ways in which body capacities, social relations and combinations of narratives get pulled into new 'articulations'.

I will come back to some of this discussion in later chapters. For now, I simply note that the study of affect is inextricably to do with the study of pattern. These are patterns which are multiple, dynamic, intersecting, sometimes personal and sometimes impersonal. Patterns are sometimes imposed, sometimes a matter of actively 'seeing a way through' to what comes next, and sometimes, like a repertoire, simply what is to hand, relatively ready-made and 'thoughtless'. It is a case of recognising too, though, that affective phenomena can often remain simply ineffable. Attempts to find order can break down as the dynamism of the phenomenon, the fuzziness and instability of any descriptions of affective states, and sheer exuberant and excessive possibilities of the body become apparent.

Power, value and capital

I have mentioned the varying durations of affective practice and their historical range. Affective practices also vary hugely in scale – they effloresce for the solitary subject, they are played out in twos and threes, they are stabilised in families and small groups, but they can also be massively scaled up. Affect can be distributed across, and engage many millions in, communal celebrations, in shared jokes, or in collective moods of lugubrious moaning and complaining, forming what Lauren Berlant (1997) calls a 'national present tense'. With this scaling up, questions about power, the regulation of affect, its uneven distribution and its value (which are relevant also in the smaller scales) become even more prominent.

In the example of the melancholic white English voices we began to see the direct resonances between affect and power. Power works through affect, and affect emerges in power. Sara Ahmed (2004a, 2004b) has developed a highly generative way of thinking about this as 'affective economy'. This focuses on how 'affective value' or 'emotional capital' comes to be assigned to some figures rather than others and to some emotional displays. Just who, for example, can take up the affective subject positions evident in Clarke et al.'s interviews with white English citizens and in what contexts is this particular lamentation and assertion of victimhood sensible? What affective practices confer 'distinction' on those who perform them and how has this changed over time? Affect powers and intertwines with cultural circuits of value as some get marked out as disgusting and others as exemplifying modern virtue (Ahmed, 2004a; Skeggs, 2010; Skeggs and Wood, 2009).

A number of those writing recently on social class, for instance, have argued that affect and the psychosocial are key technologies in class positioning and class privilege (e.g. Charlesworth, 2000; Kirk, 2007; Lawler, 2005; Reay et al., 2011; Sayer, 2005). Beverley Skeggs (2004a, 2010), for example, argues that for white working-class women, carefully traversing the terrain of 'respectability', the reflexive practice of affect has been essential for maintaining position. Explorations of affect, power and value pose, too, the issue of conformity. What is the individual's relationship with what Reddy (2001) calls an 'emotional regime'? He argues for a significant gap between the emotional rules found in any social formation and experience. Is this gap the source of emotional suffering, he asks? Are some emotional regimes worse than others?

Power, then, is crucial to the agenda of affect studies. It leads to investigations of the unevenness of affective practices. How are practices clumped, who gets to do what when, and what relations does an affective practice make, enact, disrupt and reinforce? Who is emotionally privileged, who is emotionally disadvantaged and what does this privilege and disadvantage look like? Whether this is usefully seen as a form of 'capital', an element, perhaps, of cultural capital or social capital, remains to be explored.

Wrong Turns

As I worked through the current research on affect, it was often easier to decide what I was against rather than what I was for. Flows of activity, pattern and power emerged as compelling along with the obvious advantages of theories of social practice. But much current writing on affect seemed to block rather connect necessary lines of thinking. I have already noted that in some cases the application of Deleuzian concepts of affect, understood as force or intensity, to research on the textures of affective social life has been stifling. I want to outline now what emerged for me as three, further, frustrating wrong turns. Again, the detailed justifications are in the chapters to come.

Basic emotions versus social construction

The first wrong turn I want to identify is mainly historical and appears with hindsight – it is the packaging of affect through the debate between 'basic emotions' and 'social construction'. But the effects of this framing linger, and 'basic emotions' thinking, for instance, still percolates throughout celebrated popular science accounts of emotion such as Antonio Damasio's (1995, 1999, 2004) texts.

Until quite recently it was pretty unrewarding for a social scientist to engage with neuroscience and psychology. The disconnection between social and biological analyses of emotion was almost total. Both could only talk past each other.

Throughout the 1980s and the 1990s, anthropologists and social psychologists, particularly social constructionist researchers, were finding in study after study huge variability and contingency in emotional lives, and in how people across the globe narrated and interpreted their physiological states. Psychologists and neuroscientists, on the other hand, typically dealt with only a small set of what were seen as universal and genetically determined 'psychological primitives'. The basic emotions paradigm that dominated the psychobiology of affect was a deep investment in the idea that emotion routines are programmed, that affect templates are innate residues of archaic pasts, and that the 'colour wheel of affect' falls into relatively discrete patterns (e.g. Ekman and Davidson, 1994, for reviews and discussions of basic emotions).

Psychologists and neuroscientists studied closed circuits entirely abstracted from their social contexts. As Arlie Hochschild comments (1983, p. 27), emotion was investigated 'as a sealed biological event, something that external stimuli can bring on, as cold weather brings on a cold'. Social scientists were left struggling to incorporate the body and biology since there was little biological science matching the variability they were finding in the field. Social constructionist researchers worked on what they described as 'feeling rules' (Hochschild, 1983), 'discourses' (Abu-Lughod and Lutz, 1990; Lupton, 1998), 'emotionology' (Stearns with Stearns, 1985) and local rules for interpreting emotion states (Harré, 1986). This work could make little sense of the vivacity and life of the body, while neuroscience acted as though the provocative situatedness and creativity of social life could be safely ignored. There seemed to be no biology commensurate with what the social scientist knew, while every biologist knew that affect had to be much more than a cultural script. In this context, some researchers developed 'biocultural' syntheses that might encompass both. But these typically preserved the autonomy of each level of analysis and looked for additive solutions, holding a biological 'substrate' constant, while allowing cultural variations expressive play.

The example of the dancing plague demonstrates the problems with both approaches. Basic emotions research argues that there are six (or maybe five or seven) universal primary human emotions – anger, happiness, sadness, surprise, disgust and fear – and a more nebulous set of secondary emotions. From this point of view, Frau Troffea's reactions are off the radar. Her affect doesn't fit. This doesn't seem to be a display of anger, or of grief. What were the dancers experiencing – did they feel any joy at all? But Frau Troffea's affect is surely the kind of thing a psychology of emotion should be able to encompass? It should not be a major hurdle that affect seems to be relative to its cultural context. In an important sense, modern European citizens can never fully unravel Frau Troffea's act. I am unable to enter directly into the psycho-logic of her times, be motivated as she was motivated, or to satisfactorily translate her actions into modern psychological and psychiatric accounts. This specificity begins to cast doubt on the claim that emotions come in discrete types and in basic universal forms shared by all humans across time and space.

But, on the other hand, it does not seem satisfactory either to analyse Frau Troffea's actions just as an example of 'emotionology'. The historians Peter Stearns and Carol Stearns (1985) argue that each society and historical period has its own sets of norms guiding how affect should be expressed, theories for the causes, and categorisations of different types. The term emotionology (which they coined) sums up these differing gestalts and the characteristic assemblages distinguishing particular periods. According to Thomas Dixon (2003), the emotionology that permeates Western understandings emerged quite late in its current form, between 1800 and 1850. It post-dates the dancing plagues. This perhaps explains their strangeness to my eyes.

Emotionology is interesting but too anaemic as a characterisation of the social patterning of affect. It maintains the increasingly sterile division of labour between the biological and the cultural. The concept suggests that it might be possible to analyse the cultural, mental, social, psychological and ideological elements of affect separately from the physical and biological elements. The notion of affective practice I will be advocating in this book heads off in a different, and I hope more promising, direction. An affective practice is a figuration where body possibilities and routines become recruited or entangled together with meaning-making and with other social and material figurations. It is an organic complex in which all the parts relationally constitute each other. Fortunately, as Chapter 2 will show, recent work in psychology and neuroscience, freed from basic emotions, now proposes something similar.

The rubbishing of discourse

For many people working within cultural studies (e.g. Clough, 2007; Massumi, 2002; Sedgwick, 2003; Thrift, 2004, 2008a) it sometimes seems that what is most exciting about affect is that it is *not* discourse. Affect seems to index a realm beyond talk, words and texts, beyond epistemic regimes, and beyond conscious representation and cognition. In short, it is something unfamiliar in social science communities bored with at least 20–30 years of the 'discursive turn' and with so very many unmasking investigations of the ways in which language constructs identities, subjectivities, communities, polities and histories. The argument for 'going beyond', detaching affect from the domesticating and neutering effects of discourse, is compelling. But I also want to pull studies of affect back to think again about affective meaning-making.

Some analyses of affect, such as Brian Massumi's (1996), split discourse and affect into two tracks and privilege the track of the body or the process of becoming, and the moment of impact and change. This again seems a wrong turn. Massumi draws a thick line between bodily movements or forces and social sense-making. Body activities (affectings of the body as a result of encounters) are seen as generative, potentially creative and radical, while the track of discourse (describing the body and ruminating about affect) is thought to add just the usual scripts, conforming narratives, and the subjectifications of social power (cf. Hemmings, 2005 for a review and critique). For many, discourse is seen as *taming* affect, codifying its generative force (e.g. Lingis, 1991, pp. 119–20). On the contrary, I shall argue that it is the discursive that very frequently makes affect powerful, makes it radical and provides the means for affect to travel.

Other theorists, like Nigel Thrift (2008a) and his colleagues in cultural geography (Anderson, 2003, 2006, 2009; Dewsbury, 2003; McCormack, 2003, 2006, 2007), want to build what Thrift describes as 'non-representational theory'. The target is not just inadequate pictorial metaphors for knowledge generation or Cartesian notions of the mind as 're-presenting' the world and activities of the body, although this is part of it. Non-representational theory is an attempt to get at processes that are placed below 'thresholds of conscious contemplation' (McCormack, 2003, p. 488) so that cultural geographers can describe, for example, how the senses are assailed as citizens wander the city, and how their affects (their rage, joy, disgust, malice and surprise, etc.) are automatically triggered by the ways cityscapes are engineered and built. In this vein, one recent text on political affect (Protevi, 2009, p. xii) describes the task as building a 'political physiology'. Protevi wants to pick out what he calls a class of 'politically triggered basic emotions' in which the social speaks directly to the body 'by-passing subjectivity' so that the somatic and the social are linked directly.

To be fair, Protevi does go on to think about socially distributed, affective cognition, drawing on some of the long fascinating traditions of work on embodied minds in social and developmental psychology. But, in general, the large initial claims made for the non-representational, for unmediated, pre-social body tracks, and for direct connections between the social and the somatic are radically misleading. They are incoherent as a social psychology of affect. Worse, I think, these approaches block useful and pragmatic empirical work on affect and the building of inter-disciplinary foundations for the sake of what is largely a chimera. They place some of the most random and least important affective phenomena on a pedestal and take them as generic.

I will be arguing that human affect is inextricably linked with meaning-making and with the semiotic (broadly defined) and the discursive. It is futile to try to pull them apart. An affective practice like a dancing plague recruits material objects, institutions, pasts and anticipated futures. But the main things that an affective practice folds or composes together are bodies and meaning-making. Affect, for sure, was manifested in the frenzied drumming of feet in wooden clogs. Frau Troffea's state (however we might describe it) was made visible through her 'bodily reverberation' to use a phrase from William James (cited in Oatley et al., 2006, p. 116). But, very clearly, existing narratives and discursive repertoires in terms of the supernatural battle between saints and demons, and between saints and wayward earthly citizens, were also customised and re-worked as part of this new scene, generating and reinforcing it. The dancing plague, this particular affective practice, certainly created disorder and chaos. Nonetheless, like other affective practices, it constituted an ordering of bodily possibilities, narratives, sense-making, and local social relations.

There are some major issues, of course, involved in determining the kinds of discourse studies likely to make the most useful contribution to analysing affective phenomena. The critics are right, I feel, to be sceptical about the capacities and power of broad-brush post-structuralist discourse theory in this respect. These approaches do falter in very obvious ways when faced with the dynamic affective activity of everyday life. Similarly, analyses of affective meaning-making found in ethnomethodology, conversation analysis and discursive psychology don't go far enough in the connections they make and set too many unnecessary methodological blocks. But these are not the only ways to analyse discourse, and in particular the psycho-discursive practices (Edley, 2001; Wetherell, 1998) characteristic of affective performances. Given the sustained critique of discourse theory found in the turn to affect, what is surprising, in fact, is how applicable some of the key concepts of eclectic social psychological discourse analysis (such as interrogating subject positions, dilemmas, moments of trouble, repertoires, etc.) remain for analysing affective practice.

Celebrating the uncanny

I have suggested that there is something wrong with the new scholarship on affect when it draws a thick dividing line between bodies and talk and texts. Similarly, treatments of affect focused principally on the uncanny also block pragmatic approaches to the analysis of affect.

For over a hundred years now, the aspect of affect which has most intrigued social commentators is the spread of emotion from body to body, so fast indeed that a very mysterious force seems to be involved. The extent and scale of affective transmission so impressed historians working on the St Vitus cults they chose viral metaphors like 'plagues' and 'epidemics' to characterise the flow. Early psychologists of the crowd such as Gustav Le Bon thought in terms of 'contagion' and 'suggestion' (Reicher, 2001). Recent cultural studies, equally, have been fascinated by these phenomena (e.g. Brennan, 2004). Brennan speculates that the mysterious transmitting force is in fact based on smell (as well as touch, hearing and sight). She argues that affective transmission is powered by pheromones in the air generated by one body's reaction, which automatically triggers a cascading response in other bodies. But does fear, or aggression, or melancholy spread like an air-borne virus as this work suggests? Or is it a possibility, a plan, an opportunity, an identity, a formulation of a situation, and a solution that are transmitted? As Lisa Blackman (2007/2008, 2008) notes, terms such as 'contagion', 'suggestion', 'group minds' and 'trance states' reach back into unresolved business in the history of psychology. She questions the extent to which they can be uncritically carried forward into new social and cultural theory.

Psychoanalytic writing on affect similarly frequently relies on the uncanny as a main literary mode. The unconscious is certainly relevant but how to theorise it and whether it works as a dynamic and eerie force is up for debate. Affective practice typically implicates a large, non-conscious, hinterland of associations, habits, ingrained relational patterns and semiotic links. Clearly, sometimes we are not aware of what we are doing as we do it. We only become conscious of how our bodies and minds have been recruited and entangled after the event. Affect can exhibit quite a startling degree of automaticity, too. Body states in sharp bursts often appear 'unbidden' (Ekman, 1994). They are suffered rather than acted, and the tears, blushes, fainting and jolting have their own involuntary motion. For most of us, as Damasio points out, trying to control an emotion can be as difficult as trying to control a sneeze (1999, p. 49). It seems we have some control over some aspects of what appears externally, such as facial expressions and body movements, but less control over what is happening internally (Oatley et al., 2006). Interestingly, actors and musicians trained in emotional performance are much more skilled at regulating the flow of emotion both internally and externally (Damasio, 1999, p. 50).

I will be arguing that this automaticity and the non-conscious aspects of emotions are not well explained, however, by psychoanalytic notions of a dynamic unconscious formed through repression. They are not addressed either by dividing representation from the non-representational, marking out the former as the province of consciousness and deliberation, and the latter as the province of the unconscious and the unconsidered. Non-conscious affect is not quite the same as the dynamic unconscious. There are some hugely complex puzzles to be solved around the establishment of affective habits whose origins and meanings are unclear and over-determined (such as Richard's body bumping practice in the third example above). But, I will be arguing that, although undoubtedly a powerful therapeutic technology and potentially healing craft-theory, an appeal to the dynamic unconscious is an inadequate ground for social research on affect.

I will be contrasting social psychoanalytic approaches (e.g. Baraitser and Frosh, 2007; Campbell, 2007; Craib, 1994, 2001; Frosh, 2008; Hollway, 2010; Hollway and Jefferson, 2005; Redman, 2009) with my own approach based on affective practices. A practice approach focuses on processes of developmental sedimentation, routines of emotional regulation, relational patterns and 'settling'. These routinely embed patterns of affective practices as a kind of potential. The individual is a site in which multiple sources of activation and information about body states, situations, past experiences, linguistic forms, flowering thoughts, etc. become woven together. Psychological stabilisation occurs when the 'disaggregated self', to use Reddy's (2001) terminology, 'translates' the multiple 'codes' of bodies, cognitive activity and language, consciously or more automatically, into subjective qualia, into further actions and into internal and external self-descriptions which may or may not be further translated into public accounts and narratives for various audiences. This is a very different account from, for instance, Winnicott or Melanie Klein's accounts of the psyche/soma, and from psychoanalytic accounts of affective processes such as projective identification.

A Note on Practice

Practice [is] the point at which three things converge: the law of system, the quick of activity, and the reflective gaze of value ... What if, instead of sharing a grammar, speakers shared routine ways of acting, similar perspectives, a sense of space, or common ways of evaluating speech? (Hanks, 1990, pp. 11, 13, cited in M. Goodwin, 2006, p. 264)

The concept of practice I am advocating as the backbone of my approach is eclectic. Pierre Bourdieu's (1990) work on the 'logic of practice' was in many ways the most generative source, but also Gilles Deleuze's (e.g. 1992, 2007) various conceptions of 'becoming' and 'desire', Sherry Ortner's (2006) work on 'serious games', Judith Butler's (1990) notion of performativity and also ethnomethodological thinking about 'members methods for accomplishing social life' (Heritage, 1984). There are some important differences between these approaches but a lot is shared. Theodore Schatzki (2001) outlines the very many advantages of practice thinking. This is a way of conceptualising social action as constantly in motion while yet recognising too that the past, and what has been done before, constrains the present and the future. Practice is both a noun and a verb. It is an activity and for participants (and social analysts) it is also an established reference point and site of repetition – a practice – the way I, or we, do things, and sometimes cannot help but do so again. Practice is about improvisation, it is about training, and as Nikolas Rose (1998) has powerfully demonstrated, practices that work on the psychological such as affective practices are also a form of discipline and control.

Studies of social practice tend to go backwards and forwards, in fact, between emphasising either unpredictable creativity or stifling conventionality. Bourdieu (1990), for example, or Foucault (2000), place most emphasis on how practices congeal and constrain, producing difficult to shift social formations, hierarchies, epistemic regimes and patterns of distinction. Deleuze allows much more play, while ethnomethodology takes nothing for granted and demonstrates how routines mutate, are always flexibly tailored to the particular circumstances, and thus need to be worked up again and again, afresh each time. All of these emphases have to be useful for understanding the phenomena of affect as these are often innovative and creative but also can be stubbornly lodged and painfully unmoveable.

I have taken my central term *affective practice* from Valerie Walkerdine's (2009, 2010) work on 'affective communities'. Although she doesn't elaborate a practice account, and prefers a more psychoanalytic and Deleuzian trajectory in her own thinking on affect, her work was a hugely important stimulus. Affective practice is a better concept, I think, than affective event or affective encounter because it builds in 'ongoingness' and makes one think about patterns in process. Lisa Blackman (2007a, 2007/2008), in her genealogical work on affect, distinguishes between the stream of work on spooky suggestion and contagion mentioned above and an alternative, and no less dominant stream in theory and popular culture that has emphasised emotional habits (the habits of happiness, for instance). Practice certainly pushes more towards habit than the uncanny, but it is elastic enough to guide thinking about the patterning of extraordinary, spontaneous and one-off affective activities. Sometimes affect starts from scratch, and sometimes, as Lauren Berlant (2008a) points out, we are very obviously engaged in a process of 'emotional quotation' or 'affective citation', endlessly plagiarising our own and others' past practice.

In developing this account of affective practices, I have been influenced by important and highly productive bodies of work emerging in social psychology, psychosocial studies and critical psychology (e.g. Baraitser and Frosh, 2007; Blackman,

2008, 2010; Blackman et al., 2008; Brown and Stenner, 2001, 2009; Burkitt, 1997, 2002; Campbell, 2007; Cromby, 2007a; Despret, 2004a, 2004b; Frosh, 2006, 2008; Hollway, 2006, 2010; Lewis, 2009; Middleton and Brown, 2005; Motzkau, 2009; Phoenix, 2008; Redman, 2009; Squire, 2001; Tamboukou, 2003, 2008b; Venn, 2010). In addition, I have drawn on a further, in some ways more surprising, source, one that I have mentioned a few times already. This is William Reddy's (2001, 2009) attempt to develop a theory of emotions fit for empirical historical research. Although I disagree with a number of his conclusions, he offers an incisive route through the complex cognitive psychology of emotion, along with a model of inter-disciplinary engagement. These lines of work inflect the study of affect in different ways; but, they offer more grounded approaches than much of the rest of the social sciences of affect and need to be taken up more widely.

Amongst this work, my approach in this book is perhaps closest to, and owes the greatest debt to, the elegant account of emotion developed by Ian Burkitt (1997, 2002; see Redman, 2009). Moving across a wide range of precursors, such as Spinoza, Bateson, Vygotsky, Barthes, Williams and Foucault, Burkitt argues for an analysis of emotions as 'complexes'. He suggests that an emotion complex is relational, both discursive and pre-discursive. His emphasis on relationality is vital. Following Gregory Bateson, Burkitt emphasises that an emotion, like anger or fear, is not an object inside the self, as basic emotions research assumes, but is a relation to others, a response to a situation and to the world. An emotion is above all a relational pattern and as such, I would say, is automatically distributed and located across the psychosocial field. Affect is never wholly owned, always intersecting and interacting. Given that is so, it seems to me that affective practice is the 'smallest' or most coherent unit of analysis possible for the social science of affect.

Burkitt describes how emotions rest on body responses that provoke, and turn into, feelings. Feelings, he argues, are examples of 'practical consciousness' in Raymond Williams' (1977) terminology. They are often unarticulated and inchoate senses of the pattern in a relation or in a situation, part of the affective-volitional stream of everyday life that moves us, as Vygotsky argued, to one end or another. Feeling as practical consciousness is thus a kind of intuitive 'know how', a sometimes pre-conceptual and often ineffable meaning structure, schema or 'image repertoire' that guides action. Burkitt argues that feelings are not *expressed* in discourse so much as *completed* in discourse. That is, the emotion terms and narratives available in a culture, the conventional elements so thoroughly studied by social constructionist researchers, realise the affect and turn it for the moment into a particular kind of thing. What may start out as inchoate can sometimes be turned into an articulation, mentally organised and publicly communicated, in ways that engage with and reproduce regimes and power relations.

Conceptualising these processes as examples of affective practice rather than as 'complexes', is, I think, a good way of taking Burkitt's work forward. It adds more movement and more sociality. It is not just consciousness that is 'practical' but all the elements of an affective performance. I will be arguing in Chapter 3 that there is more to the making of affective meaning than acts of 'completing'. More attention needs to be given, also, to interaction and inter-subjectivity.

The Book Ahead

There at least two possible routes through this book. First, I have tried to gather together the main lines of thinking about affect currently preoccupying social researchers, and to critically interrogate these. And so, if you want a guided tour of the field from a highly interested spectator with her own views on these thinkers and on others not mentioned, Antonio Damasio, Paul Ekman, Klaus Scherer and Lisa Feldman Barrett can be found in Chapter 2; Brian Massumi, Nigel Thrift, Patricia Ticento Clough and William Reddy in Chapter 3; Marjorie Goodwin, Jack Katz, Daniel Stern and Derek Edwards in Chapter 4; Raymond Williams, Pierre Bourdieu, Diane Reay and Bev Skeggs in Chapter 5; Gail Lewis, Sigmund Freud, Lynne Layton, Michael Billig and Christopher Bollas in Chapter 6; and Sarah Ahmed, Teresa Brennan, Stephen Reicher and Thomas Ogden in Chapter 7.

In disciplinary terms, Chapter 2 reviews the recent research in psychology and neuroscience; Chapter 3 looks at affect in cultural studies and cultural history; Chapter 4, at affect in the 'ethnosciences' such as conversation analysis, discursive psychology and linguistic anthropology; Chapter 5 examines the sociology of affect, structures of feeling and notions of habitus along with affect and social value; Chapter 6 begins a conversation with social psychoanalysis and with models of affect without a subject; while Chapter 7 continues this dialogue and brings in some recent social psychology of mass affect and work on the cultural politics of emotion.

I have tried, though, to develop an account that might do more than point out the existing landmarks. From another angle, the book could be seen as organised around explicating different threads in the tangled activities making up affective practice – the bodying, negotiating, situating, solidifying, personalising and circulating of affect – and as an attempt to develop a pragmatic overarching perspective which might ground future social research.

I wanted to understand the physicality of affect, for example, in Chapter 2 and try to come to terms with what recent psychobiology has to say about this. Does what is known about the bodying of emotion rule out the trajectory I am following into affective practice? In Chapter 3 my aim was to work out a productive approach to the making of affective meaning and to the affective–discursive. In Chapter 4, my goal was to understand how affect is located, takes shape in the moment, and is always situated in some immediate context. But, in focusing on that, one loses sight of the long-term historical play of power so Chapter 5 was then an effort to understand the sedimenting of affect, and to argue for a kind of 'affective intersectionality'. This chapter became paired with Chapter 6, focused on affective trajectories and personal histories. How does affective practice take shape not just in social formations over time but also in individuals' lives? Finally, in Chapter 7, I wanted to work out a line on affective transmission. What is going on when affect passes from one to another?

There is so much still to do, of course, to build a way of thinking to ground new research that might more easily, and less anxiously, traverse the body, the discursive, social contexts, histories, personal stories and affect's movement. Work that could, in other words, explore whatever figurations were relevant to a pressing research question without being blocked by forms of psychobiology that refuse to see connections with the cultural, or blocked by cultural studies that refuse to be interested in making meaning. It should be possible to explore the micro-organisation of affective episodes untrammelled by ethnomethodological reluctance to engage with questions of persistent social distinction and inequality. Ideally, investigations of the solidifications of affective practice should facilitate, not impede, investigations of plural subjectivities. And finally, it should be possible, too, to raise interesting questions about repetitions and personal biography without following social psychoanalysis into inherent psychological processes or into a mysterious uncanny. Indeed, these are the challenges which animated this book and which are taken up in the chapters which follow.

TWO

Bodying affect: Affective flows and their psychobiological parsing

Continuously through time, the brain is processing and integrating sensory information from the world, somatovisceral information from the body, and prior knowledge about objects and situations to produce an affective state that is bound to a particular situational meaning, as well as a disposition to act in a particular way ... (Barrett et al., 2007, p. 386)

The hilarity, the fear, the rage, the relief, the agony, the desperation, the supplication are what are most visible about those we look at. At a glance we see that the cop or the office manager is incensed, even though we find we cannot say later what colour his eyes are and had not noticed that she had dyed her hair. Indeed, the mirth and the despondency, the irritability and the enthusiasm, the rapture and the rage are the very visibility of a body. (Lingis, 2000, pp. 16–17)

According to Lingis, it is possible in a fleeting glance to gain a far-reaching sense of another's body state – their level of arousal, their degree of delight or depression, their hatred or indifference. Even if this over-estimates the ease with which affect can be read, Lingis is surely right to claim that emotions make the body visible. But what exactly is going on in bodies (and in the brain) to produce these physical states? What is the psychobiology of the exasperated cop or an enthusiastic office manager? The new accounts emerging from psychology and neuroscience may not have the elegant simplicity conventionally associated with science but slowly, and with increasing confidence, affective scientists are finding ways to do justice to the complex patterning of affected bodies and nervous systems.

The story now emerging from psychology and neuroscience is one of dynamic flows, recursive processes and flexible orderings. As I read it, the new psychobiology of affect is starting to fit with the general logic of social practice I would like to see as the main rubric for social research on affect. Psychologists and neuroscientists are beginning to offer an analysis that allows points of intersection between the ordering of bodies and the other kinds of figurations and partial patterning that organise affect.

In the last chapter I introduced some of the blocks preventing psychology and neuroscience developing socially and culturally plausible accounts, such as a reliance on a limited palette of basic emotions. In this chapter I want to continue this theme, but I also want to identify and firm up the body of work, almost a new paradigm in psychology and neuroscience, emerging in the past few years, which starts in a quite different place.

This research is commensurate with the dynamic and open character of affective practice and persuasively sketches its physical basis. These new lines of research seem robust. They are grounded in the findings of nearly ten years of fMRI and PET brain scan research, and in new psychological theory, and they endorse and encourage the integrative frame we need.

Disciplines like neuroscience offer technologies to make evident the registrations of affect upon the body. That's fascinating alone. But they also offer crucial information and perspective on what is sometimes called the 'parsing' of affect – its physical patterning, tempo and pacing. This issue of 'parsing' will be a central topic of the chapter. I aim to show this is the precise point where older psychobiological accounts fell apart, and where newer research begins to open up much more interesting and productive possibilities, smoothing the way to interdisciplinary analysis.

The first section of this chapter opens with what occurs physiologically in a burst or flow of affect to obtain a stronger sense of bodies and their properties. I will then outline the analysis of affect offered by the neuroscientist Antonio Damasio (1995, 1999, 2004). Many in the social sciences see Damasio as the acceptable face of neuroscience (e.g. Cromby, 2007b; Thrift, 2004). He is social scientists' current, number one, favourite neuroscientist. Damasio's account of affected bodies is problematic, however. His thinking is still bound up in the old 'basic emotions' metaframework of psychobiology for parsing affect. The next sections of the chapter will thus outline and critique the basic emotions legacy. The final sections of the chapter then sketch the alternative emphases emerging in the affective sciences.

The Embodied Flow of Affect

Consider, first, this account from Lisa Baraitser and Stephen Frosh of a burst of affect presented in a clinical setting:

> Occasionally I have an experience with a patient in which I literally begin to faint. It has happened more than once, and with more than one patient. The event unfolds quickly. It begins with a vague awareness that something terrible is about to occur. I sense a tightening in my chest and notice that I suddenly feel cold. I have a premonition that the patient is going to have to tell me something horrific, whether I am able to bear it or not, although the disclosure

is 'unannounced' in any other way. The patient is speaking of nothing in particular, and showing no obvious signs of discomfort and distress. And yet I am becoming aware that I am getting in a 'state'. My skin begins to prickle. I shift a little in my chair, trying to dislodge the sense of foreboding. A brief image flashes through my mind of myself collapsing. As if in response to this, a whole range of symptoms associated with fright suddenly crank up – my heart begins to beat loudly in my chest, urgently knocking the inside of my rib cage, accelerating so that I find that I am panting slightly. At the same time my vision blurs, I hear the insistent sound of blood pumping around my body, and I break out in a sweat. My face feels flushed. I start shifting more deliberately in my chair, trying to get the blood moving away from my legs, twitching, becoming agitated now, wanting to leave, thinking I may have to leave, worried that I may vomit or slide off my chair. At its peak, I believe I am not fully conscious, but have, in effect, fainted. (2007, pp. 80–81)

Baraitser and Frosh developed this example of what they call 'being in a state' to introduce themes in their own work. Like all accounts of affective activity, it is very much a worked-up description; the body here is registered through their discourse. But I want to borrow this narrative to act as a vivid prompt indicating the features that accounts of the body and affect must encompass, both when the ongoing flow of affect is intense and when it is backgrounded.

As every psychology textbook describes (e.g. Oatley et al., 2006), during a burst of sharp emotion, the body pumps out a wide range of somatic signals. Many of these are initiated in the brain stem and driven by the autonomic nervous system (ANS), such as changes in blood flow resulting in blushing or blanching, changes in heart rate and in breathing rate. There are changes in the muscles as expressions drift across the face: smiles, frowns, various forms of wrinkling and twisting. Other muscles work on posture and stance, modulating relaxation and tension, and producing the visceral clenching or calming of the guts. Within the brain and central nervous system (CNS), chemical transmitters make connections across neural synapses and pathways. Neural circuits begin to fire, rapidly conveying information.

These physical changes are accompanied by *qualia* or subjective feelings, along with other cognitions, evaluations, images, memories and appraisals of the situation. Typically, sharp bursts of affects are also action-oriented. They constitute a strong push to do something – flee, remonstrate, appeal, move closer, etc. As Clore and Ortony (2000, p. 24) describe, a burst of affect involves not just major somatic changes in the body; it also has cognitive, motivational-behavioural and subjective-experiential components. Although my attention in this chapter will be on the body, we will see that the question of how the body is patterned with mind is never far away.

How, then, to conceive of all this? A burst of affect, like the 'being in a state' Baraitser and Frosh describe, constitutes a global change in body/mind made up of multitudes of local transitions. The transitions involved are unlikely to be proceeding in a logical, linear and step-by-step fashion. Rather, current thinking in neuroscience stresses that processing is multiple and parallel (see Reddy, 2009, for a lucid account of parallel processing). Body activities refer back and forth to each other, reinforcing, inhibiting, orchestrating neurobiological flows. It is less like the unfolding of a prepared script and more like emerging forms of coalescence or partial and temporary settlings.

The cascades involved follow temporal sequences and the time latencies vary across different body regulatory systems. Changes in the central nervous system take less than a second, perhaps as little as 12 milliseconds, for the first registration of an event that might be, for instance, potentially dangerous (Daum et al., 2009; LeDoux, 1996). It can take as long as 15–30 seconds for changes generated by the autonomic nervous system such as blushing to occur (Janig, 2003). But, it may take many hours or days for the consequences to feed through into the immune system (Kappas, 2008). Being in a state is not just a moment of coalescence. It is also a moment of recruitment where body/mind possibilities and body/mind states are gathered together into a particular assemblage and unleashed, censored or regulated in social contexts.

Antonio Damasio (1995) provides an arresting metaphor to capture the changing physical patterns. He formulates affect as the impress of alterations rippling through the body, registered as differences from average states, and he uses the notion of walking on a water bed to imagine this:

> As a whole, the set of alterations defines a profile of departures from a range of average states corresponding to functional balance, or homeostasis, within which the organism's economy operates probably at its best, with lesser energy expenditure and simpler and faster adjustments. This range of functional balance should not be seen as static; it is a continuous succession of profile changes within upper and lower limits, in constant motion. It might be likened to the condition of a waterbed when someone walks on it in varied directions: some areas are depressed, while others rise; ripples form; the entire bed is modified as a whole, but the changes are within a range specified by the physical limits of the unit: a boundary containing a certain amount of fluid. (1995, p. 135)

Damasio argues that the changes associated with any particular sharp burst of affect need to be seen as just one further manifestation of the unceasing, dynamic activity of the body (cf. also Russell, 2003). The brain, and what he calls 'the body proper', are constantly active, maintaining business as usual, engaged in continuous monitoring, registering and dealing with departures from usual profiles. Emotions, for Damasio, are simply the 'top end' of the broad range of body processes involved in homeostasis which range from immune system activity, metabolic activity and simple reflexes, to experiences of pain and pleasure, to drives and motivation, and then to conventional emotions (2004, p. 45). He sees the particular engagements of the body in an affective display as a product of evolutionary history and, following Darwin's work on emotional expression, as part of a much wider range of adaptive strategies for maintaining the well-being and survival of the organism.

In affective activity, then, body landscapes, or what we could perhaps call 'bodyscapes', are being constituted and reconstituted, assembled and put together, moment to moment. Extreme events such as a panic attack, other forms of anguish and suffering, or joy and euphoria involve particularly intense cascades of physiological changes. But it seems likely these are on a continuum with what the body is doing at every point of life. In this sense, bursts of intense affect are less uncanny, eerie and weird than they may appear. They effloresce as part of broader flows and dynamic processes, registered through the ongoing, unceasing updating of body/brain landscapes. This is a useful way of thinking about the body in social practice, a flow immersed in other flows. We can begin to ask about the process of meshing as the flowing body connects with the unfurling flow of social interaction, the composition of social spaces, and the comparatively glacial flows of individual life trajectories and social formations.

Damasio's Analysis of Affect

This preliminary sketch of what might be involved in 'being in a state' opens up an enormous range of further questions about bodies and what they can do. Damasio's psychobiology of affect addressing these questions can be found in his three popular books: *Descartes' Error* (1995), *The Feeling of What Happens* (1999) and *Looking for Spinoza* (2004). His account has remained pretty much the same, although his 2004 book added some new empirical and theoretical developments, including more emphasis on cognitive appraisal in emotion. I will describe Damasio's analysis in its own terms, without any added evaluative comment, before moving to a critique of his broad background frame.

Damasio distinguishes between what he calls 'primary emotions' and 'secondary emotions', or, in his 2004 account, 'primary emotions' and 'social emotions' (p. 44). Typically, he identifies six primary emotions – anger, sadness, fear, disgust, surprise and happiness – although sometimes in his texts the list reduces to five and surprise disappears. Damasio states that for primary we should read 'innate, pre-organised and universal'. He argues that primary emotions are wired into humans and other animals and present largely preset body/brain profiles (1995, pp. 131, 149). Secondary or social emotions, in comparison, are not so strongly pre-organised. Damasio conceptualises affects such as euphoria, melancholy, contempt or shyness as subtle variations on the primary emotions. For this class of emotions, he suggests, the pre-organised biological machinery has been tuned by experience and linked to all manner of subtle cognitions producing a complex interaction. The body is not so salient in these emotions and its various manifestations are not so dominant in our attention.

Damasio is an accessible writer but his descriptions of how affect travels through the body are not easy to condense. I will approach them through an introspective example that starts as I sit here at my computer trying to develop a cogent summary of Damasio's arguments. I am finding it difficult, because there is a huge amount of material and many possible starting points. I am not quite sure which narrative is clearest. As I work on this I realise I am getting angry and irritated. I guess because it is frustrating and I am blocked in an easy flow forward.

Damasio's analysis precisely concerns the biological events that occur as the irritation I am experiencing (which could be conceptualised, in his terms, as a lower intensity variant of the primary emotion of anger) develops and unfolds, and then disappears as I start to think about why I might be irritated, get curious about that, and start writing again. Damasio suggests that my body landscape during these moments is going through a particular pattern of chemical and neural changes. He maintains (1999, p. 37) that the best way of understanding these is to divide them into three distinct stages or parts. These are 'a state of emotion', 'a state of feeling' and 'a state of knowing the feeling'.

The 'state of emotion'

The first of Damasio's three moments, the 'state of emotion', indexes what is happening immediately and physically. It is the unfolding of what Damasio understands as the preset biological machinery (or what he also sometimes calls a 'body device') that he believes exists for every primary emotion. The process starts, he argues, with the preliminary sensing in my brain of a situation demanding an emotional response. This situation is the 'emotion inducer', in Damasio's terminology, and in my example the inducer is presumably being blocked in my flow of writing. Emotion inducers might be external situations or they could be internal cognitions and thoughts such as memories of a recent event. Damasio thinks that emotion inducers then interact with or trigger the preset machinery in my brain and body like 'a key fitting a lock' (2004, p. 58). In effect, he argues that this preset machinery can be seen as a 'dispositional representation' stored in the brain/body – it is a disposition to follow a particular path in the presence of a class of stimuli, and it represents that class as an entity that requires this kind of response (1999, p. 79). Dispositional representations are 'potential patterns of activity arising within neuron ensembles' (1999, p. 79).

Damasio argues that the patterns produced by evolution in our brains and bodies are implicit, dormant and non-conscious. For the primary emotions, all humans everywhere are likely to respond to the relevant classes of situations with the same patterns. The subcortical regions of the brain in this way 'hold' a set of ready-processed recognitions, or what I guess could be called in psychological language 'archetypal meanings' (see also LeDoux, 1996).

Damasio also stresses, however, that the relationship between an emotion inducer and the pattern or dispositional representation in the body/brain will be open to a great deal of modification through cultural learning and personal history. In his later work, he emphasises this more strongly, arguing that an intelligent, cognitive and non-automatic process of evaluation and thought can intervene between what he now calls 'an emotionally competent stimulus' and the unfolding biological machinery (2004, pp. 53–7). In this way the preset biological pattern for fear, for example, can become mobilised to respond to an individual phobia or to a cultural belief system about the supernatural. But Damasio argues that these individual and social recruitments of the available body/brain patterns will be 'superposed' on top of the archaic automatic linking and presetting provided by evolution.

Damasio maintains that the unfolding neural patterns now in progress during my state of emotion will not be localised in any particular area of my brain (although some brain areas will prove much more important than others) but will be distributed from subcortical areas to the cerebral cortex to the mid-brain. The subcortical regions involved include the periaqueductal gray in the midbrain, the amygdala, the hypothalamus and the basal forebrain. These areas coordinate the further bodily responses associated with emotions such as the autonomic nervous system changes to heart rate, breathing rate, etc. noted in Baraitser and Frosh's example of 'being in a state'. In the cerebral cortex Damasio identifies the anterior cingulate and the ventromedial prefrontal regions. Each primary emotion, he suggests, will have its own distinctive pattern of neural activation. Thus sadness, for instance, 'consistently activates the ventromedial prefrontal cortex, hypothalamus and brain stem, while anger or fear activate neither the prefrontal cortex nor hypothalamus' (1999, p. 61).

Damasio argues that the unfolding of the preset mechanism involved in anger/irritation, as this affect cascades through my brain, is likely to be pretty much beyond my control at this point and beyond awareness, although an acute observer might start noticing some external signs, perhaps I start frowning or shifting in my chair. At this stage my body and brain are doing what any animal might do in similar circumstances of frustration. My body, Damasio argues, is acting out a sequence 'probably set in evolution before the dawn of consciousness [which] surfaces in each of us as a result of inducers we often do not recognise consciously' (1999, p. 37). Damasio (2004, p. 32) places particular emphasis on the claim that this 'state of emotion' *precedes* any feelings or thoughts I might develop. The pre-organised body flow and orchestrated changes in the body landscape come first, he says, because basic mechanisms of life regulation (homeostasis processes), which include emotions, occurred in evolution long before the development of the kind of brain apparatus that might enable feelings and thoughts.

The 'state of feeling' and the 'state of knowing the feeling'

The next stage in Damasio's model, 'a state of feeling', is also a biological event occurring again below the level of consciousness. Here, according to Damasio, what is going on is that my somatosensory cortices begin to form a representation of what my body and brain are doing and the patterns of activity happening both in the brain itself and in the body proper. Damasio describes this representation as a dynamic 'on-line' version or view of the changing landscape of the body, and of what is happening right now (1995, p. 144). The brain ceaselessly records and monitors, churning out an unfolding, continuing record of the body/brain landscape. Again, animals also are likely to develop 'feelings' in this sense of a non-conscious registration of body/brain states.

Damasio argues that this neural 'state of feeling' is crucial to the final aspect he wants to identify, which is the 'state of knowing the feeling'. He suggests that a final set of second order neural changes produce the last stage of knowing or being aware of the feeling (see also Panksepp, 2000, for a similar argument). Damasio claims that the 'state of knowing the feeling' arrives usually an instant after the earlier states as the last stage in the unfolding of affect. The first order and second order representations, which make up the 'state of feeling' and the 'state of knowing the feeling' respectively, are more difficult, however, to specify in terms of brain physiology. In 1999 Damasio stated that he didn't know for sure but he suspected that these neural patterns emerge from complicated cross-signalling and coordination across several brain regions. In his 2004 account, as a result of recent research, he offers a more elaborate account of the brain physiology involved (although see Rizzolatti and Sinigaglia's, 2008, pp. 188–9, critique of Damasio's physiological specifications).

With the arrival of the 'state of knowing the feeling', I now, according to Damasio, experience the full-blown psychological event of consciousness of the feeling – the subjective experience of irritation. At this point, as the state of 'knowing the feeling' arrives, self also becomes engaged, and Damasio argues that I become human in the sense that the bodily and brain process becomes connected to 'complex ideas, values, principles and judgements that only humans have' (1999, p. 35). He continues:

> It is through feelings, which are inwardly directed and private, that emotions, which are outwardly directed and public, begin their impact on the mind; but the full and lasting impact of feelings requires consciousness, because only with the advent of a sense of self do feelings become known to the individual having them. (1999, p. 36)

It is only at this point, then, in Damasio's model that the feeling could be said to belong to 'me'. Notably, Damasio seems to see 'states of knowing the feeling' as entirely individual and privately negotiated states – these are intra-psychic events rather than social events. In his later work, Damasio (2004) understands the difference and transition between the two levels of analysis and the different descriptive languages entailed in capturing the move from 'states of feeling' to 'states of knowing the feeling' through Spinoza's philosophy. He sees both neural events and psychological events as manifestations of the same process. This process produces both a physical alteration in the body and the registering of the changes in the body's physical state in the mind, in thoughts and feelings. This is what could be entailed, then, in Spinoza's claim that events in the mind form an 'idea of the body'.

The body loops of affect

Following through this sequence of stages we can see that Damasio's central argument is that the process of emoting takes place through what he calls a 'body loop'. Emotions travel through the brain and the body. The registering of this physical flow and the loop back as these changes are recorded and picked up by the brain becomes the affective experience. It is for this reason that Damasio's model can be described as neo-Jamesian. Like William James, Damasio insists that the body, including the brain, is 'the theatre' where emotions are performed and, like James, he insists that the body (in the form of neural activity in the brain and activity driven by the autonomic nervous system) precedes the feeling. The body comes first in each new affective experience. Both Damasio and James are arguing that it is our registering of the body/brain performance that comes to produce the human actuality, the experience of the emotion itself. Unlike James, however, Damasio allows for the possibility that cognitive events such as memories or other feelings might be the inducer. It is not just a simple process of *external stimulus – body response – feeling*. James' famous example suggested a sequence such as *presence of a bear – running away – observation of self running away – feeling of fear*. For Damasio, the sequence could well be *cognitive event – body response – feeling* instead.

Confusingly, Damasio also notes that body loops need not always take place physically, expanding out through the relevant parts of the autonomic nervous system producing changes such as increased heart rate and increased blood flow to the face, etc. The state of 'knowing the feeling' can sometimes come instead from what he calls the 'as if body loop'. This 'as if body loop' is a form of internal stimulation rather than stimulation from actual physical changes. The representation of the relevant body states is 'created directly in sensory body maps, under the control of other neural sites, for instance, in the prefrontal cortices. It is "as if" the body had really been changed, but it has not' (1999, p. 281).

Damasio's 'as if body loop' seems to mesh with recent research on 'mirror neurons' (Bråten, 2007; Rizzolatti and Sinigaglia, 2006). Neuroimaging studies suggest that as we watch what someone else is doing (especially if it is an intentional and/ or goal-related movement) our brains mirror the firing pattern going on for real in their brains and bodies. When we watch someone we care about in pain, or watch someone smell a liquid that turns out to be disgusting, our brains fire in the same distinctive way as the brains of those actually in pain or experiencing disgust. This research argues that as an organism moves around the world its brain is constantly preparing and holding in potential a range of relevant action patterns in relation to the objects it encounters. The brain seems to be organised around the functional goal-directed activities that are possible in particular situations or with particular objects (cf. also Rose, 2005, p. 163). I will return to this research in later chapters, as claims for mirror neurons, although contested (cf. Hickok, 2009, 2010), have been seen as evidence of the neurobiological bases of human inter-subjectivity and empathy. Although Damasio is sketchy on the details, his 'as if body loop' seems to involve a similar process of neural representation of a potential body landscape without the effort and energy required to put the body through its actual paces.

Finally, it is worth noting that although Damasio separates out in his model three stages or moments of affect ('state of emotion', 'state of feeling' and 'state of knowing the feeling'), he maintains everyday experience presents a functional continuum. This continuum is the 'running polyphony' (1999, p. 43) making up the fabric of the body/mind. It consists of continuous cycles of bodily responses, changes in representations of body states, consciousness of feelings that might lead to new bodily responses, and so on. He also emphasises that although large parts of this continuous process are non-conscious for humans, and might remain so, it is usually possible to pay enough attention to move bodily responses into the scene of consciousness. The preset biological machinery, templates and infrastructure which Damasio claims produce states of emotion are not dependent on consciousness, however.

Parsing Affect Through Basic Emotions: Unpicking Damasio's Account

What to make of this account? As I noted earlier, Damasio has been described as the 'most social science friendly' neuroscientist currently writing (Cromby, 2007b, p. 153). He is certainly a seductive and elegant guide and his account is reassuringly authoritative. In this vertiginous field, Damasio deserves his pedestal for accessibility alone. But, as others in social psychology (e.g. Blackman, 2008; Blackman et al., 2008; Brown and Stenner, 2009) have noted, if one focuses on the key concepts and arguments, the neat picture quickly becomes confusing. Damasio's reviewers and critics in neuroscience (e.g. McGinn, 2003; Panksepp, 2003) berate him both for this and for not acknowledging the work of other affective scientists. It is an odd experience interrogating Damasio's model in depth. He hides his own creativity. What is presented as a solid and neutral description of unimpeachable scientific evidence turns into something more like hand-waving. All the dots refuse to be joined.

From the perspective of social research, my concerns are: (i) his multiple and highly inconsistent answers to the question of what exactly counts as innate; (ii) the difficulties in tracking and understanding how any 'presetting' of body/brain patterns might operate in humans; (iii) the ways in which in any meaningful sense the body might 'come first' in states of affect once the importance of cognitive appraisal has been acknowledged; and (iv) whether Damasio's description of feelings as registrations of somatosensory representations does justice to their world and action orientations. This seems to ignore the ways in which 'knowledge of feelings' is also actively socially negotiated (see also McGinn, 2003 on these last two points).

A number of these problems arise because Damasio tries to combine a sensitive and radical analysis of the cognizing and conscious body with a taken-for-granted and mostly non-reflexive adherence to the basic emotions meta-framework for thinking about the parsing of affect. The basic emotions paradigm dominated research on emotions in neuroscience and psychology in the last half of the 20th century. I will suggest shortly that much of Damasio's more nuanced theory could be detached, in fact, from the basic emotions framework and sits much more comfortably with the notion of affective practices. Without basic emotions, his analysis is still puzzling in places but a lot less so, and it would seem to mesh better, too, with newer, emerging trends in empirical neuroscience.

First, though, what is the basic emotions thesis and why does it block interdisciplinary work on affect? This meta-framework takes a strong view on the organisation of affect and its chunking or parsing. It assumes that the flow of affect through bodies and brains comes patterned in relatively neat, discrete packets, bundles, programmes or templates. Each of these possesses their own distinct physiological signature, pattern of brain activation, and antecedent triggers, and each corresponds to conventional Western emotions such as 'anger', 'fear', 'happiness', etc. Such affect packets, or 'specialised neural modules' in Atkinson and Adolphs' (2005) terminology, are thought to unfold in an automatic, clunk-click, sequential manner.

Barrett et al. (2007, p. 375), illuminatingly, describe these as 'type-type identity theories' of emotion. In other words it is assumed 'that for every kind of emotion experience (e.g. the experience of anger), there is only one type of neurophysiological state'. Basic emotions are seen as universal across cultures and innate. Thought to have emerged relatively early in evolution, many of their features are seen as shared with other animals. In an evocative phrase, Panksepp (1998) describes basic emotions as 'prepared states of the nervous system' and thus as 'hard-wired' into the brain and body. Damasio doesn't quite sign up to all of these claims but, clearly, they have substantially organised his understanding of emotion.

Silvan Tomkins, whose work has been taken up so strongly in parts of cultural studies (e.g. Sedgwick, 2003; Sedgewick and Frank, 1995), set the basic emotions ball rolling in the 1960s. His student Paul Ekman and a range of other psychologists and neuroscientists, then elaborated the core argument in the 1970s through to the 1990s. Tomkins expressed his analysis of what he called 'basic affects' ('basic emotions' was Ekman's preferred term) in this way:

> Affects are sets of muscle and glandular responses located in the face and also widely distributed through the body, which generate sensory feedback which is inherently 'acceptable' or 'unacceptable'. These organized sets of responses are triggered at subcortical centers where specific 'programs' for each distinct affect are stored. These programs are innately endowed and have been genetically inherited. They are capable of simultaneously capturing such widely distributed organs as the face, the heart, and the endocrines and imposing on them a specific pattern of correlated responses. (1962, pp. 243–4)

Basic emotions research focuses on what Panksepp (1994a) calls emotional 'primes' or the 'blue-ribbon A-grade emotions' (p. 23). (Damasio's term for this was 'primary emotions' contrasted to 'secondary' or 'social' emotions.) Tomkins concluded in the 1960s that there might be eight such discrete affects: surprise–startle; interest–excitement; fear–terror; distress–anguish; enjoyment–joy; contempt–disgust; shame–humiliation; anger–rage. A number of scientists since have tried to develop more definitive lists (e.g. Frijda, 1986; Izard, 1977; Johnson-Laird and Oatley, 1992; Plutchik, 1980; and see Turner, 2000, for an exhaustive list of the lists). The range varies considerably, from the 17 emotions Ekman (1994) described in a particularly expansive moment to the more usual eight, or six, or four. Most lists, like Damasio's own list, include anger, fear, surprise, sadness, happiness and disgust, and most research has been on these. Each 'emotional prime' is thought to exhibit quite a wide range of intensity, from mild through to extreme, and thus appear in different shadings and manifestations (Panksepp, 1994b), but, as the name suggests, emotional primes are thought to be irreducible and 'pure', unique and not a mixture of other emotional states (Engelen et al., 2009, p. 26). Primes would be the emotional states that one would expect to be demonstrated very early in infants and last longest in, for instance, those disabled by some of the dementia diseases of old age (Engelen et al., 2009, p. 27).

Typically, basic emotions thinking is strongly tied to a set of presuppositions derived from evolutionary psychology and these were evident also throughout Damasio's writing. Basic emotions are thought to be 'basic' because they have evolved to deal with what Johnson-Laird and Oatley (1992) describe as 'universal human predicaments' such as loss, danger and confrontation. It is argued that a rapid emotional reaction to these predicaments would be highly functional and adaptive, preparing organisms for effective action. In a similar formulation, evolutionary psychologists Tooby and Cosmides (1990, cited in Ekman, 1994, p. 15) conclude that emotions impose on our current human circumstances 'interpretative landscapes derived from our ancestral pasts'. In other words, they suggest that humans are primed to respond strongly to particular contexts, and our emotional responses are triggered by perceptions in the here and now of 'meanings' that have been laid down by evolution.

Related evolutionary accounts from other researchers add to this the notion that evolution is conservative. As LeDoux (1996, p.125) pithily proposes, evolution works on the basis 'if it ain't broke, don't fix it'. That is, older adaptive solutions to problems in earlier stages of evolution found in other animal species are likely to be conserved and carried forward in humans. Later evolutionary processes might simply have added modifications rather than prompt a complete re-design. Paul MacLean (1990, 1993) offers the most developed argument of this kind. He suggests that humans have what he calls a 'triune brain'. In other words, our brains are made up of three distinct systems, each of which developed initially at different phases of evolution to serve different functions. These three basic systems are, first, a reptilian striatal system devoted to coordinating and scripting action and bodily homeostasis, a paleomammalian limbic system which is particularly linked to emotion and adds other self-preservation strategies such as maternal nurturance and infant attachment, and a neomammalian cortex which adds complex cognition.

As Maclean's scheme intimates, basic emotions research has tended to work with a concept of emotions as 'lower' and cognition as 'higher'. Emotion is often described as 'subcortical' as opposed to 'cortical' and as an evolutionary hangover. People are assigned a kind of 'animal nature' that is primary and 'old'. This animal nature can be subdued and modulated by cognitive and reasoning capacities acquired later in evolution. In this way, animal heritage is incorporated into humans as a building block and then distinctively human capacities are added on top.

Panksepp, for example, describes what he calls 'primitive feelings' and 'primitive affective substrates' and compares these to the 'higher reaches' of the brain and 'higher cortical processes' that allow humans to consider more alternatives. He maintains: 'When the mushrooming of the cortex *opened* up the relatively *closed* circuits of our old mammalian and reptilian brains, we started to entertain alternatives of our own rather than of nature's making' (1998, p. 301: emphasis in the original). Damasio, similarly, frequently uses the terms 'higher' and 'lower' unselfconsciously in relation to cognition and emotion but his position on this is mixed (Forgas, 2001). Work from his laboratory has also strongly questioned whether cognition and affect operate as separate systems. He and his colleagues often maintain that affect and cognition are seamless (e.g. Adolphs and Damasio, 2001), most famously in their work on the somatic or affective markers that they argue accompany decision-making.

Unravelling Basic Emotions

Although basic emotions assumptions are still prevalent in psychological and neuroscience research, it is increasingly hard to maintain this approach to the analysis of affect in the face of alternative accounts. In this section I want to look at a range of accumulating counter-claims from psychobiological research, cultural investigations and contemporary genetics.

Psychobiological arguments

Basic emotions thinking explicitly generated and implicitly guided the interpretation of a huge amount of empirical research and ingenious experimentation. Ekman's own research was on the recognition of facial expressions across cultures (Ekman, 1972, 2003; Ekman and Friesen, 1971). This work seemed to suggest that there is a core of universal emotions (although see Russell and Fernández-Dols, 1997, for one example of a number of anthropologically informed critiques). There has also been substantial investigation of how autonomic nervous system responses (such as heart and breathing rate, skin temperature, changes in blood flow, visceral responses) are bundled together and whether each bundle does present a distinct physiological signature.

Research by Levenson, Ekman and Friesen (1990, cited in Oatley et al., 2006), for instance, suggests that there do seem to be different patterns of arousal across heart rate, finger temperature, galvanic skin response and muscle activity which correlate with anger, fear, sadness, disgust, happiness and surprise. Anger increases heart rate, for instance, while disgust does not, but the heart rate increase is greatest for fear, with sadness and happiness intermediate between anger and disgust. These kinds of bodily responses in patterned combinations might indeed create their own recognisable physiological signatures. Others strongly disagree and suggest that while there is likely to be some 'bunching' of bodily responses, this 'pre-organisation' seems to be limited and variable and, in general, autonomic measures are poorly correlated with each other (Cacioppo et al., 2000; Clore et al., 2005; Davidson, 1994). As Levenson (2003,

p. 212) himself notes, the answer is likely to lie somewhere between what he describes as 'two immoderate assertions': the claim that each emotion is autonomically unique and that every emotion is autonomically the same.

Again and again, in fact, empirical research on the crucial biological hypotheses of the basic emotions framework has turned out to be equivocal and inconclusive in just this kind of way. Damasio, like many other neuroscientists, gives the impression that the basic emotions thesis is pretty much gospel and does not even reference dissenting voices (e.g. 2004, p. 302). Yet, as Lisa Feldman Barrett (2006b, p. 33) notes, 'more than 30 years ago, emotion researchers began to report that strong correlations among measureable responses failed to materialise as expected'. The psychologist and appraisal theorist Klaus Scherer robustly concluded in an early review in 1994: 'I have not yet seen a convincing *a priori* argument, let alone evidence, that establishes the existence of basic or fundamental emotions as independent and integral biological or psychological categories or mechanisms' (p. 27). And Barrett's (2006b) own impressively thorough account of all the evidence 12 years later reaches the same conclusion. She argues it is impossible to conclude that basic emotions such as anger, fear, happiness etc. can be treated in any sense as natural kinds with the properties attributed to them. The basic emotions hypothesis concerning the packaging of affect remains just that: a hypothesis.

Perhaps the most important lines of evidence come from neuroimaging studies. As I noted, Damasio argues that each primary emotion (anger, fear, etc.) has its own pattern in the brain or preset flow and in arguing this he draws on neuroimaging work from his own laboratory that seems strongly supportive. Reviews of neuroimaging studies on this question are slowly accumulating, although the patterns are difficult to interpret and prone to false positives. My colleague Johanna Motzkau has drawn my attention, for instance, to a very funny short paper (Bennett et al., 2010) investigating 'perspective taking in a dead salmon'. Neuroimaging the salmon's brain found some responses ...

Barrett and Wager (2006), discussing two meta-analyses of the existing neuroimaging research, note in contrast to Damasio's conclusion that the picture so far is very mixed. They report that there is some support across a number of studies for the role of the amygdala in fear, and some consistency in brain activation patterns for disgust, but there are also inconsistent and contradictory results. The method of presentation of the stimulus to the human participant being scanned seems to make more difference than it should do if the brain was organised around basic emotions.

Daum et al. (2009) in their review conclude that the jury is still out on whether there are discrete affects and discrete mechanisms. Their account of the latest picture from the neurobiology of affect picks out many of the distributed brain areas that Damasio also highlights, but they do not feel able to maintain specificity or innate templates for particular emotions (cf. also Cacioppo et al.'s, 2000, extensive review of the evidence, and Barrett et al., 2007). Richard Davidson (2003), in a commentary for a Special Issue on affective neuroscience in the journal *Brain and Cognition*, states firmly that one of the 'seven sins' in current neuroscience research on emotion is the assumption he associates with Silvan Tomkins that 'there is a circuit in the brain that orchestrates a cascade of responses that are specific to each emotion' (p. 130).

Cultural arguments

Other strong counter-arguments against the basic emotions parsing of affect came from the anthropologists and social psychologists working in the 1980s and 1990s on the cultural construction of emotion (e.g. Abu-Lughod and Lutz, 1990; Lutz, 1988; Rosaldo, 1980, 1984; Shweder and LeVine, 1984). The idea that affect comes in 'anger' and 'fear' type packets which are genetically inherited seems intuitively correct to Western eyes. But social constructionist work queried the obviousness of these intuitions. Early work in the 1960s consistently pointed to the importance of the context and the role of interpretation in reading body states (Schacter and Singer, 1962). Physiological arousal can be quite ambiguous, as Baraitser and Frosh's (2007) example illustrates. When this is the case, the exact emotion felt will depend not so much on the nature of the arousal but on the interpretation the context allows. Contrary to Damasio's description of the 'state of knowing the feeling', people frequently explicitly look to the situation and to others around them to decide whether it is excitement, anger or fear they could be feeling. And, of course, are continually attentive and responsive to the context and others' subsequent responses. Social constructionist work extended this point, arguing that the organisation and interpretation of body possibilities is always culturally embedded and thus the kind of universal, fixed patterns posited by the basic emotions thesis fundamentally misrepresent the ordering of affect.

Shweder (1994), in a review of social constructionist research, notes that lay theories of affective experience or 'ethnopsychologies' consistently differ across cultures. Western cultures tend to 'emotionalise' somatic and affective events (cf. also Dixon, 2003). That is, members of Western societies tend to assume that emotions are distinct and internal subjective experiences for which the individual is responsible and accountable. Emotions are placed within broader narratives that value reason and the struggle for rational control. As Shweder describes, other cultures place somatic and affective events in very different ethnopsychological frameworks, part of cultural categories such as 'bewitchment', for instance, or 'sickness' or 'moral suffering'.

It could still be the case that the somatic and affective experiences marked out within each broad ethnopsychology or cultural frame are the same or interchangeable. But this seems doubtful also. There is a wide range of evidence that different cultures organise not just their broad psychological, cosmological and natural theories of affect differently but also local accounts of immediate experiences in light of these. Some of this evidence comes from linguistic research (Wierzbicka, 1992, 1999). This suggests that the variation in emotion terms across languages is so great that there are no universal emotion concepts. Different cultures have different lexicons for somatic and affective experiences and it is impossible to match these across different languages.

These 'lost in translation' issues are profound. As Chapters 3 and 4 will demonstrate, categorisations and descriptions of experience are embedded in the everyday routines and sense-making procedures of social life. Lexical differences across cultures reflect major differences in the possibilities for moment-to-moment meaning-making which locate the nature and significance of a somatic or affective event, the consequences and implications, and, most likely, the ways in which somatic and affective events intertwine, flow and fold into each other. As discursive psychologists (Edwards, 1997) have argued, people's accounts and descriptions of emotion are part of ongoing cultural stuff. When we describe what we feel, we are engaged in a piece of cultural and often interpersonal business, tailored, for example, to rebut some accusation, persuade another to do something, establish a motive, and so on.

Cultures differ widely in what they take as an appropriate antecedent event for a somatic or affective response. As we saw, one of the criteria Ekman (1994) suggested for a basic emotion was that each emotion prime would share the same kind of antecedent conditions across cultures and within cultures. Damasio also argued that body/brain patterns have been pre-programmed to respond in the same ways to the same sorts of events. But this claim has been exceptionally difficult to substantiate. According to Shweder:

> It is a trivial exercise for any anthropologist to generate long lists of antecedent events (ingesting cow urine, eating chicken five days after your father dies, kissing the genitals of an infant boy, being complimented about your pregnancy, caning a child, touching someone's foot or shoulder, being addressed by your first name by your wife, ad infinitum) about which the emotional judgements of a Western observer would not correspond to the native's evaluative response. (1994, p. 36)

In effect, this work suggests that affective events are indexical – their meaning and definition will depend on the context. This is as true for individuals within the same culture as it is across cultures. This explains why basic emotions theorists might have found it so difficult to agree on their lists of basic emotions. As Ortony and Turner commented in 1990, there had to be something wrong with a paradigm that proposes the existence of emotional primes but then couldn't agree on what goes on the list. If an emotion is 'basic' then it should be entirely obvious; if the categorisation of affect is a cultural matter, then one can't expect categorisation to be straightforward.

One of the main difficulties with the basic emotions thesis is that, paradoxically, attempts to provide a natural history of the emotions end up denaturing affect as an object of study. As Rom Harré (1986, p. 4) pointed out, abstracting an entity – such as 'anger', 'love', 'grief' or 'anxiety' – to try to study it, also reifies it. What can be found in actual life, Harré notes, are not anger and fear *per se* but 'angry people, upsetting scenes, sentimental episodes, grieving families and funerals, anxious parents pacing at midnight, and so on'. In other words, body states are always situated and always taking place in the midst of some activity, and the medium in which they are situated is culturally and socially constituted.

If one thinks about it, it is quickly apparent that vivid and sharp bursts of classic Western affect, such as episodes of anger, fear, joy, etc., tend to be exceptional and sporadic (see Barrett, 2006b; Russell, 2003; Russell and Barrett, 1999, for similar arguments). The effort to settle on emotional primes as the unit of analysis creates an idealised set of phenomena, like the figures in a bad novel, removed from the messiness and mix of actual affect. Basic emotions are cut out from the flow of everyday cultural life, and probably quite rare 'big moments' emphasised at the expense of more banal and everyday experiences, some of which may well be fleeting, equivocal and muddled. This simplifying may have been methodologically necessary at one time as Panksepp (1998) argues, but is it still necessary? No a priori methodological principle (except perhaps the lessons from the dead salmon) seems to prevent neuroscientists from locating their neuroimaging in more nuanced, everyday affective practices, although, of course, their framings of that nuance are likely to differ from social researchers. The basic emotions thesis distils types from the flux of everyday experience yet ultimately it is that flux across *all* cultural and social situations that must be explained.

Evolutionary arguments

Some similar issues are becoming evident in relation to the evolutionary theorising underpinning basic emotions thinking. As we saw, the basic emotions tradition tends to assume a biological (and evolutionary) separation between subcortical 'lower and older' emotions and cortical 'higher and newer' cognition. Recent research, however, has moved substantially away from this thinking in line with the general blurring of the once clear boundaries between cognition and affect. Few in the affective sciences these days maintain strong distinctions between affect and cognition (see Duncan and Barrett, 2007, for a review of the neurobiological evidence for the intertwining of thought and emotion).

MacLean's view of the 'triune brain', for example, and his account of the limbic system as the area of the brain that produces emotion, now seems too simplistic. The limbic system is still given prominence in textbooks (e.g. Oatley et al., 2006) and is often described as the 'seat of emotion'. But LeDoux (1996, p. 99) argues that MacLean's arguments for a distinct 'limbic system' as the driver of emotion are unconvincing. He states: 'MacLean and later enthusiasts of the limbic system have not managed to give us a good way of identifying what parts of the brain actually make up the limbic system.' It seems, too, that more recent anatomical studies of other animal species raise considerable problems for MacLean's three-systems view of the evolution of the brain. LeDoux notes that supposedly evolutionarily 'late' cortex has now been found in reptiles. This substantially undermines the claim that some parts of the mammalian brain might operate in 'older' ways than others. As Davidson (2003, pp. 129–30) describes, researchers now conclude that: '[a]ffect is both cortical and subcortical'; neuroimaging with human subjects routinely shows that 'affective stimuli activate a broad network of both subcortical *and* cortical regions' (emphasis in the original).

As brain research has developed, what seems to have become more apparent is the flexibility and plasticity of the central nervous system. This undermines and challenges older notions that evolution and natural selection resulted in fixed action patterns (or instincts) such as the innate templates proposed for each basic emotion. Stephen Rose, for instance, describes the brain as presenting a constantly changing, dynamic architecture. This is most vivid in the developing brains of infants and children where over time neurons and glia migrate, 'locating themselves in appropriate patterns in the cortex and other brain regions, making and pruning synaptic connections with neighbours and relations' (2005, p. 146). But even mature neurons are in constant flux. Rose continues:

> Under time-lapse the dendrites can be seen to grow and retract, to protrude spines and then to withdraw them again, to make and break synaptic contact. ... If this be architecture, it is a living, dynamic architecture in which the present forms and patterns can only be understood as a transient moment between past and future. Truly the present state of any neuronal connection, any synapse, both depends on its history and shapes its future. At this as at all levels of the nested hierarchy of the brain, dynamism is all. The brain, like all features of living systems, is both being and becoming, its apparent stability a stability of process, not of fixed architecture. Today's brain is not yesterday's and will not be tomorrow's. (2005, pp. 146–7)

It was once common-place for neuroscientists to talk of human culture and consciousness as 'augmenting', 'enhancing' or 'supplementing' more primitive, basic emotional responses laid down by evolution, and the basic emotions thesis supported this logic. Examples of this perspective can be still found. Oatley et al. (2006), for example, argue in their textbook:

> Newer parts of the brain and new developments of culture did not replace these fundamental circuits of emotional readiness and experience, they augmented them. Language, in particular, has enhanced our modes of emotional relatedness. All the same we can find ourselves caught up in emotional effects that seem to have ... marks of the primitive, in systems that are, as it were, closed and impenetrable to cognitive modification. (p. 146)

Increasingly, however, other voices can be heard (e.g. Rose, 1997, 2005). These talk not of 'augmenting' but of the ways in which the evolution of consciousness and the arrival of culture 'transforms', 're-models' and perhaps one could even say 'revolutionises' possible emotional responses as circumstances require.

New Thinking on the Psychobiology of Affect and its Patterning

Increasingly, in response to these problems with the basic emotions framework, neuroscientists are beginning to develop new analytic strategies. Davidson et al., in their massive doorstop, *Handbook of Affective Sciences* (2003a), note that affective phenomena are now being analysed as highly complex assemblies of smaller parts that might be found across a wide range of diverse emotional responses. They suggest that the current focus in neuroscience is not on the putative location and functioning of whole emotions but on the ways in which 'different aspects of emotion processing are distributed in different brain circuits' (2003b, p. 5).

Emotional components are being parsed in a more fine-grain way. The general trend is towards a more molecular and distributed neuroscience approach. The search for the places in the brain where emotion or cognition or motivation happen is being superseded by investigations of integrating forms of patterning that flow across multiple brain networks to produce activity sequences that may instantiate all these psychological features. Davidson et al. (2003) focus, for instance, on the control and initiation of different forms of approach and avoidance in the prefrontal cortex. While Arvid Kappas (2008) argues that it often makes more sense to talk of 'brains in the plural' (p. 19). Parallel processing is the norm in mental and neurobiological life and more attention is also being paid now to connections between neural networks and homeostatic regulatory systems.

What is left, then, of Damasio's account in the face of these developments? Damasio suggested that the experience of emotion is like entering a zone, where the nature of the zone is determined by which one of the body's possible responses was triggered. What we are beginning to learn is that there are perhaps no clearcut zones but a process of negotiation and emergence. Equally, we do not need to accept Damasio's neo-Jamesian claim that the body always comes first in affective sequences. An affective act is not like an instinct or a fixed action pattern. It does not seem to be the case that an 'emotionally competent stimulus' or emotional inducer hits a trigger in our brains, with our minds playing catch-up, forming an idea of what the body is doing in order to produce feeling and a mental description.

It is possible that some limited classes of response might operate like this, such as fear of snakes and flinching from objects that look like snakes (LeDoux, 1996). More commonly, however, the processes of split-second appraisal and evaluation preceding bodily reactions will be interacting and finely tuned with ongoing thoughts about situations, representations of oneself in that situation, about what might count as an appropriate response, and so on. In other words, the neurobiological polyphony producing emotional body reactions (thumping hearts, sobs and screwed up faces) is not sealed off from the neurobiological polyphony that supports decisions, thoughts, complex moral evaluations, etc. Appraisal theorist, Klaus Scherer (2009), for example, describes a dynamic psychobiological architecture of interplays between conscious representations and verbal labels, split second non-conscious appraisals, action tendencies, physical responses and registrations of body states.

I don't think, then, we can quite trust Damasio's assumptions around the parsing and patterning of affect in the body. Certainly it neglects the relays with the parsing of social action, investigated by social constructionist researchers and discursive psychologists, which I will discuss in more detail in Chapter 4. What I do want to take forward from Damasio, however, is a set of emphases and a language for describing the efflorescing of body states and their flowing, recursive and dynamic nature. Running through Damasio's work (and recent psychobiology) is a persuasive image of the constantly configuring and reconfiguring body landscape. This is Damasio's 'running polyphony' made up of parallel processing on multiple levels. This can be combined with his intriguing account of affective experience as emergent from complex and dynamic body loops as physical changes are fluidly registered and represented 'on-line'.

What about the bodily parsing of affect though? Where do we go with this? What kinds of patterns and forms of order does the affected body settle into? If we strip away Damasio's working assumption of innate, ancestral templates and preset biological machinery, or rather if we judge that the arguments for these are weak, what are we left with? What seems most likely is that there is pattern but, like pattern elsewhere in human action, it is loose and often post hoc, arising in the moment of categorisation. It is the flowing and turbulent patterning characteristic of social practice and dynamic systems. Alongside his references to preset templates, Damasio refers, for example, to 'body devices', to 'body dispositions' and to 'potential patterns of activity arising within neural ensembles'. This terminology seems more apt and much more commensurate with what Shweder (1994) calls the 'whole package deal' of affect.

It seems unlikely that brains and bodies everywhere across the globe speak English and talk only of 'anger', 'fear', 'joy' and the other basic emotions in the same ways. It also seems unlikely that over time there are no patterns at all and no sedimentation or settling effects. It remains an open question, but my guess is that the body/brain acquires routines that form distinctive dispositional body/brain shapes. Just as the perfumer has to acquire 'a nose' and learn how to smell and recognise different perfumes (Latour, 2004), bodies and brains become customised through developmental and cultural processes, or through the kind of growing, setting and 'pruning' processes which Stephen Rose (2005) describes. They learn to rocket through CNS and ANS repertoires that may be quite personalised, are certainly culturally contingent, and which may become quite entrenched. The most recent psychobiological research (see Davidson et al., 2000, and Doidge, 2007, for a popular general review) stresses the enormous plasticity of the human brain, and, in particular, the plasticity in the central neural circuitry of emotion. But, it must also be the case that potential patterns of activity are constrained to some extent by neurophysiological limits in addition to what is acquired through habit and practice.

Body/brain patterning interacts in complex ways with other sources of patterning – such as the kinds of meaning-making processes I will be considering in the next few chapters. To start to introduce these broader connections, and to round off this chapter, I want to dwell a little more on recent thinking around this crucial question of the overall psychobiological and experiential patterning of affect, and compare two current dominant psychological models that take off from the demise of basic emotions. One of these comes from Klaus Scherer (2009). This is the 'component process model' he has been developing since the 1980s. The other comes from Lisa Feldman Barrett (2005, 2009) and

James Russell (2003, 2009; Russell and Barrett, 1999) and they describe this as a 'psychological construction' approach.

The psychological construction model

Barrett and Russell take a minimalist approach to any pre-ordering of affect by the body/brain. Barrett (2009, p. 1291) in fact describes emotion as a 'conceptual act', throwing most emphasis on social categorisation processes as the source of the patterning of emotional experience. Russell (2003) argues that perhaps the body/brain signals just something he calls the state of 'core affect'. Core affect is a mix of information about levels of activation, such as intense or relaxed, and levels of valence, such as pleasure or displeasure. The presenting of core affect, Russell and Barrett suggest, is turned on all the time and so we have available a constant stream of information about our changing neurophysiological states through the kinds of ongoing, body registering processes Damasio and others posit. (An account of the neurobiology of core affect can be found in Barrett et al., 2007.) What is registered, then, in sharp bursts of emotion, are big physical changes in sensations of activation and valence interpreted as pleasant or unpleasant or intense or mild. A typical transition in core affect might occur, for instance, when feeling tired (low activation, more unpleasant than pleasant sensations) gives way to euphoria on receiving great news (high activation, entirely pleasant sensation).

Pattern, then, these researchers suggest, is not so much 'spoken by' any intrinsic shaping of the body/brain but arises as the registering of core affect combines with representational processing, as the brain 'draws from its vast repository of stored representations in the blink of an eye, to associatively recombine what it has learned in the past' (Barrett, 2009, p. 1292). It is in this sense that the experience of emotion is a conceptual or an interpretive act. This view is commensurate with the claims of anthropologists, social constructionists and discursive psychologists that it is culture and learning processes, not bodies, which parse and chunk affect into recognisable and communicable experiences.

To go back, then, to the Baraitser and Frosh (2007) example, Barrett and Russell are suggesting that what orders and patterns events like 'being in a state' as particular kinds of experiences is not so much a specific sequential flow of body/brain activities but an interacting set of components in response to an antecedent event (cf. Russell, 2003). Antecedent events and their figuring lead to some change in core affect. Valence and activation level begin to rise or fall (presumably high activation and high negative valence in Baraitser and Frosh's example). Interpretive and categorising processes for the affective experience intercede ('I am scared', 'frustrated', 'interested', etc.). These may combine with an attribution for the experienced change in core affect to the general context as changes are interpreted through the problems and opportunities the context has presented ('this feeling is due to this and I need to respond in this way'). There may be an increased flood of subjective experience (e.g. a sense of urgency or confusion). Categorising and labelling will continue with more elaborated narrating such as 'yes, I am truly angry' or 'this is like what happened the other day' combined with social action and attempts at self-regulation.

This is a satisfying and plausible theory. Like all psychological models, it is an attempt to take what is known and posit modes of connection and pattern that fit the data (and like all models it changes the interpretation of the data). But does this approach fall prey to exactly the same problem that plagued the social constructionist research of the 1980s and 1990s? Has the body once again disappeared, and have we lost the autonomous physicality of affect once more? When the mind forms 'an idea of the body', in Spinoza's phrase, it seems likely that it has more to work on than core affect or valence and raw level of activation. What is the role of more specific, located information about the movement of blood to the face, for instance, or the thump of the heart? Does the 'bodyscape' present information on a wider range of varied micro-components, perhaps registered and represented through the kind of body looping process Damasio proposes? Barrett and Russell are no doubt right to emphasise that humans make sense of these body states using a large range of idiosyncratic and communal categorisations. These categorisations turn a flow of blood into an 'embarrassed blush', for instance, and the thump of the heart into the start of a 'panic attack' or 'anger' or 'just a palpitation'. The body/brain, however, might well present a larger palette of micro-affective orderings to the interpretive process, with more vivid and tailored (albeit open and flowing) physiological patterns, than Barrett, Russell and their colleagues proposed.

The component process model

Klaus Scherer's component process model develops a view on the psychobiological parsing of affect somewhere between the 'natural kinds' assumptions of affective templates found in basic emotions theory, and the looseness of core affect and psychological construction models. Scherer defines an emotion as 'an episode of massive synchronous recruitment of mental and somatic resources to adapt to, or cope with, a stimulus event that is subjectively appraised as being highly pertinent to the needs, goals and values of the individual' (2005, p. 314). He sees the mental and somatic resources or multiple components orchestrating an emotional experience as diverse. His model includes multi-level appraisal processes, stored schemata, neural events, ANS activity, body expressive activities, central representational processes, categorisation and labelling, action tendencies and motivational states. The diagram he draws of all these components in action (2009, p. 1315) bristles with multi-directional arrows to convey the complex feedback loops and interactions between these various elements.

So what kinds of patterns are produced then? The patterning of an emotional episode, Scherer argues, is dynamic and changing over time. What is experienced is the result of information integration occurring across all the multiple components. Scherer thinks that one crucial kind of integration occurs as some kind of monitoring structure in the central nervous system begins to register and represent what is being dynamically synchronised across action tendencies, motor expressions, physiological symptoms and cognitive appraisals. In a delightful phrase, Scherer argues that at this neural (and unconscious) level there is a process of 'coherence spreading' as information begins to coalesce, resulting in the formation of 'coherence clusters'.

In my terms, you could say that there is a process of settling on a 'reading', as multi brain/body/mind systems cycle and shuttle back and forth in non-linear fashions, cross-referring, and stitching together an event. This kind of coherence clustering and registration interacts then in complex ways with conscious representation and regulation, and with the communication of *qualia* or embodied subjective feelings. Scherer argues that labelling and describing the emotional experience through the categories and vocabularies available in a culture feeds into the process also. They are a kind of end stage to the process, but an end stage that can also shape the very first stage of initial appraisal.

He provides a number of examples of what might be beginning to be synchronised together, or in his words 'fused together', in the 'reading' produced as different components are centrally monitored, represented and integrated. 'Stimulus evaluation checks' which are part of early 'multi-level appraisal processes' might indicate, for instance, a situation where there is 'discrepancy from expectations and yet the event is conducive to the individual attaining their goals in the situation' (2009, p. 1311). In this situation, action tendencies and motivational tendencies will be muted and will maintain a relaxed and stable orientation. Efferent effects in the autonomic nervous system (ANS) will begin to take this characteristic shape:

> Trophotropic shift, rest and recovery; decrease in respiration rate, slight heart rate decrease, bronchial constriction, increase in gastrointestinal motility, relaxation of the sphincters; decrease in general muscle tone; relaxation of facial muscle tone; overall relaxation of vocal apparatus ('relaxed voice' – F0 at lower end of range, low-to-moderate amplitude, balanced resonance with slight decrease in high-frequency energy; comfort and rest positions; plus elements from pleasantness response (however, if a conduciveness appraisal is accompanied by plans for further action, an ergotropic shift is to be expected). (2009, p. 1311, Table One)

In other words, a kind of pattern begins to form. Scherer's model emphasises dynamic openness throughout the whole integrative chronology as well as the possibility of strong, weak and contradictory patterns. He suggests that there can be an infinite set of possible emotional episodes all with slightly different flavours, tones and nuances. Each emotional episode is like a kaleidoscope (2009, p. 1316) and each clustering on each occasion could be slightly different. But, in addition, he argues that there will be recognisable repetitions. The repetitions are what he calls 'modal outcomes'. These 'occur more frequently due to event contingencies and psychobiological prewiring' (p. 1316). Modal outcomes can be large in number, compared to the templates of basic emotions, because of the diversity of components that are being assembled each time. This then is a rather more differentiated account of pattern than, say, Tomkins' 'affect programs'.

Scherer's examples of ANS body shapes, like the one I included above, read rather like weather reports and no doubt the immense taxonomic effort required to define modal outcomes would replicate the same frustrating promise of precision combined with very apparent ambiguity. Barrett et al. (2007) point out that Scherer offers a functionalist analysis in the sense that the meaning of the situation for the individual (assessed by the stimulus evaluation checks), understood ultimately in Darwinian terms, drives the process. Scherer agrees with Barrett and Russell in understanding emotional experience as an amalgam of body signals and other forms of meaning-making, but he awards the body *per se* a more fine-grain and specific role in patterning the experience. In effect, he argues for the development of what we could call 'body buttons' or habitual body figurations that contribute their own forms of order to affective practice.

The question of the psychobiological patterning of affect (its degree, type and source) remains unsettled. In the next two chapters when I look at affective meaning-making it will become even more apparent that precise, once and for all, descriptions of Scherer's modal outcomes will always escape because of the nature of the signification processes central to the formulation of affective experience, and due to the ways in which categorisation is embedded in social activity. Even if no exact taxonomy of modal outcomes proves possible, what I find intriguing about Scherer's account is the broad balance he proposes between variability and pattern. In a situation of massive empirical and theoretical uncertainty, his account of spreading coherence, clustering, the infinite variation of affect, but with forms of familiar order, reinforces and further fleshes out my sense that flows of affect through bodies might be well described through the analogy of social practice.

Perhaps the best we can conclude at this point is that there is a subtle, relational, back-and-forth shuttling and interweaving going on at all levels of the body/brain/mind. The brain/body itself is a matrix of activities in dynamic connection that can be composed and re-composed into patterns. These patterns are then available in intersection with the registrations and patterning that result in conscious feelings. But, as the next chapter will begin to show, these feelings themselves are caught up in further complicated orderings as part of the dynamic figurations and assemblages of the person in social interaction, in social formations and throughout the history of individual life.

In her book, *Blush*, based on Silvan Tomkins' work, Elspeth Probyn (2005) suggests that we need to continually cross the domains of the biological and the social, moving beyond 'empty statements about "embodiment"' (p. 27). This chapter has tried to show how very difficult this project is. Adapting Haraway's (2004) analogy, it is like holding two pieces of string and discovering that they are just the ends of the most enormous, chaotic, knotted ball that needs to be unravelled. But I have also suggested ways of tracking these knots and my approach will be fleshed out further in the chapters that follow. I have tried to demonstrate the value of a more systematic engagement with psychological and neuroscience stories of the body than is usual in the social sciences. Without, I hope, doing too much violence to psychobiological accounts, I have argued that these are now increasingly consistent with notions of patterning found in concepts of affective practice. In this way, we can begin to extend older social constructionist analyses to incorporate the body/brain and move forward to ask some new questions.

THREE

Negotiating affect: Discourse, representation and affective meaning-making

Lacan tells his audience that they must stop pursuing the affective as if it: 'were a sort of colouration, a kind of ineffable quality which must be sought out in itself, independently of the eviscerated skin which the purely intellectual realization of a subject's relationship should consist in. This conception, which urges analysis down strange paths, is puerile ... The affective is not like a special density which would escape an intellectual accounting.' (Seigworth, 2005, p. 161, citing Lacan, 1988, p. 57)

ASB: ... I think theories of the inadequacy of language are irritating. It seems to me that language can do so much and so much more than people have ever done with it. Even when you say language is inadequate to describe experience, you are using language, and if you can invent a really good example of what it's inadequate to describe and describe it, you're still using language. But it's abstract language that on the whole is inadequate. Ordinary descriptive language is pretty good: colour words and physical words and : : :

SF: : : : rocks and stones and trees

ASB: Rocks and stones and trees. Which is why I write novels and not literary theory. (Conversation between the novelist A.S. Byatt and Stephen Frosh; Frosh, 2004, p. 147)

In this chapter I want to move on from the bodying of affect and look at affective meaning-making and, in particular, the relationship between affect and discourse. This is deeply murky territory. The complexity of affect is already evident. But 'discourse', too, is understood in multiple ways. Sometimes discourse indexes just the formal structures of language found in dictionaries or grammar textbooks.

Sometimes it marks out everyday language practice as a form of social action. At other times discourse can be defined exceptionally broadly to include social meaning-making, or signification, in all its modes including visual, tactile, aural and other sensory modalities. Discourse in this sense would cover facial expressions and gestures as well as words and utterances. In my own work I have defined discourse in varying ways depending on the research question. Here I want to go back to our earliest formulation (Potter and Wetherell, 1987). By discourse in this chapter I mean the practical (formal and informal) realm of language in action – talk and texts, words, utterances, conversations, stories, speeches, lectures, television programmes, web pages, messages on message boards, books, etc., patterned within the everyday activities of social life.

Just as there are many ways of defining discourse, there are many possible ways of understanding the relationship between the affective and the discursive. Some see a very marked distinction between the two. As noted in Chapter 1, for a large number in the social sciences, the most interesting thing about affect is that it is *not* discourse. In studying affect, it is claimed, we are accessing a lively sensual realm beyond the conventional, the cognitive and the discursive. In this view, affect as embodied intensity is more instinctive and immediate than any language-based act such as telling a story or having conversation. Discourse is identified with the *conscious*, the *planned* and the *deliberate* while affect is understood as the *automatic*, the *involuntary* and the *non-representational*. Discourse and affect are seen as having an almost antagonistic relationship. Discourse *tames* and *codifies* affect (Lingis, 1991; Massumi, 1996).

For other theorists, the relationship between discourse and affect is more blurred and complementary. Ian Burkitt (2002) suggests that discourse *completes* the formulation of inchoate and pre-conceptual subjective feelings. While for William Reddy (2001) language is a further stage in the *translating* of body states into other modalities. In conventional psychological research, language is seen as *representing* and *expressing* emotion (Scherer, 2009), while social constructionist and psychological constructionist models describe how discourse *constructs* physiological arousal, turning it into recognisable and communicable emotion (e.g. Russell, 2003).

From an affective practices standpoint, specifying the exact relationship between affect and discourse is less interesting than investigating the range and entire patterning of affective assemblages operating in important scenes in everyday life along with their social consequences and entailments. Affect and discourse intertwine in these patterns to varying extents and in varying ways. The discursive elements may move in and out of prominence as the flow of practice plays out. Sometimes they are very dominant and sometimes more peripheral.

Take, for instance, the affective practices that organise contemporary Western romantic relationships. As Roland Barthes (1979) showed in his analysis of the various 'figures' assumed by the lover, sometimes this figuration of self and other is carried and communicated entirely through glance, smile and tone. The force of words depends not on their semantic content but on the degree of stutter, the softness or loudness, and the affective force. But this affective moment could provide material, of course, for potentially endless post mortems with the loved other, or entirely privately with oneself, or with various curious audiences of friends and enemies. Spiralling affective discursive loops can be set in motion as initial affect is narrated, communicated, shared, intensified, dispersed, modified and sometimes re-awoken even decades later. When we think about discourse in this practical light, distinctions between cognitive and non-cognitive, representational and non-representational, conscious and unconscious, language and the body become less and less clear-cut. Attention shifts to how affect is accomplished and ordered, and moves away from adjudicating in abstract the exact relation between bodies and discourse, feelings and words.

To open up the issue of affective meaning-making as a substantial part of an affective practices standpoint, this chapter is organised around a critical review of two contrasting approaches to affect and discourse. One is more promising than the other, but I will argue that neither quite works. The problems with each illustrate where we need to go next. I will start with the view found in the 'turn to affect' in cultural studies and cultural geography. This strongly separates affect from discourse, frames discourse through post-structuralist discourse theory, and privileges the non-conscious and the non-representational. This work is based, I will argue, on a number of misapprehensions. Although inspiring in some ways, it is a fragile basis for social research on affect. Then, I will turn to an approach that is exciting historians but is less well known in social science – William Reddy's (2001) psychologically sophisticated account of the relationship between emotional experience and what he calls 'emotives' or discourse performatives (such as 'I feel angry'). This is more helpful, but needs a more elaborated and less individualistic account of affective–discursive practice.

In this chapter, the argument for an affective practices approach will be mostly negative, emerging through the counter-points to the work I am reviewing. Towards the end of the chapter I will try to pull together the threads, and my approach will be more thoroughly illustrated in following chapters. In brief, I will be arguing that we need an approach to discourse which is eclectic and which stresses the relational, dialogic and distributed aspects of meaning-making. This casts doubt on any simple elision of discourse with the cognitive, the conscious and the planned. I will be trying to substantiate my claim that there is usually little point in trying to decompose affective activity into its bodily and discursive constituents. Bodies and sense-making are like two sides of the same sheet of paper. So let's study the whole sheets of paper – the affective–discursive practices and affective orders of social life – and take these interwoven phenomena as our units of analysis.

Affect as Excess: Massumi and Thrift

I begin with a perspective that is especially helpful for indicating what goes awry when bodily responses and discourse melded together in practice are pulled apart in theory. This approach is particularly associated with the work of Brian Massumi

(1996, 2002) and his trenchant arguments for the 'autonomy of affect'. Massumi's emphases have been taken up widely, most noticeably by Patricia Ticineto Clough and her colleagues (Clough, 2000, 2008a, 2008b, 2009; Clough et al., 2007; Clough with Halley, 2007), in cultural geography under the mantle of Non Representational Theory (NRT) by Nigel Thrift (2000, 2004, 2008a) and others such as McCormack (2003, 2006, 2007), Dewsbury (2003) and Anderson (2003, 2006, 2009), and has been elaborated also in politics (e.g. Williams, 2010). Traces of the foundational break with discourse and representation are evident, too, in some new feminist work (e.g. Grosz, 2004; Stewart, 2007; Wilson, 2004) but rejected by other feminists (e.g. Bondi et al., 2005; Hemmings, 2005; Thien, 2005).

This broad 'school' understands affect as a lively virtual force and endorses the most general, 'post-human' definitions of affect discussed at the beginning of Chapter 1. It offers a particular, and for some scholars, highly partial reading of the philosophy of Deleuze, Spinoza and Bergson, and often combines this with some highly selected bits of neuroscience. This is a take on affect decisively formed in contestation with post-structuralist discourse theory. In this approach discourse is rarely explicitly defined but seems to be equated most frequently with formal language structures and/or the discursive formations and epistemic regimes described by Foucault and studied by post-structuralist researchers. I want to look first at the reasoning behind the break with post-structuralism.

The critique of post-structuralist discourse theory

Texts in the new cultural studies of affect typically set up a string of oppositions contrasting the domain of affect with the critical and post-structuralist modes they wish to supersede. Kathleen Stewart (2007, pp. 1–4) outlines, for instance, distinctions between:

- a commitment to 'demystification and uncovered truths that support a well-known picture of the world' versus a commitment to 'speculation, curiosity and the concrete';
- 'the notion of a totalised system' versus the 'effort to approach a weighted and reeling present';
- 'dead effects imposed on an innocent world' versus bringing into view 'a scene of immanent force';
- a focus on the '"obvious meaning" of semantic message and symbolic signification' versus attention to the 'immanent, obtuse and erratic';
- developing 'bottom-line arguments about "bigger" structures and underlying causes' versus dwelling on the ways 'in which a reeling present is composed out of heterogeneous and noncoherent singularities'.

These oppositions indicate the weight placed on affect to deliver new emphases on the fugitive, the fleeting, the sensual, and on unfolding activity. Stewart's own research presents short, polished, what she calls 'ficto-critical' accounts of random episodes of 'ordinary affects'. Disappointingly, these fail to deliver.

Without pattern, method, a theory of practice and social action, or conceptual tools for the examination of the everyday affective–discursive, Stewart offers just the fleeting pleasure of reading a beautifully crafted account of a moment in a diner or on a neighbourhood street. She loses too much as she cuts away semantics, social critique, repetition, stasis, sedimentation, regulation, pattern and coherence.

Similarly, Thrift's (2008a) 'non-representational theory' (NRT) commits itself to the study of processes that are described as 'more than language', below the 'threshold of cognition', and thus preconscious and bodily, rather than individuated, discursively mediated and constructed. In a review of affect studies in geography, Lorimer (2005) suggests that the aim of NRT is to understand 'our self-evidently more-than-human, more-than-textual, multisensual worlds' (p. 83). This is going to involve developing forms of analysis that go beyond 'a conservative, categorical politics of identity and textual meaning ... allowing in much more of the excessive and transient aspects of living' (p. 83, see also Lorimer, 2008). Patricia Ticineto Clough (2009) agrees. Her call is for a method beyond the usual trajectory of qualitative research and its focus on interpretation, meaning, signification or representation. She does not specify what this new approach will look like except that it will not be 'containing' and it will recognise that methods will inevitably 'become entangled with an immanent dynamism' (p. 49).

Massumi's (2002) account of existing critical cultural theory is savage, and, as Clare Hemmings (2005) persuasively demonstrates, pretty much a caricature. Massumi finds post-structuralist cultural theory and post-structuralist discourse theory deadening because these approaches fix bodies and subjects in cultural and social positions and code them on identity grids:

> The kinds of codings, griddings and positionings with which cultural theory has been preoccupied are no exception to the dynamic unity of feedback and feed-forward, or double becoming. ... Ideas about social and cultural construction are dead-ended because they have insisted on bracketing the *nature* of the process. If you elide nature, you miss the becoming of culture, its emergence (not to mention the emergence of matter). You miss the continuum of interlinkage, feed-forward and feedback, by which movements capture and convert each other to many ends, old and new, and innumerable. The world is in a condition of constant qualitative growth. Some kind of constructivism is required to account for the processual continuity across categorical divides and for the reality of that qualitative growth, or ontogenesis: the fact that with every move, with every change, there is something new to the world, an added reality. The world is self-augmenting. Reality "snowballs" as William James was fond of saying. Perhaps "productivism" would be better than constructivism because it connotes emergence. "Inventionism" wouldn't be going too far, for even if you take nature in the narrowest sense, it has to be admitted that it is inventive in its own right. There is a word for this: evolution. There is no reason not to use the same word for the prolongation of "natural" processes of change in the emergent domain of "culture". Is a constructivist evolutionism conceivable? An evolutionary constructivism ...? (Massumi, 2002, p. 12; emphasis in the original)

When quoting Massumi it is almost impossible to stop. His words are so evocative and dizzying. What he is suggesting is so vague, breathless and escaping.

What I want to argue is not that these critiques of existing social theory and post-structuralist discourse theory are wrong or have no value. On the contrary, they mesh well with the critical perspective on post-structuralist discourse theory adopted in social psychological research (e.g. Wetherell, 1998). This also argues that actual (agentic and mobile) discourse and meaning-making practice is not well captured in post-structuralist discourse theory. I agree with Massumi, Thrift and Stewart that it is time to take the effervescent, the mobile, the concrete, and ordinary social action seriously. But, I think one can't do this without sustained attention to discourse. What is needed is an eclectic approach that investigates how the organisation of discursive formations or 'big discourse' intertwines with the patterning of everyday, dynamic and immediate discursive practice.

The problem I feel is not that the new work on affect attacks post-structuralist conceptions of discourse; it is that much of it goes on to sever any link between affect and meaning-making. This line of cultural theory is not calling for cleverer, more flexible, and more productive analyses of meaning-making practices and their entanglements with bodies but seeks to relegate the discursive almost entirely, and in this way I believe trips itself up. The discursive is defined in the narrowest possible passive sense, not as a verb, or seen as a form of unfolding practical social action (Potter et al., 1990). This is, instead, discourse as a noun, as 'representation', or discourse identified simply with the formal structures of language in abstract. These emphases will become clearer as we learn more about the story of affect that is put forward to occupy the huge spaces opening up when critical social theory is rendered impotent.

Massumi's half-second

I will focus mainly on Massumi's work, as it has been the most obviously influential in the new panorama. One of Massumi's first steps is to privilege the body in response to the impingement of the world. He draws on research on 'the missing half-second' as a way of illustrating this, citing an account of EEG research in *Scientific American* (Horgan, 1994) that suggests a disjuncture between the body and subjective interpretations. Researchers measuring the electrical activity of the brain typically find that the brain is highly active apparently *in advance* of consciousness, seemingly organising our responses before we are aware of making any decision to act in any particular way. Measurable brain activity occurs, for example, over half a second before the voluntary movement of a finger. This research is part of a growing body of work in psychology and social psychology on 'automaticity' and what Daniel Wegner (2002) calls the 'illusion of conscious will' (see Bargh, 2007a, for reviews). The original research was conducted by Kornhuber and his colleagues (see Kornhuber and Deecke, 1965) and elaborated by Libet et al. (1983). I will come back to the details later as it is not quite what it seems.

Musing on the absent half-second, and the inadequacies of consciousness, Nigel Thrift (2000, p. 34) describes it as 'that small but vitally significant period of time in which the body makes the world intelligible by setting up a background of expectation'. Our world building and action/reaction 'software' seem to kick in early and apparently do so in such a way that we are not even aware of the delay, the recursive nature of consciousness, or even the missing half-second. For Massumi, these findings demonstrate the redundancy of subjectivity and the autonomy of the physical body and brain. He concludes:

> Will and consciousness are subtractive. They are limitative, derived functions which reduce a complexity too rich to be functionally expressed. It should be noted in particular that during the mysterious half-second, what we think of as 'free', 'higher' functions, such as volition, are apparently being performed by autonomic, bodily reactions occurring in the brain but outside consciousness, and between brain and finger, but prior to action and expression. (1996, p. 223)

This new work on affect, then, concerns the domain of what Thrift (2000, p. 36) calls 'embodied dispositions ("instincts" if you like)' seen as beyond cognition and consciousness. As a psychologist, I find it odd to read these accounts, and to see scholars from disciplines previously so critical of positivistic psychology uncritically reproducing some of the staples from undergraduate textbooks, with none of the contestation over their meaning and significance.

Quality versus intensity

Massumi develops his argument further through his own particular reading of Deleuze's philosophy, in particular Deleuze's (1988, 1992) account of Spinoza (cf. Brown and Stenner, 2009, for an alternative exegesis of both traditions and Motzkau, 2007, for a rather different reading of Deleuze). Massumi argues that a potential separation can be made between the 'quality' of an experience and its 'intensity'. Two tracks, he suggests, are set going when the world impinges on the embodied human – the quality track leads to naming and conscious awareness, while the intensity track has very different properties and is better described in terms of its strength and duration. These modes of experience, body and mind, follow very different logics and need to be described in very different ways.

By 'quality' Massumi is picking out conventional discursive and linguistic framing. The dimension of 'qualification' indexes the normal names for things, the labels people attach to affecting events as they turn experience into talk and narrative. The intensity dimension of affect, in contrast, appears to stand to one side of the usual cultural and discursive hubbub, registered if at all as a push, or as a flavour, as the white noise of physiological arousal, or as the unprocessed chaotic state of bodily happening. Massumi suggests that affect actually happens 'out of mind', beyond the phenomenological, and what is normally understood by experience. It is in this sense, then, that affect is excessive, exceeding what people can know explicitly.

Massumi consigns emotions, the older and more domestic connotation of affects, to what he described as 'the quality track'. Emotions come now to refer to how culture, discourse, consciousness, human subjectivity organise any body states that have been registered. Emotion has the 'tawdry status of the private' (2002, p. 219). Affect is more general, more obscure, less known, more interesting while emotions and feelings are personal and individual and have been extensively studied and colonised. Emotions come to indicate the moment of capture of bodily potential by the personal psychological.

Massumi uses the distinction between the quality track and the intensity track to sharply bifurcate discourse and the body. Affect, he argues, is entirely autonomous. Bodies do their own thing. Language is, actually, almost beside the point now. 'Language, though head-strong, is not simply in opposition to intensity. It would seem to function differentially in relation to it' (1996, p. 219). Indeed:

> Intensity is ... a nonconscious, never-to-be conscious autonomic reminder. It is outside expectation and adaptation, as disconnected from meaningful sequencing, from narration, as it is from vital function. It is narratively delocalized, spreading over the generalized body surface, like a lateral backwash from the function-meaning interloops travelling the vertical path from the head and the heart. (1996, p. 219)

In a similar vein, Thrift and those engaged in non-representational theory (NRT) argue that affect can be contrasted with 'representation'. Affect refers to human engagement with the world through 'the roiling mass of nerve volleys' (Thrift, 2008a, p. 7). Representation is a less lively, immediate and more reflective business:

> Ontologically, [non-representational theory] draws attention to the ways in which the world is emergent from a range of spatial processes whose power is not dependent upon their crossing a threshold of contemplative cognition. At the same time, non-representational theory challenges the epistemological priority of representations as the grounds of sense-making or as the means by which to recover information from the world ... (McCormack, 2003, p. 488)

Affect as social and as virtual potential

Affect, in Massumi's account and in NRT, may occur beyond consciousness but this does not mean that it is asocial. Massumi (2005) and Clough (2008a, 2009) suggest that new political formations and forms of governance increasingly mobilise affect, manipulating and constructing the kinds of 'affective backgrounds' people inhabit, colonising our preconscious visceral reactions. In a memorable phrase, Thrift (2004) argues that affect is 'engineered', laid down in social formations like the pipes and cables running through a city. As an example, Massumi (2005) analyses the colour-coded terror alert system introduced by Homeland Security in the USA after the terrorist attacks of 9/11. He suggests that colours in the spectrum from green (low danger) through to red (severe danger) become a kind of perceptual shorthand by which American citizens were stitched into a new affective background and neo-liberal securitisation agenda beyond everyday conscious awareness. Similarly, William Connolly (2002) argues that social and political life work on us like a film works on its audience. This engagement is not particularly cognitive, conscious or rationally considered. Rather, both films and politics engage through roller-coasters of affect: identification, investment, disgust, cynicism and immersion.

Massumi and Clough's understanding of affect both radically narrows it down to exclude conscious awareness and massively expands its domain at the same time, marking out affect as all the ways in which bodies respond to the world and to other bodies. So far, I have embedded my account of Massumi's affect in familiar human terms, within human bodies, and within subject–object ontology. However, as Anderson (2006, p. 736) points out, Massumi's affect is pre-individual and pre-personal in all senses. Bodies affecting bodies comes to include all of social and material life. For these scholars of affect, 'body' is generalised away beyond the animate obvious. A body can be a rock, a capitalist exchange relation, a cat, a philosophy, a psychotherapy group, a social movement – any whole, that is, which is composed of parts where those parts are related together in ways that can be characterised in terms of their motion, speed and rest (Baugh, 2005, p. 30; Colebrook, 2006). The subject–object distinction is irrelevant, therefore, in the analysis of affected bodies, as is any distinction between inside consciousness and outside. Affect is a post-personal force exceeding the human.

Affect is even more interesting yet. Massumi, again following Deleuze, associates it with potential, becoming and incipience. As Clough (2009, p. 43) explains, Deleuze's project returns us to delirium, chance and indifference, involving us in a temporality that is always starting up again in the midst and in relations based not in identification and recognition but in encounter with newness. If the quality track is mundanely predictable, tawdry, and stifling, then affect and its intensity keep a space open for life to erupt. Affect, unlike emotion or feeling, is something that has not yet been closed down, represented, labelled, communicated, shaped and structured. Affect is 'virtual', untamed and inassimilable, always in the process of becoming, and the leading edge of the wave of any engagement with the world before human minds get to it. Affect is virtual because it sets up and holds as possibility multiple connections and ways of being. These possibilities collapse, however, when discourse, culture, cognition and consciousness come on the scene and develop a story line. Even if affective possibilities trigger multiple story lines, affect understood as potential has faded and disappeared. The moment selection occurs, potential and the indeterminate turn into the actual and the determinate.

Massumi derives from his reading of Bergson an analysis of consciousness, discourse and cognition as selective, inhibiting multiplicity, 'black boxing' an enormous field of potential for the sake of a structured line of interpretation and action. This kind of reading of affect sustains and echoes analogies with quantum physics and decision moments of emergence, when possibilities devolve into finite and measurable realities (see Clough et al., 2007, for an example of analogies with theoretical physics, and Barad, 2007). This again is in line with the generalising of the reference of 'bodies', from human bodies to non-human bodies, to things, to potential physical and biological fields – all are inhabited by the virtual and have affective power.

What started out, then, as a relatively specific point about bodies, brains and minds stimulated by news of the mysterious half-second discovered by scientists has metamorphosed into an entire, programmatic world-view. This is powerful and exciting in the way of these things – the sense of coming close to the heart of a mystery, of veils stripped away, of connections racing in all directions. Affect, which started out as a psychological and social scientific puzzle, is now generalised into an account of becoming and emergence. It began as a term closely connected to emotions, passions and feelings, now it has become 'the perception of one's vitality, one's sense of aliveness, of changeability (often signalled as "freedom")' (Massumi, 1996, p. 229), a phenomena that Patricia Ticineto Clough (2000) describes as 'autoaffection'. It has moved from being what happens in the missing half-second to functioning rather like a generative version of the unknowable Lacanian real – the murmurings, Stephen Frosh (2008) describes, from the deep elementals beyond frail human attempts at making sense.

Some problems

When reading this work, I am often reminded of the narrator of A.S. Byatt's (2001) novel *The Biographer's Tale* – Phineas G. Nanson. This hero decided to chuck in his graduate studies in postmodern literary theory. He concludes he has been studying 'a lot of not-too-long texts written by women' (p. 1), and he is desperate instead for a world of *things* and *bodies*. He launches into writing a biography as a remedy. Predictably, he soon re-discovers that no classification scheme for any facts of life seems to hold. Personality remains enigmatic, and things mutate once more into hybrids and composites.

Cultural studies scholars such as Massumi and Thrift know these limits of classification only too well (and have been central in establishing them). But like Phineas they seem to wish to establish a new footing in something intriguingly forceful that has a refreshing physical power and intransigence. The study of affect seems to evoke (even if it will struggle to describe) a rich embodied life beyond the paper mines in which academics usually labour. As Lacan notes in the extract introducing this chapter, affect has become 'a special density which escapes an intellectual accounting'.

But in separating affect so sternly from consciousness and representation, Massumi and Thrift seem to have forgotten the composite and hybrid nature of social life they insist on in other contexts. Massumi (2002, p. 4) states that he is not a naïve realist but he seems to hanker after a grounding that cannot be argued with. Indeed, it is almost impossible to argue with him because affect in his account (the virtual) disappears as it is formulated. Even those, like Lili Hsieh, who want to celebrate the new lines of thinking about affect, worry 'lest affect becomes another God-like savior of post-modern apocalyptic politics' (2008, p. 230). Affect, she argues, over-universalises and risks ignoring the particularity of scenes and relations that have been so central to feminist analyses of the movements of power. As Deborah Thien (2005) points out, there is a hint of misogyny in this work. Affect seems to be appealing because it appears so 'masculine', contrasted with feminised investigations of domesticated emotion, and with the 'nice and cuddly'. Affect, in contrast, can be 'downright scary' (Thrift, 2004, p. 58). As Hemmings (2005) and Thien (2005) have noted, the turn to affect regularly claims to have moved beyond feminist post-structucturalist thinking without engaging with the particulars of that research in even the most perfunctory way (see Castree and Macmillan, 2004, and Tolia-Kelly, 2006, for other critiques).

There are some more particular issues. First, I think Massumi and Thrift take the wrong message from psychology and neuroscience. The rhetoric only works because Massumi elides a set of philosophical claims about the virtual and becoming with more prosaic claims from psychology and neuroscience which in fact understand affect in a very different way (see Papoulias and Callard, 2010, for a similar argument). Affect in cultural studies is in danger of being based on a (mis)take or mis-appropriation. I want to now explore this further.

My argument is not that Massumi and Thrift have fallen into errors that need to be corrected by a good dose of the real facts from mainstream psychology. My aim is to show that the kind of psychology they draw upon is not the only available psychological story. It is not even the dominant current story (although Massumi and Thrift present it as such), and, crucially, some of the other accounts available in psychology based on other kinds of metaphors and analogies lead in more useful directions. To do this task properly would require generating various histories of psychology and placing the different accounts within these. This is not the place to do this, however. I simply want to say that I don't buy the 'mashup' Massumi and Thrift offer and want to indicate what else could be argued.

Back to psychobiology

Massumi and his colleagues make three claims:

- Affect is non-conscious.
- The chronological sequence moves from body responses and then, second and later, to consciousness and cognition in a 'reflux back' to consciousness (e.g. Clough, 2007, p. 2). Body/brain responses precede consciousness (cognition and awareness) and thus can be neatly separated from them.
- Body/brain responses are thus beyond representation and cultural sense-making and are hence autonomous.

Everything else is more or less premised on this. But, as Chapter 2 demonstrated, most contemporary psychobiology takes a very different line. Current psychologists and neuroscientists maintain instead that:

- Affect has conscious and non-conscious, bodily and cognitive, elements linked in highly complex ways.
- Body/brain activity and a very simple initial form of affect may precede conscious awareness and cognition as a rapid physiological response to an external

stimulus (LeDoux, 1996) but this is highly specific and limited. Typically, affective responses are triggered by conscious cognitions (e.g. memories and perceptions) and non-conscious subjective appraisals. Usually, cognition and brain/body activity are seamlessly intertwined.

- Even the more automatic and non-conscious elements of affect involve representations of incoming information and are responses to its meaning and significance for the organism.

The picture that psychology and neuroscience typically now paints of affect is of a highly dynamic, interacting *composite* or *assemblage* of autonomic bodily responses (e.g. sweating, trembling, blushing), other body actions (approaching or avoiding), subjective feelings and other *qualia*, cognitive processing (e.g. perception, attention, memory, decision-making), the firing and projecting of neural circuits (e.g. from the thalamus to the cortex and the amygdala), verbal reports (from exclamations to narratives) and communicative signals such as facial expressions. An emotional episode, such as a burst of affect like rage or grief, integrates and brings together all of these things in the same general moment.

Klaus Scherer's definition of an emotion cited in the previous chapter summed this up:

> an episode of massive synchronous recruitment of mental and somatic resources to adapt to, or cope with, a stimulus event that is subjectively appraised as being highly pertinent to the needs, goals and values of the individual. (2005, p. 314)

The terms 'synchronous' and 'recruitment' are carefully chosen. As I showed in Chapter 2, researchers like Scherer conclude that a burst of affect requires a flowing, recursive, dynamically integrated pattern to be mobilised. This conflicts with Massumi's second assumption above in particular. Brain/body responses are autonomous only in the most limited senses and for all intents and purposes cannot be meaningfully separated from the rest of the assemblage that includes cultural, cognitive and conscious elements. As Oatley et al. (2006, p. 121) note too, many key ANS bodily responses (such as a blush) typically seem to arrive 15–30 seconds after the stimulus setting-off part of the affective response has been perceived. This is too slow to support any claim that the world impinges first on the body.

Automaticity and the non-conscious

Affective mobilisation is probably best seen as more encompassing than Massumi and colleagues suggest, but even if we see it as involving both somatic and mental resources, quality and intensity woven together, is there still ground for arguing that affect is mostly non-representational, operating 'below' conscious cognition? Like the mysterious half-second, there are certainly ample indications of the non-conscious basis of affect. The question is, what can be concluded?

These days, psychologists and neuroscientists like to put brakes on human grandiosity and stress the limits of consciousness and awareness (see Bargh, 2007a; Barrett et al., 2005; Hassin et al., 2005). The constraints on affective meaning-making are often phrased in terms of capacity using a computing metaphor:

> ... our senses can handle about 11 million bits per second ... This whopping number is largely the result of our sophisticated visual system, which can handle about 10 million bits per second. The processing capacity of consciousness pales in comparison. The exact number of bits consciousness can process depends on the task. When we read silently, we process about a maximum of 45 bits per second (a few words); when we read aloud, it drops to 30. When we calculate (e.g., when we multiply two numbers), we can handle only 12 bits per second. Compared to our total capacity, these numbers are incredibly small. If we conclude that our consciousness can process 50 bits per second ... our total capacity is 200,000 times as high as the capacity of consciousness. In other words consciousness can only deal with a very small percentage of all incoming information. (Dijksterhuis et al., 2005, p. 82)

This view suggests that much of the machinery of human life, including the functioning of affective processes, will be inaccessible. What are the implications, though? The 'unconscious', here, is the enabling infrastructure. Is the comparatively limited 'processing power' of consciousness so startling or troubling, if we can reliably access the end results of all the inaccessible processing most of the time? Can we even put these two language games, or two conceptual languages, of brain processes and mentalistic description together sensibly (Coulter and Sharrock, 2007)?

Research on automaticity builds on studies like the investigation of the missing half-second that fascinated Massumi. As noted, this study is interpreted as suggesting that much of the preparation for a social action is not necessarily initiated by a conscious intention but can begin and take shape non-consciously. More precisely, Kornhuber and his colleagues demonstrated with their EEG recordings of brain activity that if you instruct someone to flex their finger whenever they wish to during a defined period, the brain starts preparing for each voluntary finger-flexing about 800 milliseconds before the action actually occurs. Although the brain may begin responding 800 ms before the action, the main neural correlates involved in flexing one's finger such as the onset of muscle action potentials in the motor cortex appear only around 50–200 ms before the finger flexing itself (Kornhuber and Deecke, 1965; Libet et al., 1983).

In other words, there seems to be a gap of around 600 ms in which the brain is active, and during which the action is being prepared, but the action does not yet seem to have been 'willed' or initiated. Who knows, in fact, what the brain is doing during those 600 milliseconds? As Chapter 2 noted, contemporary research suggests that the brain appears to be constantly engaged in beginning to prepare likely motor sequences relevant to the emerging context. Some of these decay quickly as their relevance recedes, while others become more strongly activated and reinforced. As Coulter and Sharrock (2007) argue, there is a mass of conceptual and linguistic confusion around the interpretation of this study and immense difficulties in translating electrical activity patterns in the brain and re-reading them in the language of 'willing', 'consciousness' and 'intention'. The point to take, I think, is that action is complexly shaped and put together, and any simple Cartesian description such as 'I decided to do this, and then I made my body do it' is misleading. Thrift and his colleagues in NRT are right in this respect to be suspicious of classic representationalist assumptions but this doesn't mean that any useful line can be drawn between the 'representational' and the 'non-representational'.

Many social psychological studies in this area use a technique called priming. In a typical investigation people are exposed to a stimulus in such a way that it is registered but it is not possible to consciously perceive it. Zajonc's (1968) 'mere exposure' studies, for instance, showed participants pictures of polygons subliminally for the duration of one millisecond. This is too quick for people to be aware of exactly what they had seen. Subsequently, people were shown polygons at speeds where they could consciously process them. They were unable to say which ones they had seen already, but they showed a strong familiarity affect and preference for the ones that had been subliminally presented.

Huge numbers of these kinds of studies have been conducted in all kinds of domains. Commonly, researchers take some element of a package of cultural knowledge (described in these studies as a schema, representation, stereotype, etc.), prime participants with it in ways that don't reach conscious awareness, and then show that other related aspects of the cultural package influence what people either do next, or their subsequent judgements and evaluations. Bargh et al. (1996, cited in Dijksterhuis et al., 2007, p. 55) showed in an often-quoted study conducted in the USA, for example, that participants who had been primed with words relating to the social category 'elderly' (such as 'grey', 'walking stick', 'bingo', 'Florida') took significantly longer to walk to the lift once the experiment had apparently concluded than participants who had not been primed. Their activity, practice and sense of self had been apparently automatically re-organised without their awareness.

It is not my intention to review all this literature, or develop a critical view on it; I want to pick out two further examples of studies explicitly concerned with affect and close relationships and move on to discuss the broad implications of this line of investigation for Massumi and Thrift's approach. The two studies of interest are included in a review by Chen et al. (2007), and they demonstrate something that looks like it might be an automatic affective response. Baldwin et al. (1990) set up an experiment with groups of Roman Catholic women as participants. They were given a short passage to read describing a sexually permissive scene. Some were then subliminally primed with images of Pope John Paul II with a disapproving expression. Although not consciously aware of the disapproving Pope, the primed women reported higher levels of anxiety and tension than the women who had not been primed.

The second study (Baldwin et al., 1993) worked with participants who had 'secure attachment working models' and participants with 'insecure working models'. Secure versus insecure attachment models are assumed to derive from early childhood relationships and concern the kind of expectations people form about how they will be treated by people who are important to them. Crudely speaking, people with secure attachment histories will expect positive responses, while insecure attachment histories will lead to negative expectations. As predicted, when primed with an incomplete relationship context statement such as 'If I depend on my partner, then my partner will ...', the secure responded more quickly to positive outcome words such as 'support' while the insecure responded more quickly to negative words such as 'leave'. In other words, a particular kind of unconscious affective meaning-making seemed to be operating automatically to colour responses and perceptions.

The implications for affect as excess

What are the implications for non-representational theory and Massumi's claim for the autonomy of affect? As John Bargh points out, any strongly polarised distinction between controlled versus automatic processes, or conscious versus non-conscious, is probably too simplistic. Important social action is a mix of both. He argues:

> the features that have been traditionally associated with a conscious or controlled process – awareness, intentionality, controllability, limited capacity – do not always or even usually hang together in an all-or-none fashion, and neither do the features normally attributed to an automatic process (lack of awareness, unintentional, uncontrollable, and efficiency). Rather, the complex, higher mental processes of most interest to social psychologists are usually mixtures or combinations of these features ... (2007b, p. 2)

In a similar vein, Clore et al. (2005) point out that although most brain activity organising social action and subjectivity is non-conscious, it seems that it is always possible, when the situation demands, to pay sustained attention (cf. also Damasio, 1999). Paying attention strongly amplifies the patterns of activation, and is correlated with the experience of consciousness. It is likely then that much of what goes on non-consciously, and the kind of phenomena revealed by priming experiments, can be made conscious given enough time, information and context. In addition, it seems likely too that much of what occurs non-consciously is perhaps simply too weak, habitual and/or unimportant to mobilise the resources for more complex processing in the particular moment.

It seems to me that priming experiments can be read as parables highlighting the ways in which people swim in cultural and discursive milieus like fish in water. We are full of cultural and discursive practice – our brains/subjectivities are bathed in it – tweak one part and some of the rest is bound to follow, just as touching on one part of relational and personal histories will set off a wider cascade of habitual affective patterns. As Chapters 5 and 6 will go on to demonstrate, we seem to possess plural affective forms of 'habitus', ready to go, but also open to creative change. Habitus has automatic features, but all too clearly we are not affect automatons. Discursive practice and the kind of relational inter-subjective flows I will be highlighting in later chapters are both implicit and explicit, and the affective–discursive is both subjective and objective – in our heads and in our talk and texts. Affect, that is, comes ready wrapped.

Overall, then, I am sceptical of claims for the non-representational and the autonomy of affect. These do not rest on secure foundations. Indeed, we could define 'representation' broadly, perhaps with the similar breadth that Paul Stenner (2008) detects in Whitehead's philosophy of subjectivity. If we take representation (or subjectivity) as sense-making, appraisal, perception, action, grasping, concern, evaluation, or as organised recognition and transformation of inputs into useful information then, clearly, animal bodies and brains have to engage in representation at every single living moment. Interestingly, Damasio, whose work was considered in the last chapter, argues that representation is the main purpose and function of affect: 'affective representations map the relationship between current or future body states and past or baseline states with respect to how such changes in body state relate to the organism's survival and well-being' (Adolphs and Damasio, 2001, p. 28). As Steven Rose (2005, pp. 24–5) describes, even single-celled creatures such as amoeba engage in 'representation', converting sense data into planned movement, and can organise themselves in this way to approach and avoid. In Damasio's (2004) sense, then, they also are 'emotional'. In some ways you could argue that 'representation' or 'subjectivity' understood as practical organising activity looks almost the better candidate than Massumi's 'affect' to ground life itself if you wish to mobilise 'life' in that way. I'll come back to this question of the 'subject of affect' in Chapter 6.

To be sure, some in the affect as excess tradition and advocates of NRT have appreciated the potential problems. Cultural geographer Ben Anderson (2006), for example, tries to stitch back together what Massumi divides. He proposes a three-layered cake. There is affect itself in Massumi's sense, pre-personal, autonomous and unknowable. Then there is raw 'feeling' which for Anderson seems to include autonomic bodily responses registering that something affecting has happened such as the heat of a blush, the tension of an angry body, and so on. Finally, there is 'emotion' which consists of organised feelings, or feelings made cognitive and turned into narratives. These Anderson describes as personal and 'intelligent'. Anderson doesn't assume a linear order here or a causal direction. Rather, these 'three modalities slide into and out of one another to disrupt the neat analytic distinction. Diverse feedforward and feedback loops take place ...' (p. 737). Although Anderson's extra layer and greater clarity on feedback helps make more sense of Massumi, the psychology he offers still doesn't do enough or provide the kind of complexity required.

As Stephen Pile (2010) points out, it leaves the cultural geography of affect stuck with rigid borders within a layered body/mind with no credible way affects can impinge on raw feelings and no clear path by which emotions in the third layer can feed backwards or forwards into the first layer. We are also left with a major insolvable methodological conundrum. How to study the movements, what bodies do, and affect in itself, and how to describe what is found to the subsequent readers of the research? If the interest is in events below the threshold of representation then language is truly at its limits. As Laurier and Philo (2006) note, field work reaches an impasse when it formulates its object as unspeakable. Or, in Bondi et al.'s terms: 'How can we represent that which lies beyond the scope of representation?' (2005, p. 11). Pile makes the same point:

> affects matter – but they cannot be grasped, made known, or represented. This would appear to leave affectual geography with a problem: its archetypal 'object of study' – affect – cannot, by its own account, be shown or understood. (2010, p. 9)

Overall, I doubt the pragmatic value of violently severing parts of the assemblages recruited in bursts of affect and using a verbal scalpel to extract just the body/brain responses. It is a mistake to try to remove pre-conscious visceral perception from its usual and habitual world/brain/body/mind contexts, and to artificially freeze and isolate affect as a separate element from the dynamically integrated sequences in which these things normally operate. No easy distinction can be made between visceral and cultural meaning-making, and why should we make one – where is the advantage? I worry that contemporary readings of Spinoza's two tracks – affect (brain/body) on one track defined through intensity separated from cognition, conscious awareness and the mind on another track – have been proved misleading as social scientists continue to try to square body and mind as separate manifestations of a mysterious *Nature/Naturans*.

William Reddy's Account of the Affective-Discursive

In the last half of this chapter I want to turn to a much more grounded attempt to think about the relationship between affect and discourse. Unusually among recent social research on affect, historian William Reddy's (2001, 2009) analysis is based on systematic and respectful readings of cognitive psychological and neuro-science research. His main interest is finding a way to investigate and understand the standards and norms for emotional life applied in different historical periods. How is it that social actors are agents and yet their practical consciousness and deep feeling are pervasively socially structured? The answer lies, he suggests, in the kind of relationship that exists between affect and meaning-making.

Emotives and emotional regimes

Reddy argues that emotional expression is organised through what he calls 'emotives'. Emotives are the regulatory glue for the 'emotional regimes' that can be found in different societies and historical periods (2001, pp. 128–9). You could say that they form the kind of 'hinge' between the psychological and the social emphasised by psychosocial researchers (e.g. Hollway, 2010). Emotives connect the hazy world of subjective experience with equally indeterminate, collective social life through the semiotics of language, gesture and expression. In this way, to use my terminology, emotives figure and materialise both psychological and public life, ordering them into recognisable and efficacious shapes.

Reddy defines emotives as first-person speech acts. These can be in the present tense ('I feel angry'), or constructed around a short-term past tense ('I loved you'), or the long-term past tense ('I have always loved you'). Utterances making claims about others in the second person ('you seem angry'), or in the third person ('she must love him'), are not strictly emotives in this view, but can have some of the same effects. Drawing in part on Austin's speech act theory, Reddy claims that an emotive has both performative and constative features. An emotive is constative in the sense that it has the appearance of a description. ('I feel angry' appears to describe and summarise my subjective state.) Emotives are also performative. What this means is that an emotive is an utterance that performs an act and changes the world.

There are several ways in which emotives are performative. First, they have what Reddy describes as self-exploring and self-altering effects. An utterance like 'I feel angry' can be a moment of crystallisation. A range of confused, often fugitive, mental flowerings become formulated and labelled. This process of description changes the state being described in subtle or very obvious ways. It reflexively acts back and reconstitutes the experience as a certain kind. The moment of description in mental life alters what it describes. Someone could end up, for instance, rejecting their own initial self-description ('No, I'm not angry, I'm sad'), but this process of resistance to one's own self-description has already moved the moment on and refigured the hinterland of subjectivity. Alternatively, a person in an emotional state could find that his or her acceptance of the description intensifies a direction or trajectory in the gathering, swirling activated subjective material, or makes possible a diminution and a new direction.

Clearly, utterances that describe other people's emotional states ('you seem to be angry') can have similar performative effects as the person addressed ponders this description and responds to it. Reddy argues that emotives can often have a 'relational intent' also. This is similar to some of the features of emotion discourse noticed by discursive psychologists (e.g. Edwards, 1997, 1999, 2005). A statement like 'I am angry' directed to a particular interlocutor (a child) in a particular situation might have a very different relational aim (and thus have a very different performative force) from the same statement to a call centre worker who is trying to sell you something at an inconvenient moment. The examples I have used so far have all been discursive ones, instances of different kinds of utterances. Reddy focuses mainly on discourse but suggests, too, that an emotive could engage different kinds of semiosis. An emotive could be non-verbal, as in a ritual gesture, or an accepted mannerism for communicating affect. As the body performs this gesture (and regardless of whether the mind pays any conscious attention to the act) a similar process of performatively refiguring affective experience could occur.

Emotives, Reddy maintains, stitch people into the affective practices characteristic of the social formations they inhabit. A strict emotional regime may allow only a curtailed range of emotives. Through training and discipline the emotives that are hegemonic for the period or social group come to organise and specify the habitual directions of self-exploring and self-altering as well as the habitual play of relational intents. The performative effects of emotives and their capacity to arc back and reconstitute subjective experience can be automatic and relatively practised. People may not even be aware of how a particular description has altered their affective flow. At other times they may work hard to make the best use of these reflexive effects, using the power of emotives to deliberately and self-consciously modulate what happens next emotionally.

Reddy, however, is reluctant to assign too much power to emotives. He suggests that emotives only loosely tie the psychological into the social. Psychological affective life and public collective affective life remain distinct realms with their own qualities and forms of haziness. To explain this, I need to dwell a little more on the account he derives from cognitive psychology.

Navigating emotion and emotional suffering

[T]ranslation is something that goes on, not just between languages and between individuals, but among sensory modalities, procedural habits, and linguistic structures. This idea points not to a reconstitution of a Cartesian type of subjectivity, but toward a conception of the individual as a site where messages arrive in many different languages or codes, and where some of the messages are successfully translated into other codes, while others are not. (Reddy, 2001, p. 80)

Reddy argues that what he calls 'awake human bodies' (2001, p. 110) are engaged in processing multiple streams of information and are translating across many modalities and codes. Only some of this material is consciously attended to and is worked up to become 'activated thought material'. The self is thus disaggregated in his view. Parts of the information flow are closely attended and worked upon, other coded messages are in the process of translation, and some remain in translations that are not activated at the level of attention (or not yet). Among this patterning, as I argued in the previous chapter, some emotions might become very regular and habitual, resembling, in a phrase Reddy takes from cognitive psychologists Alice Isen and Gregory Diamond (1989, p. 144), 'over-learned cognitive habits'. But even in these cases, Reddy argues, the subjective psychological material is always richer and more complex than any emotive can grasp.

In fact, in his view, every cultural emotive will have only a limited truth-value. It is a translation into discourse and gesture of a hugely complex mass of activated, attended and non-attended, psychological material that is itself a translation of various sensory and physical modalities. This mass is continually flowing on, changing, reforming and reshaping, not least as a consequence of the attempt to grasp it in apparently suitable and available emotives. Reddy argues, however, that the affective flow is anchored by the close relationship between emotions and goals. Following a classic psychological argument, Reddy sees emotional reactions as deeply informative about where individuals are with their current projects. The experience of emotion registers blocks, successes, losses and threats.

This indeterminancy of emotives along with the tight links between human goals and emotions has important consequences. First, it means that, for Reddy, people are best described as 'navigating' their emotions, rather than, say, 'managing' them. Reddy's theory suggests that at times emotional paths will be easy to follow. There will be close harmony between what is becoming activated, the individual's goals, and the emotives available for description. There is little tension when the emotives act back to figure and refigure the affective flow. At other times, the fit between activated thought material, emotives and goals raises what I would like to call 'emotional blisters'. Reddy's scheme allows for experiential gaps and a possible lack of mesh between the individual and the emotional regime. No one emotive can ever entirely and accurately reproduce people's actual affective states. People could perhaps live with this gap between affect and representation. But, because emotions (as over-learned cognitive habits) are closely linked to the individual's goals, there is the worse possibility that emotional regimes may cause what Reddy calls 'emotional suffering'.

In other words, there may be intense conflict between the individual's goals and the favoured emotives. When the discordances are too great, what Reddy calls 'emotional refuges' might arise in a society as people seek out new spaces for expressing parts of their emotional lives at odds with current emotional regimes. Reddy is rather vague about this goal conflict, however. Does conflict arise because an individual belongs to multiple emotional communities and so has multiple, potentially contrasting emotives to hand for each goal? Or, are goals just individual, personal and pre-social? Are they always present, pre-organising the process of activation, and the translations that produce sustained attention? Do goals not have a performative language of their own? Whatever the case, Reddy argues that the possibility of emotional suffering suggests a non-relativist morality and politics.

Less conflict and suffering, and greater emotional liberty, are universal desirables, in his view. This criterion can be applied to evaluate the success of the emotional regimes found in different cultures, historical periods and within complex contemporary societies. Does an emotional regime create large amounts of emotional suffering, little, or none? Reddy argues that he reaches with these moves a kind of realist standpoint that he sees as advantageous. This is a kind of pragmatic realism (following Alcoff's, 1996, immanent realism). I would describe this as a claim that 'actual emotions will out' rather like the 'truth will out' move made by many scientists in their everyday practice to preserve realism and naturalism (Potter, 1996). Emotional regimes that consistently block an individual's goals, or consistently fail to produce emotives that capture enough of the complex patterning of individuals' psychological lives, will fail, Reddy argues. Those that are more in tune with more of the psychological hinterland will be experienced as having a greater truth-value.

Truth, falsity and the variable moralities of emotion

There are a number of problems here. For a start, as Barbara Rosenwein (2006) notes, Reddy's solution to relativism is hard to sustain. Suffering is not evaluated in the same ways among every social grouping. From a liberal North American standpoint, the degree of suffering, or the amount of work an emotional regime requires people to do, constraining and twisting their emotional reactions, might seem a good candidate for a universal standard. But for many people in many places, suffering has been highly valued as an absolute good, while discomfort is a positive sign of moral achievement. Are these people simply mistaken?

Reddy's realism is loose, of course. He is not suggesting that descriptions of affective states will ever be simply 'true' or 'false'. But he thinks that, over the long term, the more concordant meaning-making is with affective reality, the greater its value and effectiveness. I wonder, though, whether any taxonomy of meaning-making regimes as 'closer' or 'further away' from emotional 'realities' is viable in practice. Would those inside and outside the emotional regime ever agree? It seems more interesting, and important to explore when, in what social contexts, and for what purposes, gaps between affective experience and hegemonic cultural narratives become formulated by people in their daily activities. When do 'gaps' become a troubling issue for participants as opposed to analysts?

This might be highly variable even across groups inhabiting the same emotional regimes and affective contexts constructed by those regimes. What psy-technologies and technologies of the self (Rose, 1998) turn the perceived success or failure of language to signify affect into a topic, or into a main mode of self-surveillance? I want to replace attempts to decipher what is real and most valuable with practical questions about what people get up to, and how they create value in different circumstances.

Emotives or discursive practices?

My second concern with Reddy's approach is that his specifications about how emotives operate are far too sparse. Everyday discursive practice does not look like this, and a more elaborated social psychology of discursive practice is required.

For many periods of history, such as the early Middle Ages investigated by Barbara Rosenwein (2006), written records are scarce and mostly formal. Only fragmentary traces remain of the informal meaning-making of the 'emotional communities' of the period. In these circumstances, the concept of emotives alone perhaps could provide a sufficient summary of discursive pattern and practice for empirical investigations. But, even in this context, a more elaborate account of discursive practices might be useful. Reddy's formulation neglects the work available in discourse studies, social psychology and sociolinguistics which suggests the complexity of discursive action, the multiple forms of loose practical order it displays, and which provides increasingly worked over concepts for discussing meaning-making patterns, including affective meaning-making (see Coupland and Jaworski, 2008; Potter, 2007; Van Dijk, 2007; Wetherell et al., 2001a, 2001b).

Take a look, for example, at these affective–discursive exchanges taken pretty randomly from the Internet comment boards set up by the *Guardian* newspaper in the UK:

> If any MP had balls, they'd have paid for things out of their own pocket like y'know ... ordinary people.

> Oh wait, I forget, they're not 'ordinary people' are they 'cause ordinary people have things like morals and conscience. (Comment PaoloMaldini, *The Guardian*, 16/3/10)

> Paolo – To use Nicholas Winterton's words, they are a 'totally different type of people. It would do us proles well to remember that.' (Comment Mooneym, *The Guardian*, 16/3/10)

> The worst crime perpetrated by these ghastly people is this. For the price of a couple of rolls of wallpaper (Doc Fox), the cost of having Wisteria removed from a chimney (Mr Cameron) or renovating a swimming pool boiler (my own MP, Michael Ancram) they have stolen my right to vote.

> For the first time since I was old enough, I no longer feel that I can or should vote for some creature out to line their pockets at my expense.

> Thus democracy ends.

> Not with walls covered in the blood of slain martyrs, but walls covered in wall paper paste. (Comment Peerlesspundit, *The Guardian*, 16/03/10)

These postings are a nice reminder of the flavour of ordinary affective meaning-making in one of its discursive/public forms. Readers were exchanging views on a story about a UK MP (and now former Cabinet Minister), Dr Liam Fox, and his battle not to pay back £22,000 of expenses that he had claimed inappropriately. The comments could be described as an example of an affective practice of 'righteous indignation'. PaoloMaldini, Mooneym and Peerlesspundit display such delight in being sarcastic. UK readers will recall the flavour of the zeitgeist surrounding the MPs' expenses scandals. The contempt and blame were pantomime-like and extreme, the fantasies were punishing, and politicians could not atone enough. As Lauren Berlant (2005) notes, 'the post-mortem is the revenge genre of the commentary class'.

Looking at just this example of affective–discursive meaning-making alone, it is clear that people do not perform affect, and attend to others' affect, through first- and second-person speech acts ('I am angry'; 'you are angry'). It is an open question, in fact, how these kinds of first-, second- and third-person affective speech acts might feature in different sites of everyday discourse. They may be quite rare and most common in quite specialised social situations (such as child-rearing, psychotherapy clinics or courtrooms). PaoloMaldini, Mooneym and Peerlesspundit accomplish affective accounts mainly through formulating evaluative versions of events and other people's words. There is, in fact, minimal description of 'feelings', yet their utterances are certainly 'felt'.

Affect comes to life through the way Peerlesspundit formulates the MPs' actions, the examples chosen and the organisation of the descriptive listing.

Affect is conveyed, equally, through the way in which Mooneym re-contextualises, re-animates and re-voices Nicholas Winterton's words. I predict that affective meaning-making in most everyday domains might make, in fact, little distinction between 'emotives', and what we might call 'cognitives' and 'motives'. That is, speech acts formulating reasons and thoughts ('cognitives'), or action plans and goals ('motives'), will be as important as speech acts formulating emotions ('emotives'). Affective-discursive action is probably most frequently accomplished seamlessly through all three where it is more or less impossible to establish credible analytic distinctions between them. As discursive psychologists have argued for many years, the speech act is not the most useful conceptual unit for investigating actual discursive practice (Potter and Wetherell, 1987). Just as affective neuroscience is dismantling distinctions between affect and cognition, those studying affective meaning-making will perhaps need to do the same.

From individualism to affective-discursive social action

Finally, although offering a more sophisticated analysis of affective meaning-making than found in many conventional representationalist psychological models, Reddy's account shares aspects of their individualism. In his work and in psychobiology, one can find fascinating analyses of the multiple brain/body/mind translations, relays and processing that produce embodied affective responses. Yet, this dynamic modelling ends when affect goes public or becomes discursive. Complexity is replaced with relatively simple assumptions about expressive and communicative contexts. Multi-layered interaction, turbulence and flow in the head become linear, unidirectional communication outside the head.

As Michael Billig (1999a, p. 45) points out, conventional psychology (and Reddy's work has this flavour also) assumes that the human actor best resembles Rodin's sculpture of *Le Penseur* (The Thinker). Billig's analogy is brilliantly revealing. Solitary, naked, sitting on his rock, with his fist to his chin, *Le Penseur* is alone, sorting out his feelings and thoughts in his head. But is this an accurate image of what thought and feeling are like? As Billig points out, thinking and emoting are not a set of hidden processes taking place in an individual's mind emerging in uncontested bulletins like 'I am angry'. Thinking and feeling are, in fact, social acts taking place through the manifold public and communal resources of language.

'Translation', in Reddy's account, is an individual act and Reddy's 'bottom-line', in many respects, remains the autonomous individual's goals, tasks and motives. These determine in his theory what gets activated, and define the shape of any 'gap' between available emotives and emotional experience. Individual subjectivity is, of course, a major site for affective meaning-making. Individual bodies and minds constitute one place where diverse affective flows become organised for sure. But, any account that takes the psychology of the affected individual out of immediate relational contexts will be partial. In the next chapter, I will move on to look at affect as situated activity. As we examine this, we get a very different understanding of affective performance and affective sociality. Emotion arises, is signified, negotiated and evaluated in the inter-subjective moment and that social relation (along with the activity genre, and the expressive medium, as the *Guardian* material demonstrates) carries the affect, and is intimately caught up in the translation process. Affect is pre-eminently a relational and social event, and the 'dialogic' activities involved need to be at the forefront of attempts to understand affective meaning-making.

As Billig (1997a) argues, following Bakhtin (1986), even when we are truly alone, engaged in solitary rumination, others populate our heads, and we are in their company. As we emote, even sitting by ourselves on a rock, we become connected with others, rarely disconnected. The social psychologist John Cromby (2007a) describes the rich analyses theorists such as Vygotsky (1962) provide of how individual minds, and in particular the developing minds of children, become stitched into the communal affective meaning-making fabric. Vygotsky's account demonstrates, for example, how language is constitutive at 'deep' psychological levels as 'outer speech', the parent–child relation, and inter-subjective exchange are moved inside to become 'inner speech'. As Cromby (2007a, p. 107) notes, talk begins in social relations 'before becoming the abbreviated, condensed and unspoken inner speech that accompanies and metacognitively guides our actions.'

Ways Forward on the Affective-Discursive

In this chapter I have focused on two very different approaches – Massumi and Thrift's exuberant accounts of affect as excess and Reddy's impressively worked through social psychology of affective meaning-making. Both are inspiring attempts to tackle the intractable relations between the affective and the discursive and it is easy to snipe in retrospect. I am suggesting, though, that both need a theory of discursive practice. In Reddy's case, and for historical research, the potential gain is very obvious. It would complete his account to elaborate on the dynamic relational flow of language in use and its foundations in social interaction. It would clarify the patterning and operation of the emotional regimes negotiated by past and present emotional actors; it would highlight the plural and variable nature of these regimes and the close relationships with immediate contexts. Accounts of discourse practice would extend Reddy's 'navigating' beyond the last stages of 'translation' and put the agency and non-determinism he wishes to safeguard on a firmer footing. Historians would acquire, too, a way of properly thinking about the 'emotional community' and the relational and dialogic ground of affective meaning-making.

My dispute with Massumi, Thrift and their colleagues, on the other hand, is more fundamental. What is at stake is a fairly substantial disagreement about the nature and definition of affect and the best ways of tuning social research into affect. As I tried to show, this school of thought is interested in the process of 'being affected' in its most general sense. It borrows from the philosophy of Deleuze and Spinoza, who understood affect as movement, and as change as a result of encounter. In Deleuze's philosophy, affect comes to stand for 'life itself' (cf. Seigworth, 2005), understood as becoming, emergence and the plane of immanence. Discussing Spinoza, Deleuze describes, for instance, in an almost biblical manner, how an interest in the capacities of bodies to affect and be affected opens up a whole new canvas. An interest in affect means that 'you will not define a body (or a mind) by its form, nor by its organs or functions, and neither will you define it as a substance or a subject' (1992, p. 626). Deleuze goes on to argue that instead of dwelling on fixity, a focus on affect makes it possible to think about the different modes (or changes, relations of speeds and slownesses) a body might pass through. And, instead of thinking of a human (or an animal) as a subject, we can focus alternatively on the affects of which it is capable.

This is enormously valuable as a new ontological thrust in the social sciences. It dismantles the conventional distinctions between animal and human, object and subject, nature and culture and changes the conversation from about stasis to being about mobility and flow. It is exciting and influences the sense of practice I am trying to develop. But when Massumi or Thrift collapse affect as a philosophy of becoming with the study of affect as embodied, emotional social action, or when the study of becoming comes to stand in for the missing psychological dimensions in social research, it doesn't seem to work. Empirical social research has lost something useful when the study of affect in its conventional senses is conflated with Deleuze's concept of becoming or emergence. Massumi and Thrift's insistence on strictly separating affect 'in principle' from emotions and feelings, and insistence on defining affect as 'not emotion', leaves social research without its familiar, useful, inclusive terminology for emotional life as opposed to other ways of being in the world.

It seems to derail, too, all the research that attempts to think in an integrated way about the specificities of the chaining and assembling of body–brain–narrative–feeling–response–context–history etc. We need to be able to talk about the very particular nature of affective practice and have a word for it. If the standard psychological term 'affect' is co-opted to cover every kind of influence then we are in a definitional morass. As Clare Hemmings (2005) has argued, in contradiction to Deleuze's apparent intentions, Massumi's insistence on the generality and autonomy of affect actually obfuscates body–mind–body chains and movements back and forward in emotional states from physical responses to interpretations with feedback to new physiological arousal, etc. For all these reasons, I prefer to focus on affective practice as my key concept rather than affect as excess.

The problems are intensified when affect is set up in opposition to discourse, and discourse is caricatured. Researchers are left struggling with one hand tied behind their backs. We come to need a further turn back to discourse to replace what has been lost in the turn to affect! Rightly, many of us are interested in developing more dynamic, sensual and lively accounts of social life. Yet we are asked to do this with no concept of discourse, with truncated and quite bizarre accounts of meaning-making processes which both ignore and cherry-pick psychobiology, with overly simple distinctions between representation and non-representation, and so on. The consequences for empirical work on affect are woeful.

Researchers are left trying to investigate the unspeakable. In this context, Laurier and Philo (2006) argue that we need to reconsider what is meant by 'representation'. Representation does too much work in geographical and other cultural studies of affect. As I have tried to show in this chapter, it becomes generalised as a 'bad thing' elided with 'psychological', 'humanistic', 'emotion', 'cognition', 'consciousness', 'language', 'discourse', 'rationality' and 'personal life'. I agree with Laurier and Philo, we need to re-locate representation first as a particular kind of life practice and, then, as a particular kind of discursive practice in relation to other discursive practices. This does not mean a return to naïve humanism and realism or a return to analysing affect through uncritical acceptance of people's subjective descriptions of emotional states. It does involve, though, drawing on the more lively theory and account of discourse in action long available in social psychology and in discourse studies outside post-structuralist theory. This has developed its own more grounded 'non-representational' modes of analysis embedded in notions of practice (e.g. McHoul and Rapley, 2005). Without this sense of discourse as practice, and as a core part of affective assemblages, work on affect as excess remains stuck with nowhere to go except further away from the empirical which theorists seem to prize but seem unable to engage with in any useful way. All of these themes will be carried forward in subsequent chapters but particularly in the next chapter since it expands on the practical, situated and relational basis of affective performance.

FOUR

Situating affect: Interaction, accountability and the present moment

I will call this process a shared feeling voyage. This term keeps the temporal aspect in the forefront and feeling at the center. It is a kind of journey, lasting seconds, taken by two people, roughly together through time and space. During a shared feeling voyage (which is the moment of meeting), two people traverse together a feeling-landscape as it unfolds in real time. Recall that the present moment can be a rich, emotional lived story. During this several-second journey, the participants ride the crest of the present instant as it crosses the span of the present moment, from the horizon of the past to its horizon of the future. As they move, they pass through an emotional narrative landscape with its hills and valleys of vitality affects, along its river of intentionality (which runs throughout), and over its peak of dramatic crisis. It is a voyage taken as the present unfolds. A passing subjective landscape is created and makes up the world in a grain of sand. (Daniel N. Stern, 2004, p. 172)

Lori, who is originally from Georgia but has lived in L.A. for many years, prefers public transportation but must drive here routinely. When "a big new brown truck … decided to cut her off, Lori turns to the truck, 'What do you think you are doing? You know better than that!' She talks to herself and uses hand motions. She looks toward the driver in a sideways glance and then talks facing straight ahead … She does not want to lose her life over a driving dispute." But after she goes through scolding motions "she [can] drop it." (Jack Katz, 1999, p. 19)

In the previous chapter I explored various lines of thought on the relationship between affect and discourse. In this chapter I want to examine how affect takes shape in situated social activity and the patterning this contributes. The flow of affect is located in the body but it is located, too, within the flow of ordinary life. It becomes part of social interaction, caught up in social business. Lori, for instance, in the extract above, is engaged in the familiar process of 'becoming pissed off on the road' (Katz, 1999, p. 20). Her embodied actions – her hand gestures, patterns of eye gaze, exclamations and self-talk – are organised temporally and spatially. This burst of affect becomes an episode with a negotiated beginning and ending, and its own rhythm. As it composes and decomposes, it displays a 'melodic line of continuous variation' (Deleuze cited in Anderson, 2006, p. 735).

This rhythm is in part specific to Lori herself. But, as Katz argues, it is also specific to the phenomenon of road rage. It is intimately bound up with the organisation of cars and roads and their interactional possibilities. We can see, too, that Lori's affect is profoundly relational (Burkitt, 1997). The relationship established with the truck driver remains embryonic and sketchy, but it is intense, and it is there in the turn and counter-turn. Both participants are becoming figured through the duet of offence and reprimand, and the figuring is infused with gender and power. Lori, for instance, abbreviates her rage. She does not look directly at the truck driver. She seems to be scared of what he might do if the dispute were to escalate. We can begin to reflect on how more durable, persistent and complex relational matrices might organise and pattern affective practice.

In this chapter, then, I am interested in the ways in which people chunk and pattern their embodied conduct, singly and together, in the scenes of daily life. I am interested in normative sequences, in the ways in which material objects recruit, and are recruited into, the affective performances, and in the constitution of what Daniel Stern (2004) calls 'the present moment'. The patterns I will be concerned with present huge methodological challenges to social science, but they are ones that at some level are already deeply familiar to lay participants. Because we engage in affective practice all the time, every member of society possesses a wide-ranging, inarticulate, utilitarian knowledge about affective performance: how to enact it, how to categorise it, and how to assign moral and social significance to affective displays. It is the nature of this ordinary, demotic, affective action – which typically proceeds with little meta-commentary, self-awareness or reflexive fuss – which now needs to be grasped. Indeed, it is this that disappears from view when cultural studies scholars or neuroscientists take up affect as topic, and turn it into something 'excessive', or into a phenomenon that can be studied in a brain scan.

The term 'situated activity', which is the thematic hook for this chapter, comes from Erving Goffman. Goffman first noted some of the regular features of everyday affect in the 1950s in his brilliant work on interaction rituals and encounters. He defined a 'situated activity system' as a 'somewhat closed, self-compensating, self-terminating circuit of independent actions' (1961, p. 96). Not all the phenomena I consider in this chapter will fit this description, but a number do. I will be concerned with affective episodes in ongoing flows of affect marked out by participants as notable types of occasion. My interest is in moments of affective action where something distinct and recognisable happens.

Investigating situated affect requires methodological ingenuity, new knowledge technologies and excellent recording devices. There is still so much work to be done to develop these. But I will show that a preliminary reckoning can be given. I will draw on material from a wide range of what have been called the 'ethno-sciences' – conversation analysis, ethnomethodology, phenomenology, discursive psychology, critical psychology and applied linguistic anthropology. These disciplines are beginning to provide rich insights into affective practice. I will add research on the process of psychotherapy (Boston Change Process Study Group, 2003; Stern, 2004). This offers a further perspective on how affective episodes are put together in present moments and their inter-subjective foundations.

In this chapter I will be taking up 'situated' in quite a modest way. My focus will be on building an understanding of affective practice as an immediate thread of mostly ordinary actions in particular contexts. I recognise, though, that 'situated' involves wider resonances (Campos et al., 1999; Wetherell, 1998). An affective display is situated in local social orders to be sure. But it is also located in wider 'institutions of intelligibility', to use political scientist Michael Shapiro's (1992) term. Situated affective activity requires formative background conditions that are social, material and spatial as well as physiological and phenomenological; it demands collectivities who recognise, endorse and pass on the affective practice. The next chapter, then, will take up these themes and the broader ways in which situated affect circulates and solidifies in interpersonal, communal and personal histories.

Throughout this book I have been arguing against perspectives on affect that close down connections between different sites of patterning, and don't allow for intersecting figurations in their theories. Similarly, in this chapter I will be arguing for the strong necessity of developing forms of analysis that can move out beyond the specific affective moment. I will be taking issue with parts of the ethno-sciences, such as conversation analysis, discursive psychology and ethnomethodology, which block these moves.

Normative Episodic Sequences

One of the first things that becomes evident when looking at examples of situated affect is the ways in which affect is patterned in normative episodic sequences. Affective performance can display quite routine shapes. Marjorie Goodwin's (2006) wonderful conversation analytic and applied linguistic anthropological studies of pre- and early-teenage girls' social groups make this particularly clear. Goodwin analysed videotapes of girls' social activities in school playgrounds. The girls were all in 4th to 6th grade elementary school in the USA, and her examples and analyses give a unique perspective on natural, spontaneous affective practice and some of its main features.

Consider the example below. The girls, Marisol and Carla, were part of one, Spanish-speaking, friendship group Goodwin recorded. This episode was videoed while they were playing hopscotch. Goodwin has included a translation from the Spanish and a description of their actions along with a comment on the ongoing activity on the right-hand side of the transcript.

Example one (M. Goodwin, 2006, p. 39)

Marisol:	((jumps and lands on some lines))	**Problematic move**
Carla:	***OUT! OUT!***	**Out!** ((finger point))
	((replays Marisol's move on grid))	
	PISASTE LA DE AQUÍ	**Explanation**
	You stepped on this one	
	((steps on square))	**Demonstration**
	Y LA DE ACÁ	
	and this one.	
	((steps on square))	

Carla is accusing Marisol of having violated the rules and thus having lost her turn at jumping through the hopscotch squares drawn on the ground. Goodwin's investigations found that the *OUT!* cry is the standard way in which this accusation is made. It may not seem so from the bald transcript but there is a lot of affect circulating here. Carla's cry is very loud and can be heard as very aggrieved. Goodwin reports that the normal pitch of the girls' speech is between 250 and 350 Hertz, while in this *OUT! OUT!* cry, Carla's voice leaps and escalates dramatically in pitch, and she massively extends the duration of the cry for very many milliseconds. Goodwin's stills from the videotape show that Carla's utterance is backed up by a contorted facial expression and by dramatic gestures. Still in the crouching position she had assumed to watch Marisol's jumping feet, Carla points vehemently at Marisol with her arm extended out as far as it will go. She then stands up and replays Marisol's moves on the hopscotch grid illustrating what she did wrong. Although Marisol does not say anything, she is swept up in this affect. As Carla's accusing finger points at her, the still from the video shows that Marisol adopts a body stance which is in fact quite hard to describe, somewhere between a cringe, a smile and a shrug. She looks embarrassed, amused and annoyed, engaged in what looks like a local, relational, affective counter-point to a justified accusation that catches one out in an illegitimate act.

Although this is an exceedingly brief episode, many of the typical features of an affective display as part of a situated activity are evident. As Goodwin describes (cf. also C. Goodwin, 2000), Carla's moment of affect involves her whole body and her movements are intimately choreographed and patterned with her words. Her words and her body demonstrate her affective position and stance in the ongoing interaction. She is first a judge, then an accuser, and then the demonstrator of exactly what was wrong. As Marjorie Goodwin states, 'affect is lodged within embodied sequences of action. Moreover, the phenomena that provide organization for both affect and action are distributed through multiple media within a larger field of action' (2006, p. 40).

I'll come back later to the comment about multiple media and what is being assembled here, first I want to emphasise Goodwin's point that this affective display is *normatively organised* as part of socially recognised routines or affective practices. Carla's anger is not a random, irrational outpouring, or the acting out of an automatic biological template, or, in Thrift's (2008a) terms, an act of non-representational becoming. Rather, Goodwin demonstrates that it is a crafted display taking its meaning from the social organisation and patterning of the girls' usual activities. The normative organisation of affective display doesn't minimise the fact that Carla is probably experiencing intense feelings as she shouts *OUT! OUT!* It does, however, locate that intense feeling and the phenomenology within shared social life.

Like Goodwin, Jack Katz (1999) in his eclectic phenomenology of road rage emphasises the normative coherence of the affective practice he studies. He notes how road rage can embody, package and enact a number of other, related, familiar and regular affective practices such as the rhythms and routines of scolding, teaching a lesson, retaliating for a perceived slight, competition for a minor advantage, claims of entitlement and specialness, etc. Again, as Goodwin found, recognisable and crafted normative sequences turn out to be highly important. As we saw with the example of Lori, road rage has a pace to it. It has a chronology, a pattern of unfolding and a loose logic.

Ultimately this sequential organisation measures out, contains and orders the affect that seems so dramatic. Katz describes how many drivers apparently consumed by overwhelming rage seem to settle almost in the blink of an eye back into a neutral, affective passivity as their car turns off the motorway. He notes how the enraged can simultaneously engage in relatively placid conversation with their passengers while gesturing in apparent extreme violence to their fellow motorists. As Katz argues, an affective practice like road rage has at its core what he calls a 'sensual metamorphosis', a series of emotional physical changes. These are embedded in interaction routines and rituals and take shape in relation to them. They are also embedded in people's ongoing personal identity and narrative projects that pre-date and continue after any particular metamorphosis.

Affective Practices Build Small Worlds

The sequence we have just examined comprises a relatively simple affective practice. Goodwin goes on to look at other more extended and complex social practices of girls' friendship groups, such as gossip events, disputes, assessments and even the persistent degradation rituals addressed to a marginal member of one group. The picture she paints is of loosely ordered socio-political life and the 'small worlds' the girls share. Their playground lives are constituted from engrossing, persistent, repetitive but creative forms of collective activity. Affect supplies much of the texture of these practices and renders them highly involving and highly invested. But this affect is not random. Its nature and display are shaped by the girls' broader activities, determined by the unfolding sequences in which it is embedded.

Let me illustrate with a further example of persistent affective positioning taken from Goodwin's work. This is an interaction involving three girls, Angela,

Aretha and Sarah, sitting together talking. Goodwin argues that what unfolds is characteristic of the ways in which Angela is often targeted in the group.

Example two (M. Goodwin, 2006, pp. 222–3)

Angela: I-I mean like- **you** guys are like-

I don't **judge any**body because you guys know,

that like I just, you know, follow you guys.

((shoulder moves in time with words))

Wherever you guys go, but um,

Sarah: You're like a **tag**. You tag along. ((left palm

extended with arm bent towards Angela))

Basically- Angela tags along.=

Angela: So,

Sarah: That's it.=right?

Angela: So like- **Yeah**. ((shoulder shrug))

Sarah: Right Angela? Admit it. Eh heh heh!

Angela: Yeah like- whatever.

Sarah: **ADMIT** IT ANGELA!

Sarah: ADMIT IT! ((extends arms palm up to Angela))

Angela   OKAY! ((leaning towards Sarah))

Sarah: Say it. "**You::** (.) are:: (.) **I**: am **a**: (.)"

((using hands as if conducting on each beat,))

then extends hands palm up towards Angela

as if asking her to complete the utterance))

Angela: I'M A **TAG**-ALONG girl! ((jerks body in

direction of Sarah))

(0.4)

Sarah: **Good** girl! eh heh!

Angela: I'm going to **get** you! ((play fight))

Sarah: heh-heh Oka(hh)y.

heh-heh hmh-hmh-hnh-hnh-hnh!

Angela: Okay!

There is a complex act of embodied positioning and affective practice taking place here. Angela is being described as a 'tag along girl' and coached by Sarah she is made to repeat this description of herself. In being described as such, and through the repetition of the description, Angela's marginal status is also being accomplished, performed and continued.

Cultural theorist Sarah Ahmed (2004a, 2004b), whose work I will look at in Chapter 7, might argue that in these kinds of events we can see how Angela is becoming a 'figure'. Various complicated emotions are 'sticking' to Angela – humiliation, exclusion, contempt and shame – and that is how she is becoming subjected in the group. Her 'surface', in Ahmed's terms, is being constructed or impressed upon. She argues this is the way in which circuits of affective value work. Goodwin notes the non-randomness of the choice of Angela as the excluded one. This is a middle-class school, with some very wealthy parents. The group of girls is diverse in terms of ethnicity and social class, but Angela combines together two more marginal identities in this context – she is African-American and from a working-class background. The patterning of her actions, such as her practices around eating, are 'remarkable' to the other girls and become the basis of this long-term construction of her as 'other' to their more shared culture.

It might seem that we could understand what is going on here in relatively familiar post-structuralist terms as the imposition of a subject position upon Angela. No other discourse perspective would be necessary. All the detailed paraphernalia of conversation analysis and its transcription technologies turning an event into words on paper might seem rather redundant. But, as Goodwin would point out, this is misleading. If we look back at how the interaction is unfolding, and the layers added by the detail of the words, movements, turn-taking, intonation patterns and so on, we see something a bit more complicated and interesting than 'contempt', or 'exclusion', or 'humiliation'. We see, in other words, an affective practice unfolding rather than an emotion moving to 'land' on one individual. This is joint, coordinated, relational activity.

In an odd way Angela is being included through what seems to be a familiar ritual marking her difference and exclusion. Familiar practice or ritualised sequence depends on reflexive awareness about how the practice plays out and how the scene works. The transcript suggests that having done this bit of usual practice jointly the girls can move on together to something else, to play fight together in this case, and continue their chat. The interaction opens with Angela attempting a characterisation of her own conduct – she is not someone who judges anybody, she follows the other girls around – presumably she is referring back to some earlier event or conversation. Sarah seizes the opportunity, however, to develop a marginalising re-formulation of Angela's actions – this is not following, it is 'tagging along'. Angela's resigned response ('whatever') suggests this formulation is not news to her. It is not something she contests and it seems to rely on a version of who she is that is already consensual, already familiar, and available.

Looking at episodes like this in detail doesn't make them any less horrible. The point I am trying to make is the one often ignored in post-structuralist discourse theory (and in most cultural studies of affect) that affective–discursive practice is joint inter-subjective activity. To describe this episode as an example of affect, understood as a particular kind of pre-defined emotion, circulating and 'landing' on Angela and figuring her misses the human activity. Degradation is something actively done to Angela not by affect *per se* circulating but by other participants as part of their joint practice, reflecting their relational history. I will come back to these issues again in Chapter 7 (see Wetherell, 1998, for more extensive discussion of the advantages and disadvantages of post-structuralist discourse theories and conversation analysis).

Goodwin tracks Angela through many such moments in the playground and shows how over time her identity is constructed for the group through these kinds of sequences. Other researchers (Antaki et al., 2007a, 2007b, 2009) have shown how these kinds of everyday affective routines can become strongly institutionalised. Antaki et al.'s research was conducted in residential homes in the UK for people with severe learning disabilities. They demonstrated that despite government policy and forms of best practice designed to foster inclusion and empowerment (enabling 'choice' and 'voice'), the established everyday routines significantly undercut residents' actual choice and created familiar affective practices in very particular (and likely noxious) ways. Normative episodic sequences build not just the 'small' worlds of children's playgrounds, but also the affective environments of entire institutions.

The Present Moment

Conversation analytic work on filmed, naturally occurring, affective sequences such as Goodwin's studies or the work of Antaki and colleagues takes what Arlene Hochschild (1983) calls a 'fly on the wall perspective'. This is 'the fly for whom each second of human action is a long long tale' (p. 214). An event that normally proceeds at a crisp, fast pace is slowed down so that the patterning of each microsecond becomes revealed. In some respects, then, conversation analysis is the equivalent in ethnoscience to the fMRI scan of the brain in neuroscience. As I noted in the last chapter, embodied responses and affect are often presented in some 'turn to affect' scholarship as the domain of the unconscious, the automatic and the unplanned, while language is seen as the domain of the deliberate, the cognitive and the conscious. These distinctions are misleading. The kinds of patterns revealed through moment-by-moment analysis are difficult to fully articulate self-consciously at the time. Technologies such as transcription slow them down for systematic analysis. Affective-discursive patterns happen so quickly that only some of what occurs is likely to become available to be re-coded in consciousness. Yet they are 'known' and crucial to affective conduct. I'll return to the issue of the 'unconscious' of the affective–discursive in Chapter 6.

Affective-discursive patterns are crucial in part because they are the material from which people select and build more global subjective feelings of interactional and relational direction and thrust. Recognitions and anticipations of normative sequences build senses of the evaluative and moral tone of an interaction, whether we are heading in felicitous and socially sanctioned directions or towards trouble. Because they act back on feelings and narratives of personal efficacy, they contribute strongly to ongoing senses of being-in-the-world. Intriguingly, the findings from conversation analysis disrupt many lay and other assumptions about how interaction works. These are often based on literary conventions about dialogue and intentionality. But, the 'he said, she said' talk found in novels and plays, or in everyday narratives, reads rather differently compared to the transcripts of conversation analysts. Affective–discursive practice can be strange and unfamiliar when seen close up, with attempts to include more detail, yet it is in the detail that much of life happens.

This may be the site where much of human life happens, but is it the place where we 'live' in the sense in which that is often understood in Western societies? Conversation analysis focuses on the actions or moves making up an affective episode which participants have, in some way, picked up and oriented to. There is likely to be some gap, however, between how we inhabit the microseconds of social interaction and the subjective phenomenological sense of the passing moment. Perhaps we 'live' not quite in the active chronological moment of the turn-by-turn, but most strongly and personally in the narratives ruminating on some outburst of affect after it has taken place, whether these are narratives told to others, or narratives rehearsed internally to ourselves? And, if not there, then do we mostly live in a more extended present moment?

The phenomenal sense of an affective episode is likely to work through a flow and duration not exactly equivalent to the ticking of chronological time. In general terms, as Middleton and Brown (2005, p. 224) argue, '[t]ime does not break for us into tiny segments. Our duration is a continuous gnawing of the past into the present where the present is infused with the burden of a past that does not pass, does not ever escape us.' Daniel Stern (2004) argues persuasively that present, subjectively meaningful moments also involve a kind of chunking. These are gestalts of created coherence that organise various elements into a whole. He suggests the phenomenal, situated moment is likely to be between 1 and 10 seconds in chronological time with an average of 3–4 seconds. It may, of course, feel much faster or hugely slower. Exact timings are not the point. Present moments may match the 'turn units' studied by conversation analysts but they need not.

Present moments, Stern suggests, have a temporal architecture and a time-contoured shape and may include a flow that moves through various 'vitality affects' (2004, p. 36). He uses as an example, the possible affective experience of someone watching a firework rocket take off, explode and dissipate. This event is likely to be a phenomenal whole, Stern argues, with a distinctive flow through a range of microsecond transitions in intensity and arousal. The shifts in vitality affects might, for instance, start with rising arousal and expectation, followed by a sudden surge of feeling as the rocket explodes, then a fading in excitation, but a growing sense of wonder and pleasure as the display effloresces and fades away. This example assumes, of course, an observer with previous (good) experiences of fireworks who is well versed in their cultural connotations.

Stern's interest is in the strings of present moments that make up psychotherapy sessions. For me it is an open empirical question how much of his argument is specific to the affective–discursive practices of the genre and psy-technique he is exploring. Psychotherapy is a very particular kind of affective–discursive situation, not least in its masked power relations and ideological frames. But Stern's work does add important dimensions to the understanding of situated affect emerging in this chapter. As I have just described, research in conversation analysis and micro-sociology tends to focus on recurring, normative affective sequences or affective routines and rituals. Stern places more emphasis on what he calls the 'sloppiness' of affective practice. What is 'sloppiness'?

The term comes from dynamic systems theory (Prigogine, 1997; Prigogine and Stengers, 1984). This work sees redundancy and chaos as a necessary part of the process of emergence of new states. Elements are added messily to an evolving pattern such that it eventually flips into a new pattern in a discontinuous leap. Stern describes situated interaction as an unfolding flow of 'moving along' of this kind. It is an 'often ambling, loosely directed process of searching for and finding a path to take, of losing the way and then finding it (or a new one) again, and of choosing goals to orient to – goals that are often discovered only as you go along' (2004, p. 150). The affective–discursive flow in therapy is, he suggests, spontaneous and unpredictable. It works in a 'hit–miss–repair–elaborate fashion' (p. 156) with massive redundancy and 'many mismatches, derailments, misunderstandings, and indeterminancy' (p. 157).

Conversation analysis also focuses on derailments in affective interaction and the regular ways in which these are repaired, but Stern draws attention back to the bumbling along and singular qualities which affective–discursive interaction also often displays. Notions of activity circuits and normative sequences can be balanced with a stronger flavour of the indeterminancy of affective action. Often people do cycle through affective routines relatively automatically, even if each routine performance is slightly different. But, Stern reminds us that in any affective moment a number of possible lines are usually available. Affective practice, as it unfolds, closes down possible alternative activities and the 'becoming' of any particular interaction while the flow of social life eventually moves any particular affective episode or emotional outburst from present to past. Equally, Stern asks us to think more about significant, possibly one-off, moments of major subjective and relational transition, and gives a way of conceptualising the points at which some recognisable phenomenological shift takes place.

Relational Moves

Stern's work emphasises a further important theme, found too in conversation analysis and social constructionist psychology. This is the extent to which affective practice is relational. It builds (and arises from) jointly constructed relational 'realities' (Gergen, 1994; Shotter, 1993). This is evident simply in the ways in which most affect performances come in conventional pairs that get divided between people – accusation and defence, provocation and laughter, intimidation and fear, startle and surprise. We saw how Lori slipped into a familiar sequence of reprimand in response to offence and how Marisol cringed in response to Carla's outraged calling out.

Affective practices, like girls' methods of doing accusations in hopscotch, are often part of a normative back and forth. The positions taken up are responsive to what has gone before, and are often loosely paired with each other. The affective pattern is in fact *distributed* across the relational field and each partner's part becomes meaningful only in relation to the whole affective dance. This mutual shaping occurs even when there is no obvious conventional affective pair to perform. We create contexts for others as we act. Then, in reply, the other we have addressed orients to what is taking shape and remakes the context again.

Interestingly, the pairing of affective positions, normative turn and counter-turn, and processes of context-making for affective relational moves, often persist even when the affect is entirely private, self-contained and solitary. Even in a rumination rehearsed entirely in one's head, the internal affective dialogue may go back and forth in the same way with an imagined other, or within a sub-divided self as, for instance, an accusing self and a guilty self act out turn and counter-turn. As one imagines the words of another, the flow of affect might intensify and turn into a blush or a grimace. Affective meaning-making, in other words, is dialogic and typically addressed as if to someone. It is a communication.

Discussing Kendon's (1990) research on patterned behaviours in focused encounters, Stern (2004) argues that much seemingly banal ordinary interaction often consists of embryonic starts and fits of 'intention movements'. These are not completed relational moves but the mere beginnings of recognisable affective patterns. These seem rather like the moments preceding lightning strikes when sophisticated still photography shows threads of electrical connection beginning to manifest with the tallest objects in the field, before the strike completes the connection. Intention movements are abbreviated, only half-sketched and held in potential, to be completed if the interacting partner takes up the corresponding relational moves. The scene is set for participants to move into what Stern calls in the quotation which introduced this chapter a 'shared feeling voyage' and into inter-subjective, affective coordination.

Again, however, power is missing from this analysis along with any analysis of how these pairings play out in asymmetrical relations. Whose abbreviated gestures get a response and whose get ignored? Empirical research in the sociology of emotions (Clay-Warner and Robinson, 2008; Kemper, 1990), although conducted from an overly simplistic variables approach, suggests as we might expect, significant status/power effects in who gets to do what in emotional displays. While feminist discursive psychology (Reynolds and Wetherell, 2003; Seymour-Smith and Wetherell, 2006), feminist conversation analysis and ethnomethodology (Kitzinger and Frith, 1999; West and Zimmerman, 1987) and feminist linguistics (Cameron, 2007) similarly demonstrate that relational affective patterning and display are intimately bound up with perceived social category and legitimacy. As Despret (2004b) points out, there is quite a distinction between 'being available' to the other's context-making and 'being docile'.

There is quite a distinction, too, between the becomings of interaction that are authorised versus those that are 'free' just to emerge.

Chapter 2 briefly mentioned the new neuroscience work emerging on 'mirror neurons' (cf. Bråten, 2007). This suggests that an orientation to inter-subjectivity seems to be deeply embedded in humans neurobiologically and developmentally (although see Hickok, 2009, for a critical analysis). In brief, as we watch someone performing an act, our brains seem to begin to fire in such a way as to produce the same kinds of sensory-motor registrations. As Stern (2004, p. 76) comments, our nervous systems seem to be designed to be 'captured by the nervous systems of others' as we observe their gestures, facial expressions, their rising and dampening affect and then model, intuit and re-run their intentions and psychological states. As a result of these capacities, it is possible for subjectivities to intertwine, for affect to be distributed, and for affective episodes to be co-created. This also makes it possible for affects to circulate, to be contagious and to be transmitted through groups and crowds. I'll come back to these phenomena in Chapter 7.

Multimodality

The relational figurations of situated affective activity include not just humans and their particular psychologies and histories. Marjorie Goodwin's work demonstrates that the assembling activity of affective practice in the situated moment extends to encompass objects, spaces and the built environment. Equally, recent work on children and video games (Walkerdine, 2007) strongly makes the same point for animated characters, scenes and story lines. Lines drawn on pavements to represent hopscotch squares are crucial to the unfolding interaction, as are the social, institutional and spatial arrangements of play and playgrounds, whether virtual or material. Katz's work on road rage demonstrates even more forcefully that the material world is not a passive backdrop but actively enters into the organisation of the affective display.

Acts of road rage in LA require a network of motorways, tarmac, cars, places to go and things to do. More than this, the socio-material is performative (see also Thrift's, 2008a, discussion of 'automobility'). Katz describes, for example, how road rage is tightly dependent on the binary organisation of traffic. Those in cars whizzing towards us on the opposite side of the motorway or on the other side of the dual carriageway are rarely assholes. 'Assholeness' entirely depends on patterns of contiguity and common movement and, thus, occurs most often in relation to cars and drivers immediately in front of us and behind us heading in the same direction. Equally, road rage is intimately connected with the communicative affordances of the car as a self-contained, material box which organises eye contact with other drivers in particular ways and which operates like a physical extension of self. Katz describes how in some Western cultural contexts at least pedestrians rarely seem to express 'pedestrian rage'. In

LA, he reports, pedestrians tend to display an excessively polite concern with avoiding each other, minimising overly direct eye gaze and any appearance of staring, recognising the bounds of each other's space, perhaps because the communicative possibilities on foot are so much greater and more immediately troubling than in cars.

In a fascinating analysis, Vinciane Despret (2004b) demonstrates the ways in which animals as well as objects can be inducted into human affective practice and relationally shape and form that practice. She reconsiders the famous, early 20th-century case of Hans the Clever Horse. Hans could apparently count, spell and solve puzzles. When asked a question by an interrogator such as, 'What is the result of 10 divided by two?' Hans would tap his hoof on the ground five times. He stopped whenever he got to the right answer. Psychologist Oskar Pfungst, delegated to solve this mystery, discovered that Hans was only clever when his human questioner knew the correct answer. When the person asking the question didn't know the answer, Hans didn't seem to know when to stop tapping. Pfungst argued that the horse was reading almost imperceptible cues unwittingly given off by human questioners when the right answer was reached, such as slight elliptical movements of the head, states of tension and relaxation. Despret (p. 113) argues, however, that this makes Hans not stupid, but very clever indeed. Human bodies 'were talking and moving against their will, outside the frame of consciousness' and 'no one among them knew they were doing so', 'each of them, except the horse, was ignorant of this astonishing phenomenon'. Horses, due to long shared histories of interaction and domestication which make them dependent on reading human bodies, might be more skilled at aspects of this than humans themselves.

As theorists such as Donna Haraway (2004) have demonstrated, practices like the affective routines of road rage, or conventional accusations in hopscotch games, narratives in video games, or evident in Strasbourg's dancing plague discussed in Chapter 1, are the ends of much larger balls of string. They require the recruitment, assemblage and entanglement of huge social, cultural and material infrastructures. As that infrastructure develops and changes, so too will the affective practice and its meanings.

The term 'multimodality' is a reminder of some of the connotations entailed in 'assembling'. As I read it, 'multimodality' suggests a phenomenon not made up of discrete and separable elements that are ordered or put together but an integrated and organic unfolding and weaving. This interweaving displays various peaks and troughs of diverse modes of the semiotic, the material and the natural. Some of the contributing modes in any particular affective practice might become more dominant and primary at some moments. They may retreat at other moments as the practice unfolds in time. Intense body actions in materialised and spatialised contexts, for instance, might arise as the dominant performative mode early in the chronology of a particular affective practice. Semiotic modes such as narrative and story-telling are likely to become more important as the body winds down, and as the moment of strong affect is carried forward as a memory or story, with new accompanying affect.

Positioning and Accounting

I want to turn now to look at some of the more specifically discursive aspects of situated affective activity such as positioning and accounting. Discursive actions and active, reflexive representations of emotion in talk are a crucial part of situated affective practice and embodied meaning-making. As Katz argues, the study of situated affect takes off from 'the socially visible sense that a person is trying to make in the immediate situation' (1999, p. 5). Discursive psychologists (Edwards and Potter, 1992, 2005; Potter, 2004; Potter and Edwards, 2001) focus precisely on this social visibility.

Accounts are the descriptions, justifications and explanations of activities that make up so much of everyday discourse. More than this, conversation analysts, ethnomethodologists and discursive psychologists, following Garfinkel (1967), argue that accountability is a guiding principle of social life. As people talk and emote, they routinely demonstrate their implicit or explicit understanding of what is going on in the piece of social life in which they are engaged. The local order, loose pattern and method of organisation of any particular practical moment are on display, therefore. This local order is a resource that people draw upon and can orientate to, as they constitute their conduct. Analysts can go on to explicate this pattern through trying to make clear how the participants appear to be interpreting the situation turn by turn. In these ways, it is possible to build up a more detailed picture of the local cultural criteria operating for evaluating people and their activities.

Positions and positioning refer simply to the speaking standpoint and the 'character' or, in Goffman's (1981) related term, the 'footing' a participant takes up as they speak. Carla, for instance, in her *OUT! OUT!* cry considered above very obviously took up the position of rightful judge and accuser. Her footing was direct, not second-hand. She both 'animated' and 'authored' her cry. She was not animating someone else's authoritative voice, reporting for instance, that 'the playground monitor says you are out'. Overall, it is these features – positioning, footing and accountability – that make affective practice 'psycho-discursive' (Wetherell and Edley, 1999). Situated affective practices build psychologies, identities, reputations and subjectivities as they make meaning, just as they build social orders, histories and institutions.

Consider the following two examples of affective positioning and account giving. Example Three was analysed by Elizabeth Stokoe and Derek Edwards (2009) and Example Four by Edwards (1999). In Example Three, a telephone caller, C, has rung a UK mediation centre dealing in disputes between neighbours. C is elaborating her complaint about her neighbour's excessive noise to the mediator, M. Example Four is taken from a counselling session, again in the UK, with a couple who have been given the pseudonyms Mary and Jeff. In this extract Mary is part way through her story about what brought them to counselling. She has reached the point where she decided to tell Jeff about a recently ended affair, summarising for the counsellor (and for Jeff) how she sees what happened next.

Example three (Stokoe and Edwards, 2009, p. 103)

1	C:	Um:: an' some- uh- [sometimes:
2	M:	[((sniffs))
3		(0.6)
4	C:	Because I- I: have a little girl who's the s-
5		(.) ex<u>act</u>ly the same <u>age</u> actually.
6	M:	Oh ri:ght.
7	C:	Um: (0.3) an' - an:, (.) an' I usually get her
8		into bed for half past eight.
9		(0.2)
10	C:	An,=
11	M:	=Yeah.
12		(0.3)
13	C:	By that ti- a- cos I'm a single mother,
14	M:	M:mm.=
15	C:	=By that time, (0.3) I'm ti:red
16		(0.2)
17	C:	.hhh
18	M:	Yeah.=
19	C:	An' I don't have many resources left for
20		<u>co</u>:ping with things.

Example four (Edwards, 1999, p. 276)

1	Mary:	(…) so <u>that</u>'s when I decided to (.)
2		<u>you</u> know to <u>tell</u> him. (1.0) U::m (1.0)
3		and then::, (.) obviously you went
4		through your a:ngry stage, <u>did</u>n't you?
5		(.)
6		Ve:ry upset <u>ob</u>viously, .hh an:d uh,
7		(0.6) we: started ar:guing a lot, an:d
8		(0.6) <u>just</u> drifted awa:y.

For both of these examples, it is hard to deduce much about the internal or external body actions involved except through the limited information given by transcription conventions. These include the underlining of words and parts of words which the speaker has unusually strongly emphasised, pauses or delays in talk indicated by seconds in brackets, and drawn out words indicated with colons placed in the drawn out part of the word. Obviously, those present in the room or at the other end of the phone would have more information about the body actions of the participants. But I suspect even for the actual witnesses and audience the affective moment is constituted here mostly through the talk, through the discursive action of complaint in Example Three on the phone with minimal hearable body stuff, and through Mary's talk about emotion or through her narrative and representational actions in Example Four. Even so, the participants are clearly caught up in affective practice. These are affective performances.

Edwards (1997, 1999, 2005) and Stokoe and Edwards (2009; Stokoe, 2009) argue that a lot of quite complex work can be involved in an affective action. Example One presented earlier, taken from Goodwin and focused on Marisol and Carla, was pretty direct and unsubtle. Carla's positioning of herself as judge of Marisol's actions and as her accuser was hardly laboured. But much affective practice isn't like this. Participants making a complaint, for instance, have to handle what Edwards (2005) calls 'the subjective side' of complaining. People are attentive to how they will be heard and evaluated, and will try to avoid any potentially noxious identities, while claiming normatively positive positions. It is often a matter of what is not said, and what is avoided, as well as how a version of some event or experience is put together. Again, this kind of work need not be at all self-conscious or thought through. The careful positioning of self and others can be just a routine part of the practice that people run through.

Edwards argues that in British culture, to be effective, a complaint should not be an obvious 'moan' or 'whinge'. The presence of a range of lexical possibilities and affective contrasts – 'moaning', 'whinging', 'complaining', 'ranting', 'paranoid', 'biased' – tells us a great deal about the wider cultural environment regulating affective practice in a society like the UK. In this context, a successful complaint about someone else's actions should seem to be motivated by the truly awful, actual facts of their conduct rather than revealing anything about one's own character. It should hold at bay any hearable and accountable implications for the kind of person one might be oneself that might disrupt the objectivity of the complaint. Thus, in Example Three above, Stokoe and Edwards point out how C offers a category-based description of herself in Line 13 ('I'm a single mother') as she begins to elaborate her complaint. Stokoe and Edwards suggest she identifies herself in this way as part of developing a contrast with her noisy neighbour who doesn't get her kids to bed at a reasonable time. It accounts also for why she might be sensitive to the noise. She is tired for good reasons and thus C works to present herself as legitimately (not provocatively, unreasonably, or oversensitively) aggrieved.

This kind of positioning work attentive to the accountability of one's actions is not an additional or an optional part of an affective practice like complaining. Stokoe and Edwards' work demonstrates that positioning and issues of accountability are absolutely central to the affective practice as they are to all discursive practice. And, in this way, we begin to see how affect, discourse and social life are finessed together and the intimate ways in which affect is linked to convention and normal practice. Indeed, all the 'extra' discursive work which surrounds even a routine affective act like feeling a grievance and complaining about it suggests how much more complicated affect is than the simple picture painted in psychology and neuroscience of a stimulus eliciting a biological response leading to an affective expression.

In contrast to Example Three, Example Four is not an instance of a complaint; it is a version or characterisation of someone else's anger. This is not an affective display, in itself, but it is, I want to suggest, just as much affective business. A central part of affective practices consists of accounts and narratives of affect, past, present and future. In learning how to perform affect in socially recognisable and conventional ways, people also learn how to talk about and evaluate affect. This 'talk about' might take place either as a practice in itself (in acts of confession, teaching or disciplining), or it might be combined with affective displays and discursive affective actions as an integral part of a recognised, normative, more extended affective practice. Group psychotherapy sessions, for instance, often move between moments of strong emotion expressed through the bodily perturbation of tears, shouts and laughter and moments of recapitulation where the burst of affect is narrated, discussed and contextualised. The sequencing of emotional outburst with narrative re-working and consensus building around the meaning of the affect becomes a recognisable rhythmic affective practice for the group repeated over and over, shaped in light of the understanding about how therapy should proceed and what is therapeutic.

In his analysis of Mary's narrative in Example Four above, Edwards draws attention to the kinds of resources people have available for talking about affect and the positioning work these allow in relation to issues of accountability. Mary is not talking about affect during the course of an academic seminar; she is constructing a potentially highly significant and efficacious version of her relationship with Jeff in the course of couple counselling. Edwards notes how Mary's description of Jeff as going through his 'a:ngry stage' (Line 4) when he heard about her affair and her subsequent description that he was 'ver:y upset ob̲viously' (Line 6) draw on a number of common-place assumptions about emotion. First, Edwards (1999, p. 276) explains, 'these descriptions characterize Jeff's reactions *as* emotional rather than, say, as having come to a damning but rational appraisal of Mary's actions and character'. Mary has available, in other words, as all speakers of English do, the history of Western understandings and lay ethnopsychologies of emotion, including distinctions between reason and passion and a large range of metaphors for emotional states. I'll have more to say about these resources in the next section.

Edwards (1999, p. 277) goes on to point out:

> The phrase 'your angry stage' employs a notion of anger as a temporary state with its proper occasions and durations. It is a description that sets up various possible narrative and rhetorical trajectories. For example, while Jeff's anger is proper in its place, one would not expect it to go on forever, to endure unreasonably, beyond its 'stage'. Mary has made rhetorical room for something

she goes on to develop, which is the notion that Jeff's reactions are starting to get in the way of progress, starting to become (instead of her infidelity as Jeff insists) 'the problem' they have in their relationship. ... The implication Mary develops in her subsequent discourse is that Jeff's reactions should end at some reasonable point. His 'stage' is already past tense ... and he starts to become accountable for continuing to be 'upset'.

Conversation analysis, ethnomethodology and discursive psychology, therefore, in combination, describe how talk and bodies are meshed together and choreographed so that an episode of situated affect is usually some ordered combination of body actions, discursive actions, and narratives (cf Walton et al., 2004, for further strong illustration). In short, these lines of research thoroughly demonstrate that affect is a social semiotic act, stuffed full of meaning-making.

Narratives and Interpretative Repertoires

Finally, in this journey through the patterning of situated affect, I want to mention two other frequently used analytic concepts in studies of discursive practice – narratives and interpretative repertoires (Bruner, 1990; Frosh and Emerson, 2009; Taylor, 2010; Wetherell and Potter, 1988). In Edwards' example of Mary and Jeff we could begin to see how central narratives are likely to be in developing noticeable episodes of situated affect, in opening these up, or closing them down, and in making sense of past affect. It was evident too that narratives of affect mobilise shared communal and cultural interpretative repertoires of sense-making, as indeed does most talk about affect in a situated performance. These form a kind of backdrop, available to be called in to formulate and describe any instance of affect.

Some of the most interesting work on discourses and repertoires of the 'emotional self', and on the narrative canons these repertoires support, has been conducted by Deborah Lupton (1998, cf. also Averill, 1982; Walton et al., 2004, and work in cultural anthropology Abu-Lughod and Lutz, 1990). In a fascinating study, Lupton shows how people's narratives tend to focus on oppositions between natural emotion and reasoned control, for instance. The participants in her investigation constructed a taken-for-granted world in their accounts of past emotional episodes in which the control of 'natural' emotions became the mark of a rational and professional person, particularly in workplaces.

Consider this narrative from one of Lupton's participants. This is one woman's account of an argument with her boyfriend:

First I went into the bathroom, really wanting to smash something, but kept thinking that there are too many valuable things in the house I'd regret if I smashed, so I kicked a hole in the door. It felt good, but I really needed to lose control completely, like smash lots of plates, so after I kicked the door in, I didn't know what else to smash. I felt incomplete, because I hadn't fully lost control. I'd only half lost control. If I had like a big bookshelf that I could have toppled over, that would have done it for me. I obviously wouldn't allow myself to completely lose control, because my head kept coming in and saying, 'No, if you smash that, you'll regret it!' because, you know, your mother gave it to you or whatever. So I suppose I wasn't completely angry, completely enraged, because otherwise I would've lost it. (Lupton, 1998, pp. 51–2)

The narrator recruits current Western common sense about affect and its organising dialectic of emotion and control to formulate her narrative, and to interpret her psychological state. Her experience is given a very particular shape and meaning in the telling. In her narrative, her loss of control is taken as a normative feature of strong emotion, while the fact that some control was retained is taken as a demonstration that the speaker can't really have been that enraged. An interpretative repertoire around emotional control constructs the reality of the event, and that constructed reality then gives the repertoire its authority and 'truth'.

As historian Thomas Dixon (2003) argues, the history of ideas about emotion and affect since at least the 19th century in Western societies has been based on assumptions about natural emotional urges that burst out spontaneously, and are distinct from reason and thought. Dixon describes a gradual process of the secularisation of affect and its separation from religious categories and sense-making as it became widely and newly understood as a psychological event. Before the 19th century, lay theories of affect were based around different 'movements of the soul' such as 'affections', which were distinguished from the 'passions', and these were distinguished also from 'moral sentiments'. From the 19th century onwards, in contrast, emotion was 'naturalised' (and increasingly feminised). Stronger distinctions were made between reason and emotion, with emotion seen as natural, biological, feminine and primitive, and reason or cognition as moderate, controlled, masculine and rational. Emotions came to be seen as involuntary, body-based, entities which moral effort and judgement work upon. This superseded the notion that affect might be a moral act in itself, or a visitation from a supernatural agent.

Perhaps, in some ways, members of Western societies in earlier times could make more complex and subtle categorisations and distinctions than we currently manage (or maybe these were just evocative in different ways). Evaluations of people's actions focused on distinctions between 'passions' versus 'moral sentiments' versus 'affections' were, arguably, less individualistic methods of making sense, more open to the possible relevance of the entire situation and relations between participants. Indeed, what is also evident in the account above from Lupton's participant is the way in which narratives of emotional episodes in contemporary Western contexts typically organise affect as an individual production. It is not that people aren't aware of social relations, the actions of others and the effects of situations, and these are routinely incorporated into emotion narratives as causes and consequences. But, very frequently, affect is presented and constructed as something an individual does, and as something an individual owns.

As the narrative above demonstrates, people who share this common 'emotionology' tend to narrate emotional episodes from a 'heroic' standpoint. I mean by 'heroic' not that people are necessarily self-glorifying and only engage in good stories of valiant acts. On the contrary, many accounts of emotional episodes are of shameful or embarrassing moments. These narratives are heroic because, in telling their stories, people strongly own and author them, throwing most attention on their individual powers and standpoints. Their narratives, then, are like a typical experiment in cognitive psychology. Misleadingly, most attention is thrown onto what is passing through the individual's body and mind. It is for this reason, too, that qualitative research in the social sciences which relies solely on after-the-event narratives to scope out the nature of situated affect will form only a partial view.

Affective Practice – A Summary

Where am I now with the concept of affective practice? At the beginning of this book, I stated that my aim was to develop a way of thinking about affect and emotion through the notion of practice that might be generative for social research, building on previous work and borrowing from multiple sources. My argument so far has been mostly negative. I have tried to show why conceptualising affective action through the psychological schema of basic emotions, for instance, doesn't seem to work. I have argued that some recent lines of thought in cultural theory that sever affect from discourse don't seem to work either.

To the extent that there is a theory of affective practice emerging in these chapters, it takes shape as a series of orientations in contrast to these approaches, ways, for instance, of thinking about body/brain activity, about psychological events, and about everyday meaning-making. And, further contrasts with other perspectives will emerge as the book proceeds. A theory of affective practice is like a portmanteau – I am trying to argue for a set of approaches that need to be packed in the researcher's suitcase and a set of approaches that could be left on the floor. I have been trying to identify a set of points to be taken for granted such as that emotion is culturally constructed, that bodies/brains are plastic, that affect involves flows of bodily perturbation that have become quite organised, that everyday meaning-making is situated and practical activity infused (as later chapters will argue) with sedimented social and personal history, and so on.

What I have tried to do is outline the kinds of activity involved in affective practice and some of its characteristic features. But it is much more difficult to say in any neat way what an affective practice is as a distinctive object or as something concrete that one could point to. To describe a practice as affective doesn't seem to help distinguish it. In some sense all social practice is affective because all human practice is embodied and comes attached with some valence. Similarly, all meaning-making is affective. I may as well, then, substitute a word like energy or movement for affect. But, as I have tried to argue in relation to Brian Massumi's cultural theory, for instance, that does not get us very far.

As an object, then, affective practice marks out a domain that analysts or participants interpret as to do with the emotional and the psychological. The divisions between these kinds of practices and other social practices will not be clear-cut. The domains of affective practice are often those, like some of the examples in this chapter, where the body has been more intrusive than it ordinarily is. These are domains, too, as other examples in this chapter have demonstrated, where there is notable talk occurring about emotion and feelings, and domains where something personally significant seems to have occurred that someone wants to mark.

To define affective practice as this kind of thing is not hugely satisfying to be sure but it does reflect where we often are in social research, investigating activities that are interesting because of the common-sense ways they have been constructed or could be constructed. To advocate research on affective practices is not so much to decisively carve out a class of events with defined characteristics, it is a matter of advocating some ways of thinking about and investigating human psychologised activity rather than others.

The View from Studies of Situated Affect: Lessons Learnt

To round off this chapter I want to reflect a little further, in this section, on some of the approaches to affect reviewed in previous chapters in light of what is now evident. Then, in the final section, I want to consider the best directions forward and why the theoretical and methodological strictures of conversation analysts and discursive psychologists pose unacceptable limits on future research.

First, work on situated affect reinforces the concerns expressed in Chapter 2 about the basic emotions paradigm, and the ways in which it tidies up affect. Neuroscience research, as Damasio's (1995, 1999, 2004) approach exemplifies, decontextualises emotion. The context and the social situation in which an affective performance is located are 'black-boxed' and invariably are then forgotten. This may occur for vital methodological reasons – fMRI scans clearly require partial social simplicity – but the forgetting creeps over into the theory and blocks the kinds of links and connections I am suggesting are essential to understanding affective practice as a whole.

Researchers imagine and/or construct in a laboratory for a person in an fMRI scanner an idealised sequence in which some stimulus (and it doesn't really seem to matter what this stimulus is) provokes the ordered and patterned elements which are understood as 'angry', 'sad' or some other basic emotion. All attention is focused on recording the flowing body/mind processes that move the person from perception of the stimulus to a recognisable basic emotion response category. As Damasio (2004) explicitly states, the only thing that is interesting or important about the stimulus is whether it is 'emotionally competent', meaning, simply, is it the kind of thing that will stimulate an anger pattern, for example? Yet, we have seen that in naturally occurring moments of affect, flowing body/ mind processes arise in a complex relational and material field. This cannot be satisfactorily reduced to 'an emotionally competent stimulus' or 'emotional trigger' without enormous loss of relevant patterning.

Similarly, in naturally occurring situations affect does not come in particularly neat and tidy packages. Basic emotions fragment into all kinds of complicated variants. What kind of emotion is occurring (Damasio's 'state of knowing the feeling') is not left up to the body/mind to decide but is often the subject of sometimes highly consequential negotiation ('was that your angry stage or were you just being a prat?'). In the laboratory, the participant's relational field is constructed just with the researcher alone. The researcher is the one who decides that 'yes, this is anger', authorising and labelling the response. In social life, as Edwards (1995) notes, it 'takes two to tango', at least two, that is, and even when alone, others surround us in imagined and virtual forms. The identification, categorisation, labelling and narrating of affect are social activities, taking place in situated contexts in light of the unfolding business of the moment. This is how social life works in practice and despite the methodological difficulties it is important knowledge for developing adequate accounts of the psychology and neuroscience of affect.

The research I have discussed in this chapter also fleshes out the position on affective meaning-making I was developing in Chapter 3. It elaborates my claim that William Reddy's (2001) notion of 'emotives' is too limited to encompass the range and nature of everyday affective–discursive activities. Reddy argued that people express their emotions through the performative and constative speech acts characteristic of the dominant emotional regime (e.g. 'I am angry with you'). These emotives describe, perform and formulate subjective experience. We can see, though, in relation to the examples in this chapter, that it would be difficult to reduce quite subtle practical methods for doing and talking about affect into a list of declaratives. People's affective–discursive activities are manifold, and accounts in terms of speech acts miss the relationality, the coordination and the kinds of inter-subjective meshing involved in affective practice.

I hope this chapter explains further, too, my irritation with cultural theorists and critical psychologists who want to study sensuous, mobile and dynamic life but who assume that this involves moving 'beyond' the study of discourse since post-structuralist discourse theory isn't sufficiently vital. This is a wrong diagnosis. The issue is not solved by turning to the study of affect formulated as a contrast and progression from the study of discourse (e.g. Blackman and Cromby, 2007; Brown et al., 2009; Cromby, 2007a; Sedgwick, 2003). Dynamism is not achieved by abandoning the discursive.

I think instead we need to search for better theories of discursive practice and ways of thinking about the patterning of the affective–discursive in everyday life than post-structuralist discourse theories alone can offer, while holding tight to the insights from all those decades of work in cultural and critical theory. The emphasis in those theories on discourse as a noun (discourses and discursive formations) and on a kind of 'plate tectonics' view of the operation of discourse obscures human agency and practical activity. As I will try to show, my approach is genuinely eclectic. I am not proposing a flip-flop from post-structuralist discourse theory to conversation analysis but advocating forms of analysis of affective practices that can interrogate the organisation of discursive and emotional regimes as well as their practical and situated patterning (Wetherell, 1998).

Moving on from Conversation Analysis, Ethnomethodology and Discursive Psychology

I have tried to show in this chapter that the ethno-sciences offer highly generative ways of investigating and theorising affective meaning-making. These disciplines have been revelatory. They offer probably the richest ways currently available for investigating how social order is accomplished in the moment. The research of Marjorie Goodwin, Charles Goodwin, Charles Antaki, Elizabeth Stokoe, Mick Finlay and Chris Walton discussed in this chapter is only a fragment of work using videos of naturally occurring interaction as a main source of data. In the hands of these practitioners, conversation analysis is extending its usual concerns to investigate the meshing of body actions, engagement with objects, and talk-in-interaction in social activities. Discursive psychology developed by Jonathan Potter and Derek Edwards (e.g. Edwards and Potter, 1992) adds to this an approach to analysing psychological activities (memory, attribution, categorisation, etc.) as they occur in discursive practices.

But, once again, despite what they can offer, these lines of work also block integrated analysis. They are part of the problem as well as part of the solution. Many in the ethno-sciences draw a new kind of narrow circle around meaning-making and suggest methodological and theoretical strictures that prevent a flow of analysis across the somatic, the semiotic and the social.

Some hints about the nature of the problem can be seen in this often-cited dictum from the founder of ethnomethodology, Harold Garfinkel:

> For ethnomethodology the objective reality of social facts, in that, and just how, it is every society's locally, endogenously produced, naturally organized, reflexively accountable, ongoing, practical achievement, being everywhere, always, only, exactly and entirely, members' work, with no time out, and with no possibility of evasion, hiding out, passing, postponement, or buy-outs, is *thereby* sociology's fundamental phenomenon. (1991, p. 11, cited in M. Goodwin, 2006, p. 6)

Garfinkel's claim seems unarguable in some ways. I have maintained that the study of affect needs to be transformed into the study of affective practices. Understanding practical accomplishment seems central to understanding the assembling, composing or figuring of an affective episode. But is local order the *most* fundamental phenomenon? Or, even if we assume that all empirical social scientific research needs to refer back to it at some point, is it the *only* fundamental topic?

Many conversation analysts and discursive psychologists interpret Garfinkel's argument as follows. They claim that research can only explicate the ways in which participants have interpreted the world. Researchers can only legitimately study the patterns in participants' own descriptions, versions, accounts and sequences. Some conversation analysts, such as Emmanuel Schegloff (1997, see also Hutchby and Wooffitt, 2008, and Ten Have, 2007, for general reviews), eschew, then, any kind of critical commentary on participants' unfolding actions as, inevitably, this would go beyond the local order and participants' own local knowledge (Marjorie Goodwin's work, as her analysis of Example Two suggests, is a welcome exception to this practice).

For the study of affect as situated activity, this rules out commentary on the history of an affective practice and the power relations it might sustain or disrupt, which are not obvious to participants. It rules out investigations of the social implications of the broader cultural resources participants might draw upon, and the implications of their particular semiotic choices that exceed what other participants notice. It makes inadmissible past identity work that sets the conditions for current affected subject positions but is not explicitly evoked; social structural relations such as persistent patterns linked to demographies of social class or gender/race/class intersections; unremarked forms of distinction and inequalities in affective capital; and so on.

In addition to this list, discursive psychology baulks at inferring any psychological state behind discursive descriptions. Discursive psychologists (Edwards, 1997; Edwards and Potter, 1992, 2005; Potter, 2004; Potter and Edwards, 2001) argue that, in effect, we only have access to the person's version of their mental or psychological state, along with how the next speaker responds to that version. This response will indicate the kind of work the version has accomplished in the immediate situation. Statements like 'I remember', 'I intend' or 'I feel' cannot be treated, therefore, as neutral, realist accounts of what is happening in the speaker's mind. This would be to ignore the constructive nature of discourse and the kind of situated practical work that such utterances always do in social life. This methodological requirement adds, then, to my accumulating list of prohibitions: speculations about feeling states, analyses of personal order and personal history, questions about the formation of subjectivities, or about repetitions in individual actions over time not evident in the material sampled.

The arguments against these prohibitions have been rehearsed many times (Billig, 1997b; Edley and Wetherell, 1997; Wetherell, 2001, 2007; and see the debate between Schegloff, 1997, 1998, and Wetherell, 1998, and also between Billig, 1999b, 1999c, Schegloff, 1999a, 1999b, and Weatherall, 2000). Critics of the narrow focus of conversation analysis and discursive psychology have advocated more eclectic, inclusive and varied forms of analysis. The aim is a mode of research that can examine both the broader 'argumentative textures' (Laclau, 1993, p. 341) constituting a social formation *and* interaction situated in a particular moment. This style of analysis will pay attention, for instance, to how discursive threads with longer histories and conventional and communal powers weave in and out of the local order. Sometimes this weaving will occur in ways that are noticeable and remarkable to the participants themselves, and sometimes in ways that are only noticeable to social researchers. As Bourdieu has argued, we cannot understand how modern states construct objects like 'families', for instance, if we focus simply on participants' categories. These take state constructions for granted and render the reality-making processes of governance invisible (Reed-Danahay, 2005, p. 114).

AFFECT AND EMOTION

It seems to me important to remember that the intellectual apparatus and 'machineries of figuring' provided by social science knowledge technologies make different aspects of social life visible in comparison to the social practices of everyday life. This last point has also been made particularly clearly by the cultural psychologists Campos et al. (1999). They note that in one sense it must be the case, as discursive psychologists argue, that no special epistemological claims can be made for analysts' descriptions compared to participants' descriptions. Both are discursive descriptions and both thus constitute the object of which they speak. Neither the ordinary member of the public nor the research psychologist can claim neutral, unmediated access to what is 'really' going on.

If we are going to adopt a constructionist theory of meaning, then it does make sense that it should be thoroughgoing in just this way. No other theory of how language works in practice seems viable or defensible, while the very many claims for some kind of realism in the face of constructionism seem implausible when faced with the pragmatics of natural discourse use. But, as Campos et al. point out, the *epistemological* equivalence of analysts' and participants' descriptions does not mean that each description is the product of exactly the same set of knowledge practices. They come from overlapping but distinct life worlds. Thus, the kinds of commentaries which social science can offer are not equivalent to participants' own orientations and sense-making. (They are not necessarily better in every context, or 'true' in an absolute sense; they simply add new and different perspectives that are often exceptionally useful.)

In the case of studies of affect, social research might add to participants' own concerns and to their particular order-production in the moment of the broader history of a particular affective practice. The researcher might traverse, too, beyond immediate discursive practices to consider a much wider range of background conditions including commentary on physiology, geography and economics, and might locate the content of immediate narratives of affect in broader patterns of intelligibility dominant in a particular culture. I propose we can incorporate the insights of conversation analysis and discursive psychology, but we can also now confidently move on.

FIVE

Solidifying affect: Structures of feeling, habitus and emotional capital

We are talking about characteristic elements of impulse, restraint and tone; specifically affective elements of consciousness and relationships: not feeling against thought, but thought as felt and feeling as thought: practical consciousness of a present kind, in a living and interrelating continuity. We are then defining these elements as a 'structure': as a set, with specific internal relations, at once interlocking and in tension. Yet we are also defining a social experience which is still in process, often indeed not yet recognized as social but taken to be private, idiosyncratic, and even isolating, but which in analysis (though rarely otherwise) has its emergent, connecting, and dominant characteristics, indeed its specific hierarchies. These are more often recognizable at a later stage, when they have been (as often happens) formalized, classified, and in many cases built into institutions and formations. By that time the case is different; a new structure of feeling will usually already have begun to form, in the true social present. (Raymond Williams, 1977, p. 132)

... personality has to be seen as social practice and not as an entity distinct from 'society'. Personality is what people do, just as social relations are what people do, and the doings are the same. (Robert Connell, 1987, p. 220)

In the previous chapter I looked at affective practice as a lively, situated communicative act. I was trying to elucidate the performative patterns in affective episodes and their moment-by-moment organisation. The multimodal flows involved in Lori's road rage studied by Jack Katz (1999) were a good illustration, as she screwed up her face, wagged her finger, and then stifled her display, afraid of the consequences. I noted the kinds of social and material configurations that make affective moments like these possible, but my main concern was with the here-and-now of affective action and affective–discursive meaning-making.

In this chapter I want to pay more attention to persistence, repetition and power, and the continuities threading through these kinds of situated moments.

This chapter and the next are paired. In this one I am concerned with how affective practices sediment in social formations. How, for example, do characteristic distributions or profiles of affective practices arise which distinguish members of dominant social classes, reinforcing their privilege? How do workplaces, institutions or historical periods acquire distinctive affective flavours? In the next chapter, I will be concerned with questions about the sedimentation of affective practices in individual lives. How does a personal affective order emerge over time, and the potentially large colour-wheel of affectivity reduce down to compose individually distinctive repertoires?

As Connell notes above, these two sets of questions about social formations and personal histories reflect different standpoints on the same psychosocial matter. They are inseparably linked. One angle produces social history, the other social psychology. This typically doubled relation between personal affective habits and affective social conventions – between personal history and social history – can be seen in the ruminations below from the crime novelist P.D. James. At the age of 89, James was reflecting back on her own emotional preferences in an interview conducted by journalist Penny Wark:

> 'One faces things by oneself and there they are. You deal with it', she says, baffled by the 21st-century taste for sharing pain and eschewing privacy. 'I feel that I have a responsibility to the dead, for what my husband might not want to be told. I don't think that I should make money by writing details of private pain or private difficulties which my children will find hurtful' .... 'We now have a world in which people write their diaries on Facebook for millions of other people. To me that is incomprehensible. There is something rather sad about children who may not be making relationships at school getting home and blogging. When a child is run over you see all these toys and flowers piling up, then they have counsellors to deal with their grief and you see them all hugging each other and crying on each other's shoulders.'

> She remembers a day during the war when a recently married colleague heard that her husband had been killed. James said she was sorry and suggested to her supervisor that the girl might like to go home. 'She said, "No, she's got a job to do. She won't want to do that." I felt if she went home she'd have her mother or somebody to comfort her and I still think she should have been allowed to go home, but I don't think that woman was callous. I think that she thought that's what she wanted, to get on with the job.

> 'But the idea that we'd all go up to her and hug her – I do find it a bit creepy. I like emotional reticence. I accept that for many people who have appalling experiences psychologically they are probably better if there is someone they can share them with, but I can't imagine myself getting any comfort from being counselled.' (Wark, 2009, pp. 4–5)

James is recalling here an affective life rather different from the affective life of many contemporary middle-class British citizens. As Ian Craib notes, 'there are fashions in emotions and ... people come to talk about the fashionable ones' (1994, p. 90). What 'feels right' at the time turns out to be historically quite specific.

The connections between personal affective histories and social histories are obvious but this doesn't make them easy to investigate. I'll be arguing in the course of this chapter and the next that the same types of theoretical problems plague attempts to analyse both personal affective order and social affective order. Raymond Williams, writing in the 1970s, was clear on the key challenges. He argued that any patterns (his preferred concept was 'structures of feeling') effervesce and are difficult to detect. Affective solidifications are slippery, first, because social and personal life flows on and is endlessly evolving, so that it is often only when a structure or pattern is changing and disappearing that its grip becomes evident. Second, as P.D. James describes, structures of feeling are embedded in practical consciousness and usual streams of activity. Feeling routines are simply what people do, Williams argued. This doing can be in broad daylight. But in an important sense, too, we live our practices quite obscurely, often not fully knowing the choices made and the implications.

For these reasons, the identification and stabilising of persistent affective patterns in a social or personal formation can require a lot of retrospective constructive work. But this work is also constitutive of the phenomena it describes and inevitably over-simplifying. When a psychotherapist, for instance, traces out the affective repetitions in an individual life, or when a sociologist or historian traces out the structures of feeling for a generation or community, they risk constituting and solidifying the practice as they describe it. The narrative of affect emerging from the reconstructive work becomes itself a template and guide for organising future practice. It creates (and can institutionalise) what it tries to describe.

One of the central challenges confronted, then, in this and the next chapter, concerns how much neatness to attribute to affective configurations. How tidy and robust are the patterns in personal and social affective practice? To what extent do individual lives, social affiliations and affective practices line up in a determining gestalt? If, and when, they align, how do these regularities come about? Williams' preferred term 'structure' in fact seems infelicitous once we have grasped the import of his other arguments. 'Practice' seems a better rubric for the kind of open, flowing articulations he proposes. But, how are practices stitched together and with what levels of inconsistency, movement and heterogeneity?

In contemplating these questions, I will discuss a number of theoretical leads. I will focus on affective practice and social class because some kind of selection is necessary, and such interesting and important lines of work are becoming available in this area. There is so much that could be covered in this chapter, from the gendering of affective practices, and changing patterns in emoting femininities and emoting masculinities, to much less frequently explored issues around, for instance, the affective practices of colonisation, whiteness and migration. My concern is less with documenting the changing particularities of different affective practices, or what Reddy (2001) calls 'emotional regimes', than finding useful ways of theorising the distributions of affective practices in social formations for future empirical research.

In this chapter I will take up Bourdieu's (1984, 1990, 1998) work on habitus as a dominant and generalised answer to questions about how the social ordering of affective phenomena might occur. I will look in detail at recent work from feminist scholars such as Diane Reay (2004, 2005) and Beverley Skeggs (2004a, 2004b) on emotional capital and the relationship between affective performance, social class and social value which extends Bourdieu's thinking. This sociological research explores who is affectively privileged, who is able to 'bank' large amounts of 'emotional capital', and who 'naturally' seems to produce valued affective styles, avoiding abjection and contempt.

I will be arguing, though, that the concept of habitus assumes too much affective order and I will be advocating instead what could be called an 'affective intersectional' approach. I will also suggest that analysis is being impeded, even in the most recent sociological research, because the implicit psychology of the affective social actor underpinning this work is incomplete. The chapter begins, however, with Bourdieu's classic concepts (see Burkitt, 1999; Crossley, 2001; Jenkins, 1992; Reed-Danahay, 2005; Swartz, 1997, for useful reviews).

Habitus and Embodied Dispositions

Following his general take on social practice, Bourdieu maintained that social life is simultaneously subjective and objective, driven forward by human activity but in an ordered rather than random or arbitrary fashion. Social action, he argued, is both a scene of agency, improvisation and strategy and a scene of repetition, constraint and routine. This dual logic reproduces and also gradually transforms existing social relations and power figurations. As Norbert Elias (2000) and Marcel Mauss (1979) had concluded before him, Bourdieu saw the concept of 'habitus' as the key to understanding the paradoxical combination of openness and structure.

He argued that past practice becomes embodied in social actors so they acquire a kind of sediment of dispositions, preferences, tastes, natural attitudes, skills and standpoints. These dispositions then guide future conduct. In this way, the past becomes carried forward, flexibly but inexorably, into the future. Except under conditions of severe social and material restraint, social actors are, potentially, mostly free to act differently; but our socialised inclinations and available knowledge drive us to do what comes most easily, and thus rework and reproduce what has been done before. As some possible lines of action are practised, and other possibilities atrophy, habitus takes shape. Potential lines of action and reaction that are not socially supported or resourced recede, becoming less and less available, and no longer even imaginable. Means and the perception of ends become in this way organically tied together and self-entailing.

Children acquire habitus partly through direct conditioning and training in homes and schools, in part through observation and modelling. As Andrew Sayer (2005) argues, however, habitus can't result just from a process of conditioning. Habitus also arises through intelligent and reflexive adaptation to new circumstances. It is reinforced by the churning over of internal conversations inside the head (Archer, 2003), as people ponder and suffer angst over the patterns in their lives, make resolutions and resist the forces that seem to be moving them in what feels like the wrong directions. New members of social formations such as children and migrants must practise in order to accomplish locally recognised ways of life and turn them into habits. Habits can harden over time and often become so taken for granted that their very existence disappears from view. Then it will seem that the world is just like this, always has been like this, and should always be like this. But, habitus is both the 'weight of the world', in Bourdieu's terms, and a process of active self-creation and new instantiation. The social actor can lightly touch on what is usual, play with it, cite it but not act it, inflect it, combine it with other practices, and so on. As contemporary psychological studies also make clear, socialisation is life-long and thus the scope for acquisition of new ways of being and the disappearance of old ways.

For Bourdieu, the dispositions of habitus were reflective and unreflective, corporeal, practical and cognitive. As noted, the 'feel for the social game', what he called the *illusio* (1990, pp. 66–7), can be so encompassing, so total, and feel so natural, that the investments and identifications are not even apparent. Crucially, Bourdieu argued that habitus becomes written into the body. It is as much a physical as a mental process.

Habitus is indicated in body *hexis*, for instance. That is, it is evident in posture, familiar gestures and mannerisms, looks, ways of inhabiting space, accents, and so on. Past practice and social location are embodied in an over-developed muscle, in the callous on a writing finger, in a cringe and timorous stoop, or in a confident stride and a braying voice in a London street. But, the habituated body is more than a list of modifications to individual parts. It is a set of integrated coordinations and patterns. It is a set of 'complexes' in Bourdieu's terms (cf. also Burkitt, 2002). As Bourdieu describes, these patterns are tied into social prompts.

> There is no better image of the logic of socialization, which treats the body as a 'memory jogger', than those of complexes of gestures, postures and words – simple interjections or favourite clichés – which only have to be slipped into, like a theatrical costume, to awaken, by the evocative power of bodily mimesis, a universe of ready-made feelings and experiences. (1984, p. 474)

As a result of the connection between the complexes of the body and social prompts the body becomes mimetic. Just as I apparently cannot help myself from opening and closing my own mouth when guiding a mouthful of food towards the mouth of a baby in a high chair, the body cannot help itself rehearsing what Bourdieu describes above as a 'universe of ready-made feelings and experiences' when prompted by a familiar situation. The body, Bourdieu states, is a 'memory-jogger' and in this way an 'accomplice' of social reproduction, encouraging and moving the individual towards some imagined futures but muting others.

Affect and Habitus

This emphasis on mimesis suggests that Bourdieu saw emotion and affect as mainly conservative forces. This is an interesting hypothesis and worth exploring further. Emotions are conservative in Bourdieu's view because they force the individual back into established practice, and reinforce the power of past practice. Thus, when faced with a situation threatening a social trajectory and the ongoing projects favoured by the dispositions of habitus, an individual might feel intense anxiety. This anxiety imagines the failure of these projects and rehearses an anticipated outcome. In this way, it massively increases the push of habitus and people's obedience to the social world their affect has presumed.

Emotion anticipates and thus increases the likelihood that the past will be reproduced.

> Emotion, the extreme case of such anticipation, is a (hallucinatory) 'presenting' of the impending future, which, as bodily reactions identical to those of the real situation bear witness, leads a person to live a still suspended future as already present, or even already past, and therefore necessary and inevitable – 'I am a dead man'; 'I am done for.' (Bourdieu, 1990, p. 292)

For Bourdieu, emotions more than anything seem to carry the unreflective or non-conscious aspects of habitus. They present the crunch point at which social agents discover they cannot help themselves, and re-enact past practice without knowing why, or without necessarily being willing to do so. Bourdieu maintains that emotion is not representational knowledge that can be 'brandished', or the self-conscious following of a script from memory. Affect is something the body does; it is pure action. As Nick Crossley (2001) points out, for Bourdieu, social actors 'are bound to social fields by a strong affective grip' and feel the 'weight' of the cares and concerns generated by these social fields 'with a great emotional intensity' (p. 102). Furthermore, those who transgress the boundaries set by habitus can provoke 'visceral, murderous horror, absolute disgust, metaphysical fury' (Bourdieu, 1984, p. 475, cited in Reed-Danahay, 2005, p. 111).

Bourdieu's account of affect remains sketchy (see Probyn, 2004b, and Reed-Danahay, 2005, for thoughtful exegeses of his few direct statements). Exactly how affect operates is left for the most part unelaborated. As Probyn points out, Bourdieu ignores the potentially disruptive quality of emotion. Affect can also jolt us into a new scene, she suggests, as well as into repetitions of old scenes. It is not clear when affect reinforces habitus and when it might bring about change. Reed-Danahay argues that Bourdieu blurs distinctions between cognition and affect (knowledge and feeling) in his work. In this way we could say he anticipates and he is commensurate with some of the new directions in psychobiology and neuroscience discussed in Chapter 2. But as Reed-Danahay also describes, Bourdieu pretty much uncritically endorsed the bio-cultural model of emotion dominant in his period. Affect for Bourdieu seemed to divide into a set of raw and universal biological responses – part of the natural human bedrock – and something which in its more complex amalgams such as love and honour was culturally conditioned.

This impression is confirmed by Bourdieu's general position on 'libido' as dissected by Crossley (2001). Bourdieu (1998, p. 78) saw libido as biological. It is an 'undifferentiated impulse' which becomes differentiated and organised in social fields. Biological libido pushes people to care, invest, identify and generates passionate feelings. But what they care about will be given by their habitus. As Crossley points out, this unspecified biological impulse is vague in the extreme. He proposes to replace it instead with the 'desire for recognition' (2001, p. 102). To my mind, though, this is not much better. An effective and elaborated social psychology of affective embodied practice is needed to fill this gap.

I will come back to this missing social psychology later. For now, I want to follow a little further the relationships between affect, habitus, class and social value, first again in Bourdieu's own work, but then in more recent sociological research.

Cultural Capital and Social Distinction

At the heart of Bourdieu's approach is his exploration of the ways in which the embodied dispositions of habitus are tied to social relations, social class and social positions, and thus to forms of distinction and opportunities:

> Habitus are generative principles of distinct and distinctive practices – what the worker eats, and especially the way he eats it, the sport he practices and the way he practices it, his political opinions and the way he expresses them are systematically different from the industrial owner's corresponding activities. But habitus are also classification schemes, principles of classification, principles of vision and division, different tastes. They make distinctions between what is good and bad, between what is right and what is wrong, between what is distinguished and what is vulgar, and so forth, but the distinctions are not identical. Thus, for instance, the same behavior or even the same good can appear distinguished to one person, pretentious to someone else, and cheap and showy to yet another. (Bourdieu, 1998, p. 8)

People display their social value through their habitus. In particular, Bourdieu argued, it carries their cultural capital.

He saw cultural capital as a kind of privileged aesthetic sense, appreciation and understanding, as sets of tastes and preferences. Cultural capital is objectified in forms of property (books, works of art, CDs), and usually marked and validated by credentials (university degrees and specialist skills). Parents who possess cultural capital typically have a keen investment in passing it on to their children (Reay, 2004). Bourdieu argued that like other forms of capital, cultural capital has an exchange value. Thus higher education certificates usually translate into differential positions in job markets.

Bourdieu assumed a strong, unifying relationship between types of cultural capital and social class. As a result, the working class, for example, would be distinguished by a set of shared communal dispositions, values, cultural tastes, forms of expertise, and so on which would be relatively sharply distinguished from the habitus of the middle classes. In effect, habitus and cultural capital operate rather like a self-fulfilling prophecy (Swartz, 1997). Distinction is there in part because it is imagined to be there and thus the prophecy is made reality. Bourdieu had a clear vision of the relative arbitrariness of social distinction and its relational basis. The important thing about beer versus champagne, for example, is not so much the intrinsic qualities of each but their relation to each other and the circuits of value, scarcity, difference and social distinction created.

Bourdieu's (1984) own empirical research in the 1960s in France supported his predictions about the relationship between social class, habitus and cultural capital to the extent that he felt able to draw maps of the contemporary social and symbolic space. He drew connections, for instance, between drinking ordinary red wine, liking football and accordion playing and being a skilled worker or farmer. This nexus could be contrasted with being a technician, liking light opera, and voting for the left, or with being a university professor, liking chess, piano and whiskey, or contrasted with being an industrialist, liking horse riding and champagne and voting for the right. These different kinds of habitus constituted distinctive social, material and psychological spaces. The first group (of men) had low volumes of both economic and cultural capital; the second group were mid-level on economic capital and on cultural capital; the third group had high levels of overall capital but a much greater extent of cultural capital than economic capital; while the last group were also high on overall levels of capital but, unlike the professors, were high on economic capital and short on cultural capital.

As Bourdieu makes these links between habitus and social location, what is happening to affect? Again, it seems likely that affect will solidify the social relations of class just as these relations solidify forms of affect into embodied habitus. Bourdieu highlighted relatively non-intimate correlates of class such as occupation, voting histories and leisure pursuits. In recent years, however, a number of social researchers, in particular feminist scholars, have extended Bourdieu's work and developed rich accounts of affect, social class and social value demonstrating that it is not just cultural goods which are unevenly distributed but perhaps also affective practices (cf. Charlesworth, 2000; Illouz, 1997; Kirk, 2007; Lawler 1999, 2000, 2004, 2005; Layton, 2006; Lucey and Reay, 2000; Lucey et al., 2003; Reay, 2004, 2005, 2008; Reay et al., 2011; Reay and Lucey, 2003; Rogaly and Taylor, 2009; Sayer, 2005; Skeggs, 2004a, 2004b, 2005, 2010; Tyler, 2008; Walkerdine, 1991, 2009, 2010; Walkerdine and Lucey, 1989; Walkerdine et al., 2001).

Affect and Social Value

This work has deepened our understanding of the broad relation between affect and social value sketched in very general terms by Bourdieu. Illuminating research from relational psychoanalyst Lynne Layton, for instance, begins to paint a much more specific picture of how emotion and social value might lock together in everyday experiences. She starts with an anecdote:

> I needed a garden hose and took a friend shopping with me to a store called Ocean State Job Lot. As we left the store, my upper-middle-class friend looked utterly disgusted and said, 'That place gives me the heebie jeebies.'

I tried to find out what she meant, what emotion 'heebie jeebies' describes for her, but as I asked and it became clear that the emotion had to do with a disdain not only for the lower-class goods in the store but for the lower-class shoppers, shame set in and she refused to keep talking. (Layton, 2006, p. 51)

Exploring this further and interrogating the experiences of others, Layton begins to highlight the kind of affective grip involved in habitus and its power. An emotion like the 'heebie jeebies' indicates how taste, distinction, social position and affect intertwine. The origins of people's investments and powerful likes and dislikes often remain obscure, yet these prove deeply motivating, propelling us in and out of life-styles and consumption patterns, leading us to flinch away from some situations while gravitating towards others.

The affects involved are anything but banal. As Imogen Tyler (2008) has demonstrated, differences and distinctions between 'people like us' and 'people not like us' can evoke intense affects of disgust and contempt, provoking extreme emotions of shame and humiliation among the dominated and those made abject. Beverley Skeggs gives this example of a rant from Germaine Greer against 'chavs' and 'Essex girls':

She used to be conspicuous as she clacked along the pavements in her white plastic stilettos, her bare legs mottled patriot red, white and blue with cold, and her big bottom barely covered by a denim mini-skirt. Essex girls usually come in twos, both behind pushchairs. Sometimes you hear them before you see them, cackling shrilly or yelling to each other from one end of the street to the other, or berating those infants in blood-curdling fashion ... The Essex girl is tough, loud, vulgar and unashamed. Her hair is badly dyed not because she can't afford a hairdresser, but because she wants to look brassy. Nobody makes her wear an ankle chain; she likes the message it sends ... she is not ashamed to admit that what she puts behind her ears to make her more attractive is her ankles. She is anarchy on stilts, when she and her mates descend upon Southend for a rave, even the bouncers grow pale. (Greer, 2001, p. 8, cited in Skeggs, 2005, p. 966–7)

Greer constructs a scary, incomprehensible and unseemly femininity. She seems to envy the anarchic energy she imputes to the 'Essex Girl' but also reproduces long histories of middle-class fear and disgust directed at the working-class woman figured as vulgar and out of line. Skeggs (2005, 2010) has documented how white working-class women often figure in this way, defining what she calls a 'constitutive limit' – constructed to mark the boundaries of middle-class propriety, demure affect and good sense. As Stephanie Lawler (2004) has argued, any 'affective good' seems to be achieved through repudiation. The 'good' can often only be identified and claimed as one's own distinguishing characteristic if some other group is assigned the 'bad'. This is perhaps most evident in the relational ordering of masculinities and femininities (cf. Hollway, 1984), but is now coming into view for social class relations also.

Affect and Social Class

The experience of class in a country like the UK, then, is not just about the kind of classic territories which Bourdieu mapped: going to the dogs versus riding to the hunt; shopping at Fortnums versus shopping at Aldi; voting Labour versus voting Tory. Class, recent research maintains, is lived at the level of the gut, through what Reay (2005) calls its 'psychic economy'. Indeed, the affective patterning of class and material inequality might well end up being more persistent and important in maintaining difference than any other associated regularity such as voting preference or leisure habits. Because class is relational, the psychic economies in Reay's sense are intertwined. Affect follows, regulates and composes social relations and social value. Hinterlands of exclusions, vicious differentiations and pockets of pride, fear and envy are created (Sayer, 2005) along with sets of comparisons and subjectifications blighting life chances (Charlesworth, 2000; Rogaly and Taylor, 2009; Walkerdine et al., 2003).

Class position generates a specific affective style. Reay, drawing on Andrew Sayer's work, proposes, for instance:

> We can map out a psychic economy of class where a combination of arrogance, satisfaction, contempt and pride constitute an exclusivist middle-class position in the social class field and a mix of guilt, defensiveness, empathy and conciliation go to make up the 'middle-class egalitarian' (Sayer, 2005). Similarly a varying combination of resentment, envy, pride and anger constitute the solidarist fractions of the working classes while their more individualist peers are characterized by a mix of deference, envy and shame ... (Reay, 2005, pp. 913–14)

In recent years new empirical work has focused particularly on the affective styles composing the habitus of the British white middle classes. For Skeggs (2004a, 2004b) the affects of this group reflect the ethos of 'possessive individualism'. She argues that the middle class is marked out by a deep-seated commitment to self-improvement, deferred gratification and to accruing more and more 'property in the self'. These ambitions are particularly evident in middle-class parents' practices in relation to their children who are encouraged to acquire a wide range of qualifications, forms of knowledge and experiences found in music lessons, gap years, private school education and multiple 'A Level' qualifications which can then be 'banked', setting them up for life. This acquisitive attitude is taken to be normal and moral, used as the standard for judging other social groups.

It is not only the middle class, however, who generalise their very particular affective practices as a universal ethical prescription. Skeggs (2004a) argues that recent social theory makes this mistake also. She suggests that recent sociological research on individualisation, for instance, mis-recognises the basic middle-class model of self just described, and its typical affective practices, as a general trend. This work (e.g. Giddens, 1991) claims that the historical trend in late modernity is towards more emotionally open, exploratory, reflexive and 'worked over' selves, and is thus moving away from more traditional, older communal identifications and the more stoical and controlled affective practices of previous generations. Skeggs (see also Walkerdine and Bansel, 2010) argues that what might appear to be the emergence of a new kind of 'late modern' individual and affective subjectivity is in fact just the usual middle-class self, and thus theory once again rewrites the working class as deficit.

Other new research on social class and affective styles has examined more closely the class fraction Reay (2005) described as 'middle-class egalitarian'. Reay et al. (2011) examined a large sample of white middle-class parents in the UK who had made 'against the grain' school-choices for their children. An 'against the grain' school-choice involves sending children to local comprehensives with comparatively poor positions in school league tables as opposed to following the more usual 'fortress' middle-class strategies of choosing private education, moving house into up-market school catchment areas, or searching out schools where children would be 'at home'. Reay et al. argue that these middle-class 'fish out of water' ended up, however, often reproducing key aspects of their own habitus despite their best intentions.

For this group, the cultural property acquired for their children and accumulated in the self came to include cosmopolitanism and familiarity with the 'exotic multicultural other', fitting their children for more global futures. Reay et al. report that the result was a greater social mix in schools but little social mixing. These researchers describe, too, how discourses of 'brightness' found throughout the school system became a kind of affective defence for the parents. The privilege and distinction which middle-class children carried into their new environments ensuring their success were typically understood as due to the 'specialness' of the child and their intrinsic talents. This research, then, suggests how entrenched and persistent cultural capital can be. It also paints a vivid picture of the affects of the middle-class going along with that – the anxieties, desires, defences, the conscientiousness, the competitive jostling and the sense of entitlement to feelings of contempt.

Emotional Capital

Does it make sense, then, to add 'emotional capital' to the growing list of capitals in the social sciences (economic capital, cultural capital, social capital and symbolic capital)? Would this be a useful way of capturing the sedimentation of affective practices in social formations and its uneven consequences? Are there affective practices that add value and which could be exchanged for other kinds of capital such as greater material wealth? Do some affective styles offer a leg up just like owning a house in London or New York or a big bundle of shares?

A concept like 'emotional capital' suggests that some affective styles (made up of particular combinations of affective practices) offer some groups an advantage. It raises the perturbing possibility of potential affective 'arms races', as socially disadvantaged groups struggle to attain the affective styles of the 'distinguished', only to discover that some other forms of affective manners have become the new emotional capital.

In a thoughtful analysis Reay (2004) argues that if emotional capital exists, it operates in a rather more complex way than other kinds of capital. Reay attributes the first use of the term to Nowotny (1981). Nowotny suggested that emotional capital (e.g. love, care, affection, patience, empathy) is something that women possess and that men and children appropriate. Like Arlie Hochschild's (1983) notion of 'emotional labour', it is not necessarily the individual possessor of the capital or the emotional labourer who benefits, and who can convert expertise and emotional productivity into other gains. Instead, employers, men and children who can draw on the emotional investment of workers, wives and mothers may be often more clearly the winners. Reay argues that mothers' emotional invest-ments in their children are in fact exceedingly complex. Reviewing findings from her own research, she suggests that 'seemingly positive emotions could sometimes have negative repercussions for children, while apparently negative emotional involvement could spur children on academically' (2004, p. 62). Mothers' anger and anxiety could push their children to succeed, while in other cases it simply produced highly anxious children. Mothers were treading what Reay describes as a fine line between empathy and over-identification.

Perhaps, then, as Illouz (1997) argues, emotional capital lies in the capacity to manage emotions and navigate calmly through emotional storms, as opposed to being overwhelmed by distress and strong affect? Illouz associates this capacity with the new middle classes who have become familiar with psychological tech-nologies and skilled in working on the self. Again, Reay suggests, it may not be this simple. She reports data from her research with UK-based, black mothers. This suggests that these women's experience of racism in schools encouraged strong angry affects that were, in fact, beneficial in supporting their children. Here, being calm in the face of intense provocation would not have been effective.

Reay's conclusion is that emotional capital is not defined by the affect itself and its routine methods of unfolding. It will be a complex outcome of situated patterns, and thus highly dependent on who is doing the emoting, the context, local norms and expectations. It is these things that determine whether a par-ticular affective practice accumulates value, other forms of capital and privilege. Reay notes that class is relevant here in a broad way: it will be more difficult for those without cultural and economic capital to marshal what may be required to turn strong affect into something positive and beneficial, while those with many cultural and economic resources are likely to be able to better tolerate short-term emotional suffering in the service of some long-term goal to realise the benefits of deferred gratification. The working-class mothers Reay studied tended to be more concerned with their children's immediate emotional well-being. They were less willing to compromise this for later potential gains that might be difficult to realise or may never eventuate.

In general, as Skeggs (2004a, 2004b) points out, Bourdieu's notion of cultural capital is unhelpful as a description of working-class life and affect. His theory of working-class habitus mainly stresses lack and deficit. The notion of emotional capital is likely to intensify this. For Skeggs (2004b, p. 87), Bourdieu provides an excellent description of how the middle classes make themselves through possessive individualism, and 'how the game is played to middle-class advantage'. But, '[a]re the working class always lack, beyond value, without value, resigned and adjusted to their conditions, unable to accrue value to themselves?' Skeggs argues that Bourdieu's theory recapitulates middle-class positionings of the working class. For both Bourdieu, and for the middle classes, working-class affective culture is seen as a mix of 'bad choices', failure, pathology, and as signs of 'moral lack' according to the standards of the middle-class individualised self (2004b, p. 91).

Skeggs suggests that, unacknowledged by Bourdieu and other recent social theory, the working class might experience a different relation to affect and to self compared to the middle class. This could not be described as building emotional capital in any conventional sense because there is no 'trading up' to create surplus value. For the middle classes, Skeggs argues, affects are mobilised as part of exchange relations. Affect and identity are caught up in complicated strategic work to create and maintain a valued self that might achieve, and then hold on to, valued social locations. For the working classes, in contrast, affect is pure 'use-value' rather than exchange-value. This is emotion for its own end in authentic response to social conditions. Features of working-class life such as anti-authoritarianism, humour, rage, indignation at unfairness, and communal loyalty are forms of affective energy performed not to accrue value but for their own sake as responses to social injustice due to accidents of birth and social location. I think, however, the division Skeggs makes here between authentic and reactive practice contrasted with inauthentic and managed practice is problematic. I will come back to this point below.

An Overview and Some Problems

This chapter began at the point at which ethnomethodology and the other approaches considered in the last chapter started to fall silent. My focus was on persistent patterns in affective practice found across social formations and how best to theorise these. The research I have examined in this chapter has pursued two related lines of enquiry. Investigators have looked at how affective practice enters into social relations, regulating, mediating, conserving and disrupting the status quo. We can see that affect can maintain, increase and diminish power, influence and social value. Affect can function, too, to construct and mark boundaries and reject the 'other'. It can work to keep people in line as their anxiety and fear, for instance, push them to conform. Here affective practice is studied as social activity, woven in with other social practices, with potentially mixed effects and impacts.

The second, intertwined, line of enquiry followed the territory originally sketched out by Raymond Williams. This is the notion that affective practices sediment so that, for a generation, a social class, a gender, a national or regional group, a particular period of social history, etc. one can find ways of performing affect, or an affective habitus, which have become characteristic, and which define the flavour, relations and habits of that group. Here, affect is seen in some ways as more like a possession embedded in the individual, as part of their unthinking everyday repertoire.

For both kinds of research, but particularly for the latter line of work on habitus, it is worth exploring, first, in a bit more detail the social psychology implied here. What is being assumed about affect and the emotional social actor? The second challenging issue concerns the complexity and heterogeneity of people's actual social locations and affiliations. Does the research do justice to these? Examining these two problems will lead me to try to move in the last section of the chapter to an alternative 'affective intersectional' approach.

The social psychology of affective practice

I want to argue that sociological research on affect and emotion is in danger of developing a model of affect and the emotional social actor that is too static and bound up with traditional, 20th century, psychobiological accounts. Social actors are presented as operating like jukeboxes. Press the right buttons and the affective tunes appropriate to status, position and habitus will blare out. Middle-class competitiveness will burst discordantly into life while for some factions of the working class the only tunes are deference, envy and shame. People are treated as affect automatons, emoting and being taken over by affect, not being able to help responding, but not quite understanding why.

Affective practices (like the range of affective tunes in the jukebox) are assumed to come in neat, recognisable, standard, basic emotion-style packages. Particularly for Bourdieu, these emotion packets are reactions rather than actions, fixed biological patterns rather than assemblages or recruitments. These are responses rather than practical methods for performing, re-animating and re-configuring social relations. Skeggs reinforces this jukebox tendency when she divides affective practice into authentic and inauthentic types and then conflates these with social divisions.

Bourdieu, especially, carries over a particular legacy from biology. Indeed, it is easy to read emotion as 'natural' and corporeal. It is then also easy to treat it as rather different from other kinds of social practice. Affect is presented as a kind of practice that is always unreflective and non-conscious, and which is never planned, self and other regulated, narrated, agentic and negotiated. The famous duality of practice – it is subjective *and* objective, open *and* evolving, constraining *and* 'could be otherwise' – gets forgotten.

I want to suggest that research on affective practice and social formations needs to move to a more elaborated and complex account of the nature of affect and

the emotional social actor – treating affect actually as practice. A more promising starting point is appreciating that the palette of affect is likely to be highly varied. Affective actors are not social dopes, knowing just a few tunes, or pushed and pulled by basic emotions, as theories of habitus often seem to imply. Sometimes it will be the case that an affective performance is best described in jukebox terms as the unfolding and reiteration of an unbidden, long-term, embodied habit. Sometimes instead, though, people's affective practice will be highly self-regulated and modulated. Probably more usually it will move variably along these dimensions in a complex changing mix as an affective episode is put together in concert with the performances of others. Similarly, everyday affective practice will bear a variable relation to judgements of authenticity. Sometimes affect will be deeply felt, and sometimes it will be more obviously 'performed'. It is unlikely that just one social group knows how to be strategic and only one social group knows how to be authentic.

The affective canon, then, which becomes characteristic of a community, a social group, an institution, or a social formation, is likely to be a mix of different manifestations of affective practice as well as varying in content and in typical distributions. Some of the canon composing a particular habitus may work, for example, through aspirations, regulating through setting ideals of self-control or dramatic display. It may include playful affective routines involving ironic and reflexive mimicry, and sometimes core distinguishing affective practices will just operate in the expected, taken-for-granted, unarticulated and self-evident ways. As Andrew Sayer (2005) argues, and Chapter 4 demonstrated, affective practice will usually be open to moral and normative assessment, and thus will be woven together in subtle ways with people's usual communal methods for describing, accounting for, and judging self and others.

A more complex social psychology of affect, and more attention to affect as practice, will enrich sociological work on the ways in which social formations are configured, come to power and dissolve. The second challenge I want to raise is perhaps not so easily tackled.

Heterogeneity and plurality

Habitus as a concept is tied to social groups and social categories. In this way it predates the growing emphasis on complexity of positioning which is increasingly becoming a staple of identity studies. Can habitus (habituses perhaps) be plural? What would that look like? As a white, middle-class, able-bodied, female academic in her 50s, a migrant to the UK from New Zealand, how many different types of habitus do I move through in a typical day? Is there a habitus or structure of feeling that goes with each distinct social position? Or, is my habitus, and its characteristic affective practices, singular but a particular, partly idiosyncratic, partly shared composite or amalgam of my diverse range of social locations? If it becomes too particular then how much do I still share with others as a collective structure of feeling? How fragmented and heterogeneous can a habitus get and still count as a habitus?

One recent, large-scale investigation of British cultural tastes and social class (Bennett et al., 2009) suggested that habitus is more complex than Bourdieu's theory predicted. This study emulated Bourdieu's attempts to map social class, tastes, preferences and leisure activities. It discovered that cultural capital in the contemporary UK is more overlapping and less differentiated than Bourdieu found for 1960s France. Habitus is now less likely to be automatically unified, coherent and homogeneous. It is not clear, though, whether the social world is just more fragmented than it used to be in the 1960s, or whether the theory was wrongly pitched in the first place. Surveying the patterns in their data, Bennett et al. (2009, p. 2) emphasise that they are left in no doubt that 'class counts' but they go on to say 'we are equally certain that class does not always count more than gender or ethnicity'. These days 'distinctive forms of cultural capital are also associated with gender, ethnic, and age divisions, which interact with each other and with class-based forms'.

We need to add to Bennett et al.'s list other regularities in positioning, not just those based on the standard identity categories. Particular workplaces, occupations, peer groups and various institutional affiliations, for example, are likely to add further layering to affective practices and to possess their own noticeable and distinctive ways of being. As many have noted, one of the difficulties with Bourdieu's notion of habitus is that it can seem over-deterministic. As Sayer (2005, p. 3) argues, if there is a 'logic' to the social patterning of something like class-based styles, this is 'as likely to involve slippages, blockages, non-sequiturs and wishful thinking'. In fact, I want to predict that affective practices will routinely effloresce over the conventional, demographic boundary-lines of class, gender, ethnicity, religion and nation, communal life and personal life. The associations between organised affective practices and social groupings will not be tidy, and this lack of neatness will be important in understanding the ways in which affective practices travel and change.

It must be the case, indeed, that as soon as identity got complicated in both theory and in life (Wetherell, 2010), habitus would lose any simple classificatory power. As mobility and globalisation have increased, it has become more evident that many social actors, even those traditionally seen as the most fixed in place such as the English, white, working class (Rogaly and Taylor, 2009), live within a nexus of exceedingly complicated intersections between resources, histories, futures, investments and identifications.

There is also the challenge of understanding and creating room for what Lauren Berlant (2000) calls 'minor affect' (see also Probyn, 2004b). The concept of affective practice stretches to encompass both conventionality and unconventionality. It is not just about the hegemonic, or the most powerful conventions, and not just about 'winning ways' and 'winning feelings'. Berlant posits in her writing on intimacy a 'wild energy', 'drive' or 'mobile attachment' that can create a wide range of affective spaces. Some of these, she argues, are predictable, conventional and concrete. These are the spaces and practices people can return to again and again, which can be controllable and can seem to be built 'just for us' (pp. 5–6). Here, she states, we can feel at the centre of own lives and can feel as if we 'have a life'.

Other figurations of affect, however, do not enjoy such solidity:

> these have no alternative plots, let alone few laws or stable places of culture in which to clarify and cultivate them. What happens to the energy of attachment when it has no designated space? To the gestures, glances, encounters, collaborations or fantasies that have no canon? 'Minor' intimacies have been forced to develop aesthetics of the extreme to push these spaces into being by way of small and grand gestures, the wish for normalcy heard everywhere these days. (2000, p. 5)

As Chapter 3 argued, there are problems with 'wild' definitions of affect. But Berlant compellingly describes how affective practice can be dominating and stupefying and also creative. Affective practice can disempower in the guise of empowering, but it can also be genuinely novel and generative, as Deleuze (1994) suggests, enriching and enlarging and renewing. In some way analyses of affective practice over long historical durations must keep open all these possibilities.

Affective Intersectionality

It seems clear that the study of affect in social formations needs to go 'intersectional' just as the study of identity has gone intersectional (Phoenix and Pattynama, 2006). For identity, this has involved focusing research on the ways in which different threads of social relations, points of identification, and identity-making practices meet and wind together. This intertwining may be either in the context of an individual life, in a particular site, in an institutional scene, or in a moment of trouble and conflict, or to sustain privilege or create abjection. It may produce either 'liveable' or 'unliveable' conjunctions.

A similar intersectionality for affective practices and social formations will involve recognising that people are likely to be able to mobilise (and be mobilised by) quite wide-ranging and diverse repertoires of affective practices closely linked to context. There are likely to be complicated mixes of affective repertoires available to any one individual or social group at any one moment, including some affective practices that are widespread, for instance, and which are very stable, and some which are very local and exceedingly transient, specific to particular workplaces, to some families, to a few streets for just a few months, and to quite particular historical moments. Just as with identity, however, this doesn't mean that people do not get stuck, or differ in their positions in relation to circuits of affective value. I suspect this 'sticking' will be strongly site- and context-specific. The affective positioning around middle-class, 'against-the-grain' school choices investigated by Reay et al. (2011), for instance, looks like one site and context where this happens *par excellence*.

Like 'structure' for Raymond Williams, 'intersection' is not quite the right word for what I am advocating. It is too static a description of the complex mixing of affective practices found in social formations and individual lives which we need to investigate. Stabilised affective practice and affective necessities emerge as fragmented and heteroclite subjectivities form and engage in the plurality and polyphony of shifting social relations. Social psychologists (Billig et al., 1988; Wetherell and Potter, 1992) have argued that, in fact, it is this polyphony and the dilemmatic nature of contemporary ideologies that keep people in line and preserve social order. In other words, contemporary common sense naturalising and justifying privilege is a patchwork or kaleidoscope of contradictions and fragments that refuse to cohere. People navigate this patchwork, customising it for their own purposes, sliding from one repertoire to another. This, Billig et al. suggest, is how common sense works rather than the meek trotting out of singular and coherent belief systems pre-dumped in people's heads.

If, as many studies of discursive practices have demonstrated (e.g. Wetherell and Potter, 1992), sense-making in classic ideological territories such as justifications of inequality and racism is organised patchily in this way, then it is also likely to be the case for affective practice and the particular knotty forms of its sedimentation we need to investigate. Dilemma, trouble and contradiction in affective practice might prove good starting points for discovering consequential patterns in practical distributions. A focus on plural affective practices will perhaps offer a more encompassing way of understanding the combinations, competitions and exclusions that result in the affective styles of those who are entirely confident of their power, the styles of those whose 'lives [are] devoid of social consecration' (Charlesworth, 2000, p. 6), and those who are somewhere in between.

I am not wanting to claim, however, that it is always wrong to begin, as research on habitus typically seems to do, with a sample based on a social group, on one identity, a social class, one nation, etc., or a combination of two or three of these things. Sometimes the editing down of the complexity of affiliations and social locations to answer specific research questions about affective solidification, structures of feeling, and persistent affective practice is crucial. The research I reviewed above on social class and affect shows how this editing of identity can work. It can be revelatory to try to line up identity, affect and social location. But perhaps it is time now, after a generation of thinking about habitus and structures of feeling, to re-consider solidifying affective patterns in ways that also focus on sites, scenes, actual practices and contexts of use, and the messiness of social life. The next chapter will pursue some of this thinking further.

SIX

Personalising affect: Relational histories, subjectivities and the psychosocial

The processes of subjectivity are over-determined and contextual. They interact with, partially determine, and are partially determined by many other equally complicated processes including somatic, political, familial, and gendered ones. Temporary coherence into seemingly solid characteristics or structures is only one of subjectivity's many possible expressions. When enough threads are webbed together, a solid entity may appear to form. Yet the fluidity of the threads and the web itself remains. What felt solid and real may subsequently separate and reform. (Jane Flax, 1993, p. 94)

But I'm losing track. As I said, what I was thinking about Mum was that day at Betty's. The medal ceremony starts and we all have one eye on the t.v. so as to be sure we catch it. We see the men standing at the sides of the individual podiums: What way do they go? From gold to bronze or the other way round? Whichever way the gold medal winner stands in the middle and so that was Tommy. Anyway when they are all on their podiums and the US anthem is playing – we see the fists rise up, as if in slow motion, not a hand across the chest or both hands by their sides but two black hands above two slightly bowed heads and two white hands held down by the guy's side. And as though coordinated by some invisible force, as each of us saw that symbol and felt its power, we jumped up, as if one, and as our fists rose above our heads – all 12–13 of us – and yelled, 'yes! Black Power, Black Power', as we leapt to our feet and the floorboards of Betty's suburban semi- trembled under the weight of our energy, our pride, our delight.

You were with us – or more like you were with that white boy from Australia, or was it New Zealand? – who acted in solidarity with Tommy and John by refusing to salute and wearing a badge showing his support for them.

'Uh, wit' your bad self, and say it loud I'm black and I'm proud.'

And we did and we were. You saw that Mum didn't you and laughed and cheered.

But it was far more complicated than simple gestures of solidarity – I mean, as I've been saying, in the confines of intimate life – it was far more messy and ambivalent, wasn't it Mum. I mean we all were together, and you and Paula and Pauline and Pat, all of you had black children and had been sharing your lives with black folk for at least twenty years by that time hadn't you?

So it wasn't about separation, was it Mum. I mean you – we, were all living together but it didn't mean that all racial cleavage and antagonism disappeared from our lives, did it.

[...]

I mean we have some stories to tell about that kind of thing, that proximity of love and racism, the simultaneous closeness and distance, the us-ing and them-ing inside the family. (Gail Lewis, 2009, pp. 13–14)

In this chapter I want to try to understand further the emergence of individual affective styles and trajectories. How do particular affective connections, routines, ways of emoting and making meaning come to order individual lives and become dominant or 'winning' styles? As life continues, affective practice seems to become customised, becoming less diverse, more predictable and pre-figured. Some emotions become usual, while other affective possibilities become exceptional or even apparently impossible. Process becomes perhaps better described as a 'standing wave', in Blackman et al.'s (2008, p. 19) phrase, a kind of sticking and regimentation. The personalisation of affect is a product of relational histories made up of repeated interactions, narratives and habitual body routines. The social valuing and differentiation discussed in the last chapter are turned into flesh.

The complexities involved in understanding personal affective orders are illustrated in Gail Lewis' (2009) magnificent article 'Birthing Racial Difference', the source of the extract above. Lewis stages in this paper a conversation with her mother to evoke and analyse experiences of mixed-race mother–child relations. She demonstrates some of the repetitive affective patterns forming the texture of her relationship with her mother and the subjectivities these provoked. Lewis was born in 1950s London. Her mother was white and her father had migrated to London from the (British) Caribbean in the 1940s. Her article is a compassionate analysis of her mother's history and the experience of mixed-race family life in times of intense racial antagonism.

This article is so much better read in the original than re-described. Lewis shows how the intimate affective practices of care and love and the ordinary hates and confinements of family life intertwined with the ambivalence arising from her mother's fight against, and at times weary capitulation to, the shame and disgrace projected by outsiders and other family members on to a white mother of black babies. Lewis' mother is pushed 500 different ways in this account. She is caught between maternal love and strategic disavowal of her daughter, patterns of solidarity/inclusion and difference/exclusion that reverse according to the context, fierce responses to those attacking her and protectiveness to her children versus acquiescence to the norms of the times.

This account persuasively reinforces the messages emerging from the last chapter. Personal history, subjectivity and affective practice develop in social relations. The social orderings of the affective routines of family life are vivid and sharp in this case because the particular social circumstances are dramatic and pressing. But this intimate connection between the personal and the social is present in all lived affective trajectories. This work reminds us why conceptions of a singular affective habitus fail, along with simple 'jukebox' models of the psychosocial actor, and why it is necessary to think in 'affective intersectional' ways. Lewis describes complex psychosocial patchworks coalescing, travelling and continually re-forming. As Jane Flax (1993, p. 108) argues, psychosocial order is 'a shifting and always changing intersection of complex, contradictory, and unfinished processes'.

What forms of thinking, then, about subjectivity and the psychosocial can catch the weave of pattern and the solidifications of relational, affective and social practices, as well as encompass fragmentation, creativity, re-formation and happenstance? This chapter will critically examine two main kinds of arguments about the nature of the affected subject. As I move between them, I will be trying to put together a kind of 'goldilocks' psychosocial theory for investigations of affective practice in individual lives that learns from both sources.

The first approach I will consider is one that more or less abandons subjectivity altogether. This is the thrust in recent cultural and political research to analyse affect as lines of force without a subject. There are some claims that are shared here with the approach to affective practice I am trying to develop. Like theories of affect without a subject, notions of affective practice also stress what could be called the 'impersonal personal'. Affective practice resembles discursive practice in this respect. The playwright, Dennis Potter, tellingly noted, for example, 'the trouble with words is that we don't know whose mouth they have been in' (cited in Maybin, 2001, p. 68). The same is true for affect. Affective performances, like words and language, are personally owned (and can feel intensely so) but are also trans-individual and collective. They come bearing the traces of past usage and past contexts. Like theories of affect without a subject, I recognise that it is often useful to move past the individual as the traditional unit of analysis to focus instead on practices that subjectify. But, unlike these theories, I also want to explore further the specificity of subjectivity and psychosocial practice as forms of figuring with their own, very particular, contributions.

The second approach I will consider comes from psychoanalysis, particularly relational psychoanalysis, and requires more lengthy discussion. This perspective, in contrast, does focus on the specificity of subjectivity. It offers useful ways of describing the fragmented, inconsistent and heterogeneous nature of individual affective patterns. It gives insight into what Graham Dawson (1994) calls 'self-composing' and into persistent methods of self-ordering. One can gain an understanding of the subject as a meaning-making generative, the activity of the personal 'phantasmatic' and the constant, scrappy, deeply felt, articulation and

AFFECT AND EMOTION

construction of subjectivity through affective routines. But I will suggest that this approach rests on a theory of the dynamic unconscious and a way of thinking about the psychological that is incoherent and too cut off from social practices. Psychoanalysis creates obfuscating psychological mysteries that weaken attempts to forge a genuinely psychosocial style of analysis.

In fact, both the approaches considered in this chapter – psychoanalysis and theories of affect without a subject – ignore the kinds of immediate, banal and everyday human efforts involved in affective practice and discussed in Chapter 4. The advantage of focusing on practice is that it demystifies the social psychology of subjectivity. I will try to show how it highlights the day-to-day, relational, interactional and self-regulatory work typically written out of psychoanalytic accounts.

Affect Without a Subject

I described in Chapter 3 the view of affect emerging in cultural geography, cultural studies and in political theory. This construes affect as 'becoming', as unspecific force, unmediated by consciousness, discourse, representation and interpretation of any kind. For Patricia Ticineto Clough (2008b), for instance, 'affect only registers at the imperceptible pre-conscious, pre-individual scale of measure' (p. 140). Inevitably, then, this analysis rests on a kind of anti-humanist negation of subjectivity. Subjectivity becomes a no-place or waiting room, through which affects as autonomous lines of force pass on their way to somewhere else. To get more of a handle on the theory of the subject and subjectivity entailed here, I want to look at two formulations of this general position, one from cultural geographer Nigel Thrift (2008b), and the other from politics researcher Caroline Williams (2010).

Not surprisingly perhaps, for both Thrift and Williams, psychology as normally conceived becomes redundant (see also Hsieh, 2008). For Thrift, the study of subjectivity is actually the study of geography, or, for Williams, it needs to become in part a kind of 'physics of the body' (cf. also Protevi's, 2009, 'political physiology'). Thrift imagines human subjects as bemused and wandering, perennially scratching their heads. He suggests the human slogan could be 'I don't know what got into me'. We are assailed, he maintains, on all sides by events that we don't originate, don't properly own, but that modify and re-configure us. People are like lurching, semi-animated crash dummies, albeit ones with proprioceptive sensations stimulated by what Thrift calls 'extrapersonal loci' (2008b, p. 84).

Commensurate with the thesis of the autonomy of affect and the slant of non-representational theory (described in Chapter 3), Thrift argues that analysis should focus on lines of force, intensity, modification and difference which stratify, organise and pass through living and inanimate bodies. It is in this sense that psychology becomes geography. It becomes an investigation of the forces and vectors moving through humans causing affected states. Thrift wants to go back, in fact, to older Aristotelian definitions of psychology as the science of the soul or the principle of life. To properly study the principle of life, psychology will need to generalise its subject matter to include, for example, parrots, tool-using New Caledonian crows, and what Thrift calls 'nature actors' like oil. In other words, psychologists should accept that there is nothing particularly special about human beings. The proper topic is super-ordinate. It is the mobile configuring of power across a range of processual and temporary instantiations.

People, then, are 'waxing and waning territories of interest and desire' or 'mimetic soups' (2008b, p. 85), through which subjectifying shocks and lines of force pass. Thrift suggests the following images for the person and the psychosocial actor:

> In this conception, persons still exist but as much looser allocentric formations with porous boundaries over which they have only limited control. The geography of each person consists of numerous layered subjectivities flowing through them, modulated by a particular characteristic style that we might understand, as a way of composing, as soulful compositions, even as art-forms. A person becomes a shifting ensemble of states that are received and passed on, states over which that person rarely has much in the way of direct control but which can be modulated in the passing in such a way as to produce nuances or even, at the limit, quite new forms of going on. (2008b, p. 85)

Politics researcher Caroline Williams (2010) takes a similar line. For her, too, psychology is superseded. She associates psychological investigation with a conventional model of political subjectivity and with the traditional humanist subject, both of which, she argues, have led to a dead-end. The conventional model posits a rational, cognitive or thinking subject. It focuses on political actors who are motivated by emotions and feelings deriving from their particular, personal psychological organisation. Williams wants to get beyond this. Again, her aim is to identify 'processes without a subject' (2010, p. 247). Following Spinoza, she suggests: 'There can be no *psychology* of affects but only a necessary study of the mechanisms and forces contributing to the shaping of political bodies, subjects and collectivities' (Williams, 2010, p. 253; emphasis in the original).

Again Williams finds inspiration in Massumi (2002), and in his thesis of the autonomy of affect, inflected, however, by further thorough reading of Spinoza:

> I argue that it is to Spinoza's distinctive conception of affect that we must turn to theorise this nexus of problems. For him, affect is conceived as both a power to affect and be affected, and the political body is itself the elemental site of transformation and production. Affect is also de-subjectifying in an important respect as for Spinoza it is also a kind of force or power that courses through and beyond subjects. Thus, it cannot easily be inscribed within the borders of subjectivity. For Spinoza, affects are forms of encounter; they circulate – sometimes ambivalently but always productively – between and within bodies (of all kinds), telling us something important about the power of affect to unravel subjectivity and modify the political body. Indeed, I aim to demonstrate here the ways in which Spinoza's thought is deeply relevant for thinking beyond the subject, calling us to think about the structure of affect and the agency of bodies in new and exciting ways. (2010, p. 246)

Hauling Back the Subject

As I noted, an analysis in terms of affective practices endorses some of these lines of thinking about the subject and subjectivity, and, certainly, the critique of traditional humanist psychology, if not the conclusions drawn from that critique. But my approach also moves in some quite sharply divergent directions. Like Thrift and Williams, I am sceptical about traditional expressive models of individual personality and character that see the subject as the integrated and originary centre of experience. I have been similarly educated by older post-structuralist emphases and have learnt how to trace out the ways in which people are subjectified, or constituted and formed as they engage in practice, taking up and inflecting already available positions. In this sense, as Denise Riley (2005) argues, passion is impersonal. Practice draws attention both to a transpersonal 'ready-made' we confront and slip into, as well as to active and creative figuring. Routines do in some sense 'land on' people and 'subject' them. And 'forms of encounter' or social relationships arrive with the affective slots for actors already sketched (in this situation you do superiority, I do abasement and deference, or *vice versa*).

Equally, like Thrift, I do not expect subjectivity to be coherent. Subjectivities arise in the plural, in shifting and patterned, often clashing, ensembles. Could we ever claim one unified and integrated 'subjectivity' or character in the singular? As Gail Lewis' (2009) work alone demonstrates, experience and psychic life are built up from multiple, and often contradictory, practices with sometimes quite irreconcilable internal rhythms, patterns and effects.

On these points we agree; where I differ from Thrift and Williams is that I am much more interested in the individual person as a very particular and specific site of transformation and pattern-making, and in understanding the personal affective history of this individual. Thrift refers in passing to the person as having a characteristic style or a distinctive way of composing ('a way of composing, as soulful compositions, even as art-forms', 2008b, p. 85). He gives us, though, no way of thinking about this further. How do we grasp the ongoingness of a particular subject, their repetitions and continuities, and the ways in which their present practice intertwines with their past practice? What can we say, too, about human specificity and the distinctiveness of human psychology? Are human affective practice and human psychology literally indistinguishable from the practice and psychology of a talking parrot?

More broadly, I find it quite difficult to work out where I am in relation to ideas of affect without a subject because they are so incredibly vague about the ensembles or states that constitute subjectivity. No one seems to be able to say what the affecting forces consist of. Indeed, if these forces are beyond representation and imperceptible, as Clough suggests, then they are forever fugitive. Nothing seems to be added to them when they pass through human bodies so the specifically human and the psychological are always irrelevant forever and ever. Subjects are constituted but this work of constitution seems to have no consequences for analysis, or for political life, because concrete subjects and their actual actions are uninteresting. Rather, analysis turns back again and again to the scene of unspecified affect, to unspecified forces without a subject, to what is in some baffling way prior to the subject and outside any instantiation.

I do accept that psychology is an acquired taste. It is a discipline with a problematic history, which is hard to engage with. I can see the advantages in re-defining psychology as geography or as a new kind of physics. But the critical points made in Chapter 3 are still relevant. These accounts do not work, in any sense, as plausible theories of human affective action. The cul-de-sacs and mistakes this leads to are very evident in the details of Williams' account. She is forced to rely, for example, on introducing Damasio's (2004) outmoded evolutionary position, which I discussed in Chapter 2, to support the received view of the autonomy of affect, and to bolster Massumi's view of affect as following a different track from conscious representation and interpretation:

> ... extricating affect from any essentialist position that seeks its naturalisation as an emotion or feeling attributable to a conscious subject. This is not merely because, as neuroscientist and Spinozist Antonio Damasio also notes, much of our emotional experience takes place 'in the theatre of the body under the guidance of a congenitally wise brain designed by evolution to help manage the body'. (Williams, 2010, p. 250)

The histories of social psychology and feminist research across the social sciences demonstrate that a focus on emotion, consciousness and the psychological subject does not necessarily naturalise or essentialise (Hemmings, 2005). I would argue that these traps are currently more of a danger for theories of affect without a subject, as Williams' uncritical acceptance of Damasio's conservative evolutionary psychobiology demonstrates. As Chapter 2 showed, Damasio's assumptions about basic emotions, unlike recent feminist work on human emotion, really are essentialist. The vagueness and confusion of Massumi's account of affect, endorsed by Williams and others, its lack of specificity and psychological naïvety, risks, I think, undermining rather than sustaining critical political thought and action.

Paul Stenner (2008) has argued that this kind of theory of the subject is, in fact, a mis-reading of the process philosophy of, for example, A.N. Whitehead, on which it is in part based. Stenner argues that Thrift and similar theorists overly 'flatten out' distinctions between human and non-human entities and turn the affected subject into simply a 'reactive ensemble of body parts' (p. 93). In contrast, Stenner notes Whitehead's conclusion that 'regions of activity' like humans, single cells, vegetable life, inorganic aggregates, etc. have to be seen as quite diverse and specific modes of assemblage or organisation. Humans offer a kind of high-grade complexity as coordinated systems, or as sites combining what Whitehead described as 'societies of actual occasions'. Other forms of life (e.g. trees, frogs and cats) are also coordinated systems too, of course, but each form of life presents a distinctive kind of continuity and creativity:

> For Whitehead, this coordinated stream of personal experiences is to be thought of as yet another instance of a society of actual occasions. Each occasion of experience is a self-realizing event that becomes and then perishes.

Each occasion has its direct 'inheritance' from its past and its anticipation of what it will become in the future. Each occasion is a concrescence of many data into the unity of the subjective form. However, for Whitehead, what is distinctive about the grouping of such personal experiences into societies is that the assemblage is purely temporal with no spatial dimension in evidence. It is purely a matter of one occasion of experience following another and giving rise to another, and so forth in a temporal chain. Whitehead calls such a purely temporal society a 'personal' society and he calls the occasions that occur within it 'presiding' occasions (Whitehead, 1933/1935, p. 263). The enduring entity associated with such a society is a person conceived as an enduring percipient. (Stenner, 2008, pp. 105–6)

It is not my intention to follow Stenner into a more detailed description of Whitehead's account of the subject. But, it is interesting to note that the philosophical sources sustaining arguments such as Thrift's can also open the way to thinking more extensively about human specificity. Whitehead's approach, in common with notions of practice, focuses attention on the flow of activity and on temporal succession. For Whitehead, the flow of experience accompanying activity has no 'space' of its own, but nonetheless exhibits endurance, persistence and repetitive ordering as the various occasions composing subjective experience anticipate what will come next and, in particular, are guided by past 'self-realising events'. Overall, this gives a practical way of thinking about human distinctiveness.

If accounts of affect without the subject flatten out subjectivity, and neglect the specificity of human practice, then can psychoanalysis offer more useful perspectives? What do these approaches (from Freud to object relations theory) have to say about the distinctive forms of pattern-making which human subjectivities contribute to affective practice? My interest here is in what could be called 'social psychoanalysis' or in those lines of work that operate 'outside the clinic' (Frosh, 2010), and which can be found in various guises in psychosocial studies, cultural studies and sociology.

Moving to Psychoanalysis

Sociologist Sasha Roseneil (2006) argues that social psychoanalysis disrupts the blandness of contemporary sociological accounts of social actors. It delivers a view of the conflicted, ambivalent and suffering individual struggling to live adequately in what are sometimes harsh social circumstances, plagued by disappointments, failures of relationships, and constantly unsettled by the gaps between actuality and fantasy (see also Craib, 1994). If Thrift suggests that the person is like an artist bringing skilful composition, or perhaps simply personal nuance, to affective practice, social psychoanalysis suggests something darker, something specifically intra-psychic, which is more powerful and transforming. Memory, imagination and cognition actively work on social experience contributing their own logics to emotional life. The person, it is argued, is much more than a gateway or site through which affecting forces jostle, to be then transmitted on to other human receivers. Instead, a rather massive and distinctive re-working of the social is thought to occur as it passes through human subjectivity.

Social researchers (e.g. Rose, 1998) following Deleuze, sometimes propose that human subjectivity can be seen as the 'folding' of exteriority to make up a 'pocket' of interiority (Blackman et al., 2008). The logic of subjectivity is thus the logic of the social. The bends, twists and kinks in subjectivity are the bends, twists and kinks evident in the social materials (and the lines of practice) taken over as one's own particular subject-hood. The act and moment of subjecting oneself to the social creates subjectivity, or a kind of declivity in ongoing social flows, and a personalising of practice. For social psychoanalysis, in contrast, subjectivity is a much more strongly delineated specific site, space or place – it is the 'internal world' of the individual or their 'inner psychic life'. The formation of such a space involves much more than the temporary and contingent working up of some of the flow of social practices as personality.

In social psychoanalysis, the intra-psychic (the psychological processes making up inner life) and the social (what is internalised and worked on) are seen as irreducibly different phenomena. The psychic and the social are assumed to operate on different logics. These are different kinds of processes 'hinged' together (Hollway, 2010) to co-constitute experience and the psychosocial actor. This way of thinking permits the possibility of psychological depth as opposed to the continuous equivalent surfaces posited in metaphors of 'folding'. Social material enters 'the inner world' but like light passing through a prism it gloriously (or dreadfully) emerges again in a remarkably transformed state. As Nancy Chodorow (1999, p. 2) puts it: 'powerful unconscious inner realities and processes shape, enliven, distort and give meaning and depth to our experience'. Personal meanings around affective actions and feelings will thus be substantially different from social and cultural meanings.

I want to argue that social psychoanalysis is both right and wrong. Right because it provides some substantial ways of thinking about the personalising of affective practice and the distinctive consequences of this personalising. Wrong because it pins its accounts to archaic psychological theory and consistently overpsychologises affective practice.

Social psychoanalysis tackles important questions and issues typically brushed aside in models of affect without a subject. It fleshes out the events and processes that ideas of habitus discussed in the last chapter assume but never quite explicate. It suggests that who performs affect, and their particular history, matters, and offers ways to think about this mattering. But, I think it is also the case that the dividing lines between the psychic processes and social processes are much more blurred than social psychoanalysis suggests. The metaphor of an intrapsychic world with its own distinctive and irreducible processes hinged with social processes is misleading. To follow through on the affective intersectional understanding I began to formulate in the last chapter a different approach is needed. We need an approach that can work with polyphonic and heteroclite subjectivities taking shape in complex, unfinished and plural social relations.

To explain what I mean both about the insights generated by social psychoanalysis and the blocks this perspective also creates, I want to go back to some of the territory first covered in Chapter 3 and think again about the non-conscious or unconscious aspects of affective practice and how to make sense of these. I also want to consider in more detail the notion of a personal affective idiom or a personal affective order and personal history.

The Unconscious of Affective Practice

We know that affective practice often unfolds relatively automatically with little conscious monitoring. Like other forms of habitual talk and social action, it often emerges 'unbidden', very quickly, too fast for the kind of thoughtful strategic planning novelists often attribute to their characters. We just act and this action usually turns out to be recognisable, communicative, reflexively related to the ongoing flow of others' actions, and jointly coordinated with them. We move in and out of 'knowing' what we are about during this flow. Through acts of 'paying attention', which are sometimes strenuous scenes in themselves, we can move into conscious feeling and the narrating of affect and into forms of construction, describing and remembering. These look like acts of 'retrieval' but are in fact new forms of social action.

It also seems clear, too, that affective practice, like other forms of practice, rests on a large unarticulated hinterland of possible semiotic connections and meaning trajectories (built around the discursive, the visual, the tactile, etc.). What we do is non-conscious in the general sense that these possible meanings and significances exceed and proliferate what can be grasped and articulated in any particular moment. There can always be a new, alternative, currently unfelt and unformulated, way of figuring what we are about. These webs of semiotic connections are genuinely psychosocial. They depend on the resources of shared languages and sign systems, cultural and historical repertoires, but worked through personal histories. One thing leads to another and some of the possible trajectories and lines of connection are well travelled and others are creative and new, just for this occasion. The affective hinterland always escapes entire articulation. It exceeds any particular connected act of affective meaning-making.

This kind of 'affective unconscious' supports the affective repetitions that, for Bourdieu, made up the embodied dispositions of habitus discussed in the last chapter. Affective routines, relations and connections learnt early seem particularly persistent. People become caught, for instance, in what they and others may perceive as self-sabotaging repetitions. Affective practice sediments and solidifies in individual lives. We can, as a result, be surprised by pattern, not because it is deliberately pushed out from consciousness, but because we have not yet had the chance to formulate the conjunctions in just this way, or to engage in the kind of reflexive reconstructions required. Our affective performance bears a complex relation to our past affective practice and relational history. As Whitehead described (Stenner, 2008) each new 'self-realising' activity builds within the contexts and routines set by past self-realising activities. What comes 'naturally' and 'spontaneously', then, refers back to past histories.

The non-conscious characteristics of affective practice I have just described are well known in psychoanalytic practice and elegantly evoked there. The kind of unconscious or non-conscious I am highlighting is reminiscent, for example, of the realm of the 'unthought known' suggested by psychoanalyst Christopher Bollas (1989). As with the non-conscious connections popping up in the priming experiments of experimental social psychologists discussed in Chapter 3, there is no necessary impediment to making further meaning, no particular block on making sense in some way. Attention is limited, there is too much experience occurring on too many levels to process it all, and what we do know, what we can articulate, and what we are most familiar with, depends on our particular relational histories and the needs and creative pressures of the moment.

Bollas provides a compelling phenomenological description of affective meaning-making as an inevitably incomplete process of gathering together the 'tattered fabric of being':

> Can I characterize the nature of my inner experience during such moments of being lost in thought? I know I cannot. They are not clear. For every image there are several practical and unrealized movements toward image. For every visualization there are a multitude of unvisualized yet assumed images that contribute to the feel of dense imagining. For every contemplated word there are scores of other words which never reach consciousness but which have been part of the movement of language. And so the account continues, with each and every element that goes into the making of self experience. (Bollas, 1995, p. 66)

Just as experimental social psychology and neuroscience propose multiple, non-conscious activations, registrations and responses that spread out in the moment, Bollas argues that some potential meanings and links get pulled out of the shadows and conjured together. They turn into what he describes as moments of 'condensation' or 'psychic intensity' as connections and associations are made with some affective force, only to dissipate, as one element within the condensation becomes the trigger for new associations, and psychic life moves on. He describes, for example, his own associations on seeing an advertisement for Philip Glass' opera *Akhenaten*. His train of images and affects move from a memory of seeing the opera and 'all that "went into" that evening' (1995, p. 49), to a memory of a papier mâché model his son made of the Nile, to a memory of a friend whose brother-in-law plays for Philip Glass, and so on.

This is a useful way of thinking about the social psychology of the habituated affective social actor. Bollas suggests an image of the individual moving through the world, and pulling it into shape in familiar but not necessarily clearly articulated ways, leaving a trail of always escaping material behind. In Donnel Stern's (1997) memorable phrase, much experience remains relevant and guiding, but 'unformulated'. It could be formulated, turned into narrative, pondered over, communicated and discussed but has not yet and may never become available in this way.

Both Bollas and Stern see this 'gathering together' process in relatively benign terms. Judith Butler (2005) takes a different view. She deduces a constitutive and frustrating limit on self-narration and intelligibility. She argues that the very conditions for instituting subjectivity will remain unconscious or unknowable in a basic sense. We can never grasp and describe the entire texture of the relational and discursive fields that preceded us, and that formed the creative context in which 'a person like us' took shape. This is a 'pre-history which has never stopped happening' (p. 78), but which escapes articulation. The feeling worlds we now inhabit derive from affective routines and relationships we will never grasp in entirety and exceed what can be told. Our angle on our own affective history will always be partial, and, as many have noted (e.g. Rose, 1986), 'identity' in this sense inevitably fails.

Repression and the Dynamic Unconscious

The unconscious I have sketched out here for affective practice could be seen as a less psychologised version of the psychoanalytic unconscious proper. In fact, I have alternated between the terms 'non-conscious' and 'unconscious', treating them as equivalent. For social psychoanalysis, in contrast, the two are distinct, and the unconscious is always qualified as 'dynamic'. I want to suggest that it is at this point that social psychoanalytic theory becomes unsustainable.

The dynamic unconscious is assumed to be formed through repression understood as a distinctive psychological or intra-psychic process. I will look, first, at Freud's classic account of affect, representation and the unconscious and then very briefly at Lynne Layton's (2004) relational psychoanalytic approach as one example of attempts to socialise the dynamic unconscious before returning to continue arguing for a practice-based view.

For Freud, affect was defined as physical, forceful bodily energy that could be measured quantitatively (see Baraitser and Frosh, 2007; Frosh, 1987, 2003; Green, 1977, for useful commentaries). For later mid-20th century psychologists, as Chapter 2 showed, bodily excitation was thought to divide into different types that could be parsed as six or seven different basic emotions. Freud's categorisations were less elaborate and more superordinate. Circulating energy divided simply into life instincts aimed at self-preservation or death instincts aimed at destruction.

Freud argued that in the usual flow of human life, quantitative bodily energy or affect becomes bound up with qualitative ideas and representations, memories and thoughts. The experience of a feeling or emotion, then, typically arises when bodily states and energies are put together with habitual thoughts, subjective states and patterned responses. According to Jan Campbell (2007), the life instincts are forms of affect that have been bound, contained and channelled in this way while the death instincts are destructively and chaotically unfixed, not contained in developed patterns of meaning, whether conventional or idiosyncratic.

Crucially, for Freud, the binding and unbinding of affect and representation was open to the play of repression. Unacceptable material would be repressed from consciousness, becoming unthinkable and unspeakable. It would remain powerful (in fact could become even more powerful) as a kind of goad, but the subject would remain entirely unaware of what had been repressed. In this way, the links between an affect (a bodily push) and an idea could become severed or dissociated. Bodily energy, such a state of sexual excitation for instance, might be linked to a forbidden category of person (such as a family member, or some generally unsuitable social object perhaps of the 'wrong' gender, age or social class background). In this case, the representation associated with the affect, the idea of its object, would be repressed. Freud argued that the affect would still be felt, and would circulate in the individual's psychic world, but it might well become displaced, for instance, onto another object or emerge as a hysterical symptom.

Freud, and his later followers, thought the existence of a dynamic unconscious (or a reservoir of unknown and unacceptable thoughts, ideas and affect/representation links pushing for expression) explained some familiar experiences. There might be a process of 'splitting' so that the emotion that should be linked to some memory or narrative or experience goes missing or gets repressed – the affective charge that should power and infuse a story or a memory has been flattened and the associated trauma, for instance, is not experienced or communicated. Similarly, Freud saw anxiety as a signal of repression at work. The affect or bodily excitation and forceful energy was still present and circulating, felt as anxiety, but the psychic context and the meaning-making had been repressed so the individual was simply aware of the tension, combined possibly with a dread of public collapse as the unacceptable affect/representation pushed hard for release.

Socialising the Dynamic Unconscious

In recent years, a number of social psychoanalysts have tried to re-work this concept of a dynamic unconscious formed through the repression of instinctual material and pushing for release in ways that are more commensurate with social theory. Relational psychoanalyst Lynne Layton (2004), for instance, defines her position as she takes issue with feminist psychoanalyst Juliet Mitchell's (2002) continuing adherence to Freud's model and to notions of 'drive'. Mitchell, like Freud, argues that the unconscious is built from prohibitions on desire and from the universal elements of cultures such as incest taboos – sons should not have sex with mothers and daughters should not have their father's children. The unconscious arises because some affect must be actively and constantly repressed. Mitchell emphasises the effortful and painful blocking of wishes, desires and reactions required to produce the mostly 'civilised' and socially adapted individuals that practice theorists such as Bourdieu assume. Her attention is focused on the inevitability of irrationality and adaptive failure and on the cracks appearing in social life from the distortions introduced by repression.

Layton (2004) agrees with Mitchell that there is a defensive and selective process at work so that only some affective meaning-making arrives at consciousness. Unlike Mitchell, however, Layton sees the dynamic unconscious as built from historically contingent social relations rather than universal prohibitions. It is, thus, what Layton calls a 'normative unconscious'. The content is local and is socially and culturally mediated. This unconscious derives from the internalisation of relational repertoires during childhood and the living out of the patterns presented to the child by homophobic and racist capitalist societies mediated through family life.

A normative unconscious still counts as *dynamic*, in Layton's view, and involves active repression because it is still distinguished by conflict. It creates neurotic symptoms and intense suffering of a stronger degree than ordinary, or common or garden, unhappiness. Crucially, the unconscious is dynamic in her view, rather than simply non-conscious or pre-conscious, because it results in repetition compulsions. People, she argues, become trapped in non-creatively reproducing damaging affective routines that derive from the societies they inhabit and the ways these were mediated in past relationships.

In a later article, Layton puts it like this:

> [O]ne's relational repertoire derives from one's own particular way of making meaning of and interweaving experiences that have been narcissistically wounding, traumatizing and humiliating, with experiences in which one has felt recognized and acknowledged as a subject who has his/her own separate thoughts, feelings, wishes, etc. … [These] problems … are often sequelae of the way that hierarchies of gender, race, class, sexuality operate in any given culture. It is my sense that social hierarchies are most psychologically damaging because they require a splitting of human capacities (between genders, races, classes) that, in health, ought to be integrated rather than split. (2007, pp. 148–9)

Questioning the Dynamic Unconscious

Psychoanalysts disagree, then, about the status and origin of what is repressed, but they agree that the psychological process of repression forms the unconscious. The unconscious, then, is always dynamic. As Hollway and Jefferson (2000, 2005) explain, this suggests that the social actor engaged in affective practice will inevitably be a 'defended subject'. There is the ever-present possibility that affective action and experience are not what they seem because something hidden and mysterious will be operating.

This, of course, imposes severe limits on social analysis. It draws attention away from the organisation and normative logics of the unfolding situated episode, context, interaction, relation and practice and on to a hidden, determining, individual, psychic logic instead. People's emotions and responses will need skilful interpretation as they will not know what they do or why. The audiences for social psychoanalytic research (if not the participants themselves) will need to be told the real meaning of the presented experience, and informed about the real nature of the participants' feelings, revealed through extensive conversation with an authoritative analyst who can form an opinion as to what is being repressed.

Much social research interprets 'beyond the text' in this kind of way. It is part of the value that social science adds. But ideological critique or discursive deconstruction focuses on conflicts in the *cultural* resources available to people to make sense of their situation and on the play of power. The interpretations social psychoanalysts such as Layton or Hollway and Jefferson develop presuppose and re-negotiate the very personal substance and most intimate self-understandings of their research participants. This leads to some obvious methodological and ethical quagmires (Wetherell, 2005). The problems, though, are not just moral and practical. When one thinks about it in more detail, the entire notion of repression becomes implausible.

Repression and the consequent formation of a dynamic unconscious have been powerful ideas for so long, we tend in social research to take them for granted as natural facts of human life. But this model is in many ways an archaic conceptual apparatus and psychological theory. Michael Billig (1999a) argues that when you look at it closely the concept of repression turns out to be radically underspecified. Its explanatory force evaporates.

Freud proposed the existence of a mental process that results in people not knowing or registering certain wishes, feelings and desires. This blocking or repression suggests a possibly semi-conscious process of self-monitoring and actively putting material out of mind, but also that people could end up puzzled by their affect. Repression can work so effectively, and the meaning become so disconnected, Freud suggested, that the person has no sense at all of what else they might feel, other than what is immediately conscious, even if others around them might be able to hazard a guess. Because Freud had a 'quantitative' or hydraulic model of human drives, he assumed that the energy of affect would not go away but would appear in some way or other. Thus, a sexual drive toward a non-admissible object will be deflected onto another object, turned into a symptom, expressed in a dream, or in a slip of the tongue.

Billig convincingly demonstrates that Freud completely fails to explain how this repression might happen. Freud offers no explanation or psychological theory at all of how repression works. Gaps and digressions open up in his writing at the moments when readers might expect him to elaborate on this psychological process. Indeed, what kind of psychological process could this be? Some kind of active agent in the head, unknown to the conscious mind, continually processes all psychic states like a benign father and selects some to censor. These states then effectively disappear into some kind of hidden holding area of the brain/ mind, but continue to be active, and thus continue to have effects. So, does the brain/mind do this innately? What is the process by which some psychic contents become inadmissible?

Billig argues that there is likely to be a much more plausible and mundane social process at work than the kind of obscure psychological sequence Freud assumed. Repression is part of the surface social psychology of everyday life, and it is a mistake, in his view, to understand this as an indicator of depth, hint at puzzling mysteries, and enigmas; even if it leads to engrossing stories, and increases the authority and power of the detective psychoanalyst who can uncover the mystery and reveal the truth.

Billig suggests that repression is a discursive practice. (Perhaps we could say now it is a self and other regulatory affective–discursive practice.) It is evident in the normal process of 'changing the topic', moving away from things that one does not want to talk about, or think about even in the privacy of one's own head. He points to the extensive discursive training in the rhetorical arts of repression and 'changing the subject' which parents provide for their children. Indeed, children are endlessly asked to practise repression. The skills of not attending to, ignoring and blocking out some reactions to situations, feelings and impulses, just like skills in navigating conversation, are well-practised techniques, acquired early and used very frequently.

This alternative reading suggests that we are all constantly negotiating and managing affects, our relations with others, habits, emotional repertoires and emerging situations. This negotiation and self-management, however, is social psychological in the fullest sense, infused with culturally specific techniques for self-regulation as distinct from the private, internal, psychic machine Freud proposed.

Billig goes on to re-analyse and plausibly re-interpret Freud's case studies (such as his work with 'Dora') in this light. Billig is not arguing that affective meaning-making and the communication of affect are never demanding or free of trouble. 'Changing the subject' can be full of conflict and anxiety. Choosing not to think about something, choosing not to feel afraid or angry, for example, and avoiding 'looking bad', can involve effort and may not be successful. Affective meaning-making, however, needs to be seen not so much as an act of natural expression, an instinctual push that can be blocked by a defence like repression, but as an act of selection and construction. It involves 'emotional labour' in Hochschild's (1983) sense, and this labour is often historical, habitual and non-conscious, if not dynamically unconscious as Freud claims. In addition, as Chapter 2 concluded, it now seems a mistake to try to divide out bodily energy from its practical organisation. Is affect ever 'unrepresented' or 'unbound' in some sense? What are the consequences for Freud's theory if the physical is always/already organised?

Support for Billig's reworking, and for placing more emphasis on training and the everyday patterning and positioning of relational life, comes from detailed case studies of affective settlement in individual lives. One such is Lisa Capps and Elinor Ochs' (1995) investigation with Meg, a married mother of two children, in her mid-30s, who suffered from severe agoraphobia. Following through and analysing hours and hours of interviews, observations and recordings of Meg's life and her everyday interactions with her husband and children, Capps and Ochs developed with Meg a strong sense of the ways in which her panic had become what we could call a kind of affective habitus or a repetition compulsion. It arose over and over again in particular kinds of interactions, sustained by Meg's sense-making around each episode, and her ossifying narratives.

In a sense there was a kind of 'unconscious' here. Meg's troubles and suffering were intense. Her affect felt beyond her control and mysterious, arising apparently spontaneously, irrationally and randomly. It led to major conflicts between her wish to conform to social expectations and what she felt she could do. But a psychoanalytic account of this panic as a manifestation of a repressed dynamic unconscious would miss the main thrust of its operation. It was much more productive and illuminating (if banal in comparison to the psychodramas constructed by psychoanalysis) to look at the patterning of Meg's actual everyday social relations. Knowledge of the subject positions other family members, and Meg herself, created over and over again was particularly revealing and helpful for changing Meg's affective practice.

Affective Character Types and Phantasmatic Histories

Just as I am sceptical of the psychological theory underpinning repression, I am sceptical too about other depth psychological processes posited in social psychoanalytic accounts, such as projection, splitting, transference, projective identification, etc. (Wetherell, 2003). I will come back to some of this critique in the next chapter in the context of ideas about how affect is transmitted from one person to another. To round off this chapter, though, I want to look at one more example of how potentially intriguing and important social psychoanalytic leads about the patterning of personal affective trajectories are undercut by over-psychologising.

One of the most powerful contributions of social psychoanalysis is to show how people and their habitual affective practice construct realities and figure the world. Those influenced by Melanie Klein argue, for instance, that patterns in individual affective practice arise from an unconscious 'phantasmatic' (Dawson, 1994) made up of imaginings of relationships, phantasised scenes and habitual preoccupations, passions, positions and standpoints that organise affective experience and interpretation. (Because these are unconscious patterning scenarios, Klein used the term 'phantasy' to mark a difference with conscious 'fantasy' or daydreams.) Klein's account could be seen as filling out Whitehead's overly philosophical description noted earlier of how past occasions of subjectivity figure present and future occasions. From an affective practices perspective one would expect that any such phantasmatic (to borrow the term for the moment) would be highly diverse, heterogeneous, contextual, closely related to other social practices, changing and plural.

But, because social psychoanalysis gives such a prominent role to psychological processes as the organising principle for the ways affective hinterlands are carried forward, the plurality evaporates and individuals fall in these accounts into simple homogeneous affective types. All the potential variety and figurative potential of individual affective practice gets reduced. Indeed, famously, in Klein's case, overarching pattern will be determined by very early infancy and the ways in which innate processes are engaged at the very beginning of life. Klein saw, for example, individual affective phantasmatics as structured by universal movements between paranoid-schizoid states characterised by splitting and projecting and depressive states characterised by reparation. The affective subjectivities carved out in very early infancy constitute meaning-making generatives that are deeply scored by innate psychological processes. This is a psychological model that is hard to sustain on closer examination.

Again, Lynne Layton's (2002) work can be used to illustrate the problems that arise when the psychological principles of psychoanalytic theory are applied to analyse the multifariousness of affective practice. I described Layton's analysis of the kind of dynamic unconscious that might underpin a socially generated affective habitus. She also suggests that certain kinds of habitus will create particular pathological psychologies. There will be strong correlations not just between affect, social class and social value of the kind I examined in the last chapter but also between social formations, habitus and psychological type. Specifically, the dominance of neo-liberal doctrines in American society will produce a very particular dynamic unconscious, affective habitus and psychological style.

The ideological environment of neo-liberalism, Layton argues, puts extreme and unhealthy emphasis on the free and independent individual. It creates a context in which dependency on others, lack of agency and autonomy, indeed relationality and connection, in itself must be repudiated. When one style of affective being is so strongly encouraged, there is scope, in Layton's view, for a particular kind of dynamic unconscious conflict as socially undesirable traits are actively repressed. She maintains that a kind of social perversion and severe narcissistic character problems result.

Narcissism, in these terms, is a disorder whereby attachment capacities and needs are split from needs and capacities for agency and autonomy. Narcissistic individuals oscillate between unrealistic grandiosity and excessive self-deprecation, rigidly dichotomise social categories into us versus them, and find it difficult to experience empathy for self or for others. America becomes a society in Layton's view, not simply full of narcissistic individuals, but with an affective habitus dominated by psychological processes such as projection. The qualities and needs rejected in the self are projected onto those defined as lesser and other. Affective practices, in this view, indicate and are mediated by unconscious dynamics. An affective habitus is powerful because it becomes embedded as character and as a psychological type.

I don't find this account of contemporary North American affective characters persuasive, although I do think it is important to try to trace out the profiles of affective practices facilitated by certain social niches such as privileged neo-liberal sensibilities, or by particular 'emotional regimes', to use Reddy's (2001) term. I am not convinced that a focus on character types is going to be an insightful way of summarising these profiles. These are the patterns of practice not of personality.

In effect, Layton returns us to the kind of 'type' social psychologies that dominated mid-20th century thinking, when notions such as the 'authoritarian personality', for example, were developed to explain the popular appeal of fascism. Her account suffers from the same problems plaguing these earlier evocations of types and also overly simplistic 'jukebox' models of habitus and affective practice. Whichever way we try to twist and turn such idealised characters, there turns out to be too much variation in actual practice and trajectories and the 'type' dissolves. As Gail Lewis' account of relations with her mother, which introduced this chapter, demonstrates, the trick must be to develop complex affective intersectional analyses of pattern in personal affective trajectories.

Towards 'Light' Relational Subjectivities

My discontent with models of affect without a subject developed by researchers such as Thrift and Williams was that these gave no way of thinking through human and personal specificity. They failed to explain the particular kinds of figuring processes involved when people develop persisting affective repertoires over time. What happens when the subject becomes a site where affective practice sediments and takes on some typical, if complicated and constantly re-figuring, forms of order? Affective biographies seem to involve more than adding personal nuance or styling. The human is a different kind of activity and site of patterning compared to Thrift's 'nature actors' like oil or talking parrots.

In any particular life, such a strong sense emerges of the richness of the potential interpretations, feelings, associations and actions set up by the brain/body, subjectivity, the discursive milieu and relational field. At any given moment 'we' emerge from that, rather as Bollas describes, configured in a selective and sometimes 'intense' way. The history of this personal configuring is crucial in what gets repeated. Affective meaning-making taken up and practised will become habitual and 'primed' over time. Similarly, relational configurations such as contempt and abasement or adoration and narcissism set what may become familiar repertoires in place. Along with disciplinary techniques of self-monitoring, self-control and practices of repression, this will constrain future affective practice, creating contexts and situations encouraging repetitions.

Social psychoanalysis, and its vast storehouse of clinical examples, is rich in accounts of precisely this kind of patterning. At its best (e.g. Hollway, 2010), this work gives a highly developed analysis of the histories of relations that form human subjectivity, demonstrating just how entangled 'self' and 'other' become. But, from the beginning of this chapter, it was also evident that a productive account of the personalising of affect would be deeply attentive to social ordering, and would need to presume a kind of affective intersectionality, explaining the sorts of patterning indicated in accounts such as Lewis', for example. On these points, social psychoanalysis seems to falter. The potential for a social psychology of the process of affective settlement in individual lives is undercut by simple notions of type and by reference to an armoury of depth psychological processes. I have tried to show that there are no easy dividing lines between autonomous psychological and autonomous social processes (hinged or unhinged). Instead, my hope would be to explore the formation of pattern in people's affective lives through practices that cannot be deciphered into separate 'psycho' and 'social' lines.

A rich auto-ethnography, like the analysis Gail Lewis develops, shows the effects of the unconscious and figuring processes as I have tried to re-formulate these in practice terms. In a similar vein, studies such as Capps and Ochs' investigation of Meg, supported by Billig's re-theorising of processes like repression, strongly indicate the advantages of re-locating depth psychological principles as everyday affective practice. Other studies (e.g. Frosh, et al., 2003; McAvoy, 2009; Phoenix, 2008; Phoenix et al., 2002) have also developed fascinating, new, psychosocial modes of analysis, examining participants' personal and relational histories in ways that are attentive to personal specificity without being overly psychologised. These lines of research demonstrate how people gather themselves together in the context of available but not always articulated affective hinterlands and previous relational histories. They show how we form diverse and heterogeneous patterns of personal idioms and plural, personalised forms of affective habitus. These are social but not reducible to social location or even to any simple criss-crossing pattern of multiple identities.

In sum, what I am moving towards, then, is positing a kind of 'light' or 'minimal' subjectivity as a basis for research on affective practice (see also Blackman, 2008; Despret, 2004b). What I mean by this is an approach that sees subjectivity as an organising site contributing pattern and order to affective practice. But, as I have tried to argue, this subjectivity comes lightly endowed. It is not pre-packed with a raft of innate psychological processes, and with large numbers of pre-organised routes, but with a relational capacity, and tendencies towards figuring and gathering. These 'blank' subjectivities gain their textures, shapes, potentialities, repetitions, creativities, and find their limits in relation to animate and inanimate others. This, then, is what the human 'region of activity' in Whitehead's terms (Stenner, 2008) might look like. It is perhaps all we require.

SEVEN

Circulating affect: Waves of feeling, contagion and affective transmission

[A]ffective transmission is never simply something one 'catches' but rather a process that one is 'caught up' in. Its complexity is revealed through the linkages and connections of the body to other practices, techniques, bodies (human and non-human), energies, judgements, inscriptions and so forth that are relationally embodied. Happiness is never therefore singular (a property of the individual), or a contagious force which you might catch in a particular spatial and temporal location. This problem of communication is revealed by attempts to produce happiness, which either reify emotionality as a set of practices of the self or are directed to moments of happiness which just seem to arrive. Rather, happiness discloses the wonder, ambiguity, mystery and inexplicability that our attempts to know fail to catch and bring to life. Perhaps the question of happiness should be directed to the question of how to live with the unknown, the unresolved, and the limits of autonomy as a performative ideal. (Lisa Blackman, 2007/2008, p. 29)

... it is also an examination of the more general logic by which, in a season of high passions, we produce a calculus of public affect and emotion, usually without knowing it, and in a way that suggests massive analytic disrepair in our conceptualization of political attachments. (Lauren Berlant, 2005, p. 1)

Moving through communal affective atmospheres, or riding waves of public feeling, can feel like swimming in the sea and passing unexpectedly from colder regions to warmer zones, from a top layer of water warmed by the sun into more chilly regions. Picking up a newspaper, turning on the television, or talking to someone on the bus, you can find that you are suddenly shifting from one affective zone to another, swept up, for example, in frets of communal anxiety and panic, by the warm ooze of sentimental pity, or the benignity of a shared joke. In a similar way, groups of people are said to manifest affective aura, physically palpable to the outsider entering the room. With a flick of the page, a change in channel, or a shift into another conversation, one can sometimes surface somewhere else, in a different affective region or affective practice. Each wave of communal affect exerts a physical grab, as our bodies begin to enact anger, or compassion, or shake with laughter, and as we become positioned in relation to the available figures, narratives and affective possibilities.

Metaphors of floating in affect, affective atmospheres, auras, riding waves, etc. are seductive, but are these the best ways of understanding how people move in and out of affective practices? In this last chapter of the book, I want to look more closely at the transmission of affect. I am interested in how affect circulates. The explanatory stakes are high, particularly for political scientists seeking to understand the rapid shifts that can take place in the demos as old orders cease to 'feel right' and alternative fantasies of 'the good life' begin to engage populations. Lauren Berlant (2005) describes just how hard it is for intellectuals to come to terms with the shifting force of collective affect. She notes that we are trained to believe that good arguments matter but social and political change seems more frequently based on emotional valence. Berlant finds the humanities and the social sciences in 'massive analytic disrepair' when it comes to addressing such phenomena. What would a practical theory of the circulation of affect look like? This is the question for this chapter.

Finding a productive way to talk about affective movement is central. Most scholars stick with 'transmission' as their preferred term (e.g. Brennan, 2004). Transmission doesn't feel quite right, however. It suggests that a self-contained packet of emotional stuff is being transferred wholesale from one body to another. Often what is more interesting is the rapid, implicit and explicit, negotiation process through which we jointly begin to figure the affective moment we are in, and what should happen next. Although it is the term I will use, 'circulation' suffers from similar problems if it implies that affect is an ethereal, floating entity, simply 'landing' on people. Would it be better to use the terminology of 'contagion' and 'suggestion' dating back to late 19th-century psychology?

As Lisa Blackman (2007/2008) explains in the extract above, an affect like happiness is not something we 'catch', like catching a cold. Becoming happy is about being actively 'caught up in' a process or a practice. Affect is not a contagious virus. In an illuminating set of genealogical investigations (2007a, 2007b, 2008), she traces out the framework of contagion and suggestion and the impact of these ideas on William James, Henri Bergson and Gabriel Tarde. Blackman warns scholars embarking on a new 'turn to affect' who are looking back to this earlier work for inspiration against performing a simple flip-flop from one intellectual formation to another. Moving from theories emphasising the self-contained, rational, liberal individual to theories focused on contagion, suggestibility, mediums and telepathy is tempting, but ignores some of the particular history and implications of these ideas.

As Blackman points out, a more sophisticated theory of affective transmission is needed than either the old models of suggestion and contagion or the 20th-century social psychologies of 'social influence' based on distinctions between 'conformity' versus 'independence', and notions of 'reasonable' and 'unreasonable' suggestion (see also Motzkau, 2009; Reicher, 2001; Turner, 1991; Turner et al., 1987 for similar arguments). I will be arguing that thinking in terms of affective practice offers the most productive way of understanding the passing of affect from one to another, forming what can seem like pulses of energetic relation. Affective practice is something that can be encountered as a pre-existing given – and at that point it may feel as though we are entering a 'zone' or an 'atmosphere' – but it is also something that is actively created and needs work to sustain. The circulation of affect inevitably brings us back, therefore, to those key questions about where affect is located, the permeability of bodies and minds, and to the analysis of affect as social action.

This chapter will follow up a number of promising leads and sources. Relational psychoanalysis, for instance, offers a reasonably developed model of how affect can move from one person to another through its work on unintentional and unconscious communication. The feminist literary theorist Teresa Brennan (2004) provides an interesting, albeit frustratingly patchy, account (she died before her book was finished), while Sarah Ahmed (2004a, 2004b) provides an impressive cultural politics of the circulation of affect. These approaches range widely from face-to-face (body-to-body) transmission, to groups and crowds, to second-hand seductions into large-scale cultural affective practices. I will try to be attentive to the specificity of these different modes, but I will also be arguing that some of the same kinds of processes underpin both small-scale and large-scale circulations of affect. An adequate account of one is relevant to the other.

None of the three perspectives I will be examining is satisfactory alone. We need a broader interdisciplinary approach. Any particular instance of the circulation of affect, whether occurring in consulting rooms, parliamentary committees, football stadiums or in the message boards of the Internet, involves understanding a raft of processes: body capacities to re-enact the actions of others; the developmental infrastructure of inter-subjectivity; the power of words; the affective–discursive genres personal and social histories provide which channel communal affect; inter-subjective negotiations; consideration of the cultural and social limits on identification and empathy; and exploration of practices of authorisation, legitimation and resistance, not to mention analyses of the containing institutions, spaces and media of circulation.

The question of the limits on affective transmission is particularly crucial, and almost entirely neglected in the new turn to affect. On this topic, developments in the social psychology of social influence and crowds (Reicher, 1984, 1987, 1996, 2001; Stott and Reicher, 1998) offer some incisive ideas about the boundaries of affective 'contagion'. Social psychology has a rich history of work in this area – coordinated action could be said to be the defining problematic of the discipline – and I wish I had more space to mine conventional research on social influence. Overall, the approach I will be recommending is more prosaic and mundane than other current alternatives developed by Ahmed, Brennan and relational psychoanalysis, less taken up with what seems uncanny and spooky. This doesn't mean that I think the transmission of affect can be dismissed. On the contrary, the fact that affect does circulate, and that affective practice can be communal, is crucial to the very possibility of collective action and to sociality and polity.

The Problem with the Metaphor of Transmission

I want to begin first by explaining in a bit more detail why I think 'affective transmission' is a highly misleading way of conceptualising what occurs when affective practice engages more than one, and becomes 'supra-personal' or 'transpersonal'. The metaphor of transmission turns a phenomenon that is actually highly pervasive and banal into something overly mysterious and 'special'. Teresa Brennan (2004, p. 3) describes affective transmission as taking place, for example, when the emotions and energies belonging to one person enter into, and become lodged, in another person. Even this relatively bland formulation suggests something uncanny – how can a physical state move from one person to another? How can anger held in one body break out in another body? Presented thus, it seems to involve a kind of magic.

If we think about some everyday examples, however, the mystery dissipates. I see, for instance, an expression of anxiety pass over your face as we are crossing a busy road and I simultaneously realise that I have become fearful. We pause in mid-conversation, realise the traffic lights are changing, and we both start to run to avoid the speeding oncoming cars. A group of civil servants are sitting in a meeting listening to unwelcome news on projected cuts and anger flashes around the room. It is palpably there, not owned by any particular individual, reactions polarise as angry response succeeds angry response. Millions of people watch their national teams play in the World Cup. Most are cast into despondency. A few million, though, leap around the room, laugh and stand taller. All the time, in other words, people are orienting their conduct to each other, constructing contexts for mutual action, and developing shared foci and frames which guide what seems like the appropriate thing to do next. As an affective practice emerges, or as we enter into an ongoing affective practice, we begin to engage with interpersonal and collective ways of figuring situations, with the affective positions offered by conventional relational duets, and our bodies begin to respond.

There is a lot that needs to be understood about these simple daily activities but it probably doesn't help to see them as uncanny or work them up rhetorically as startling. Brennan presents the fact that affect is distributed and can spread from body to body as a new ground-breaking discovery that disrupts notions of the self-contained individual. This is equally misleading. There is so much work already available in neuroscience, social, developmental and cultural psychology and in the ethno-sciences more generally on inter-subjectivity and coordinated action. This work has long questioned psychological self-containment. Brennan preserves her critique (and claim for a new discovery) by ignoring this material, but at quite a cost. Paradoxically, her emphasis on transmission ends up re-instating forms of individualism that have been unpicked more thoroughly elsewhere.

The individualism inherent in notions of affective transmission is clear in this description of unconscious communication from Freud, quoted by Christopher Bollas:

> In a startling and far-reaching metaphor, Freud likened the analyst's reception of the patient's unconscious to a radio set receiving a transmission. 'He must turn his own unconscious like a receptive organ toward the transmitting unconscious of the patient. He must adjust himself to the patient as a telephone receiver is adjusted to the transmitting microphone. Just as the receiver converts back into sound waves the electric oscillations in the telephone line which were set up by the sound waves, so the doctor's unconscious is able, from the derivatives of the unconscious which will be communicated to him, to reconstruct that unconscious, which has determined the patient's free associations.' (Freud, 1912, pp. 115–16, cited in Bollas, 1995, p. 10)

One can imagine Freud with his hand cupped to his ear listening to his patient lying on the couch, straining to hear through the crackle, but patiently decoding the message. Again, however, this type of formulation idealises acts of affective communication and renders them strange. Affective practice ceases to become mutual activity. This is partly appropriate for the consulting room, but even there it is only somewhat accurate. Like encoding and decoding models of communication more generally, 'transmission' assumes a slow and frozen world peopled by cardboard cut-out figures. Those figures are essentially solitary. They are essentially separate, laboriously engaging with each other, digging out nuggets of affective meaning to transmit. No wonder shared affect seems puzzling. Any sense of the interactional context is missing, let alone the broader social context, or feel for the interrupting liveliness of social life, its fragmentary, fast pace, and the pervasive ever-present possibility of changing the scene and re-negotiating what just happened.

It is not just the definition offered by Teresa Brennan, therefore, which mystifies the circulation of affect. She is in tune with the long history of psychoanalysis, from Freud onwards, which has made the uncanny the main rhetorical mode for reporting on affect. It results in fascinating and entertaining case reports for sure. But as I tried to describe in the previous chapter, drawing on Michael Billig's (1999a) arguments, the formation of the unconscious through psychological processes such as repression is assumed but never explained, and remains entirely obscure. What does it mean, for example, for Freud's unconscious to 'listen in' to his patient's unconscious? What kind of communicative activity is this?

To explore these kinds of issues further, I want first to critically examine Brennan's account of 'chemical entrainment' in light of some recent social psychological and psychobiological investigations, then go on to interrogate accounts of affective transmission in relational psychoanalysis, before concluding with Sara Ahmed's cultural politics of emotion.

Crowds and Vigilantes – A Story of Chemical Entrainment?

One of Brennan's (2004) main concerns is with the affective phenomena emerging in crowds and groups. I suggested earlier that passing through public life can be like floating in the sea through warmer and colder layers of water, moving through regions of affect, which enlist us for a time, physically take over our bodies and then release us. That sounds like a rather benign process. In contrast, what many external observers note about crowds and about mass affect is their frightening extremity; it can seem less like surfing the waves like a fish and more like drowning.

Consider, for example, the 'Paulsgrove protests' studied by Jessica Evans (2003). This was a wave of action against suspected paedophiles that took place on a deprived estate in Portsmouth on the south coast of Britain. As Evans describes, locals were responding to an anti-paedophile campaign launched by a tabloid newspaper, the *News of the World*. The newspaper began publishing photographs of suspected paedophiles, campaigning for their locations to be released to the public. This strategy not only sold a lot of newspapers but also sparked off a number of local man-hunts and misidentifications. The righteous indignation, or 'manufactured rage', as some saw it, of the Paulsgrove protestors led to the torching of cars, the firebombing of flats and the hounding out of individuals across the estate.

Commentators on Paulsgrove and other similar episodes around the country reached for the handy armoury of 'contagion' and 'conflagration' to make sense of what was seen as mob violence. Observers were particularly impressed by the speed and rapidity of the mobilisation as rage passed through the estate. This impressed Gustav Le Bon, too, in his early studies of crowds and mass action in the 1890s. What was the mechanism behind this suggestibility? As Stephen Reicher (2001) describes, Le Bon didn't offer an explanation so much as moral censure. He saw crowds as irrational, a site where an atavistic 'racial unconscious' takes over, turning civilised people into barbarians and shifting people into more primitive and less evolved modes of response. Le Bon thought that the individual becomes submerged in the crowd and conscious personality becomes swept away. Individuals in crowds become highly suggestible, unable to resist the flowing affect, even if it leads them to actions they would not contemplate when alone. We are back again, in other words, to the uncanny.

Describing these lines of argument, Teresa Brennan (2004) also notices that Le Bon (and indeed some later research on crowds) does not actually explain the affective transmission noted. Crowd theorists evoke 'contagion' but can't seem to progress further than that. Brennan's own explanation for suggestibility and affective transmission is a novel one. She is interested primarily in the contribution of the senses and, in particular, the sense of smell. She argues that affect becomes distributed across bodies through a process of 'chemical entrainment' and this is how emotion can pass from one to another. Individuals are not self-contained, she proposes, rather we are open to being re-organised chemically by others' reactions. Physiology provides a direct 'unconscious' route along which affect can travel. Brennan gives as an example walking into rooms she describes as rank with the smell of anxiety. She adds: 'I breathe this in. Something is taken in that was not present, at the very least not consciously present, before. But no matter how thoroughly my system responds to the presence of this new affect, it is the case that something is added' (2004, p. 68).

The chemical agent she identifies as responsible (on a relatively cursory review of the literature) is the pheromone. A pheromone is a chemical emitted by one body that causes the release of hormones in the blood of another body, leading to a change in the body state and to feelings and action. Pheromones are known to trigger hormones connected with human sexual behaviour, for example. In Brennan's view this kind of chemical entrainment combines with other forms of 'nervous entrainment' as milling bodies touch and bump into each other and begin to move in rhythm through chants, for instance. Visual stimulation is important also in Brennan's account, although she is keen to dethrone vision and the image in favour of the other senses usually neglected in cultural research. Bodies might begin to align with each other in patterns of joint nervous action in response to aggressive scenes, for instance, or in response to the aggressive facial expressions of others.

To be honest there doesn't seem to be much evidence beyond limited aspects of sexual behaviour, and less clearly for testosterone and aggression, for the claim that pheromones and chemical signals could be the missing, mediating link in affective contagion. It is not my intention, though, to review this literature or even take issue with Brennan's account of it. If we are seeking a physical and 'infra-structural' basis for affective communication, then extensive recent work on 'mirror neurones' and on the developmental psychology of the emergence of inter-subjectivity offers a more robust perspective, although aspects of this account, too, are contentious. I will discuss that work in more detail shortly.

Here, I just want to argue that Brennan's account fails (and indeed is a step backwards) because she does not solve Le Bon's problem. She, too, is unable to explain the limits of affective contagion and indeed the crucial sociality of affective communication. Even if I accept that my body is open to being 'entrained' with others, why do I sometimes go along with the affect others display and why do I sometimes resist? Why does others' anger sometimes provoke anger in me, but also just as frequently anxiety, laughter, indifference, or sadness? Equally, why do bystanders on London streets watching dramatic and violent protest not feel impelled to emote with the demonstrators? Are their noses blocked? As Lauren Berlant (2008b) points out, transmitted affect can simply have no consequences at all. There is flatness rather than sparking and flaring. We can't assume a perfect mirroring relation between an affective atmosphere (Brennan's rank smell of anxiety) and emotional states. Often we guess wrongly what others are feeling and we are incompetent at reading the atmosphere. Then, too, what Berlant (p. 4) calls the 'work of the normative' intercedes 'in apprehending, sensing, tracking, and being with, the event'.

The Limits of Affective Contagion

Stephen Reicher and his colleagues Clifford Stott and John Drury (Drury and Reicher, 1999; Reicher, 1984, 1987, 1996, 2001; Stott and Reicher, 1998) have developed an extensive social psychology of crowd dynamics and affective contagion in recent years. One beginning point for this work was appreciating that many accounts of crowd psychology come from outsiders rather than insiders. These outsiders usually also have an ideological agenda of their own which is opposed to the aims of the crowd. Thus Le Bon, for example, was writing at a point of extreme anxiety among the ruling classes of the period about the threats of the new 'mass society' and the dangers posed by revolutionary mobs (cf. also Blackman and Walkerdine, 2001).

Many accounts of contagion and suggestibility remove the crowd from their social and political contexts and erase their social practice, turning normative forms of collective social action into pathology and rendering the crowd mysterious. Contagion comes to seem the only plausible explanation. To go back to the Paulsgrove protests – Stephanie Lawler (2004) compares representations of the Paulsgrove women at the heart of the protests with media representations of a demonstration by a group of middle-class London women mobilising in Balham against the building of a residential centre for serious sex offenders. As she notes, the latter were sympathetically portrayed in the press as vigilant, while the former were simply vigilante. Lawler documents the vilification of the Paulsgrove women in the newspapers. This became, in fact, a classic case of the crowd viewed from the outside.

The attacks proceeded through familiar gendered and classed codes. Typical descriptions of the Paulsgrove women included the following:

> Each evening scores of mothers all with their children, emerge from their homes clutching bags of crisps, fizzy drinks and bottles of alcopops, to gather around spiky-haired, heavy-smoking Katrina Kessell. Demonstrators, ranging from mothers pushing prams to tattooed teenagers ... (Martin, *Daily Telegraph*, 10 August 2000)

> There on TV were the mums (no dads), faces studded, shoulders tattooed, too-small pink singlets worn over shell-suit bottoms, pallid faces under peroxided hair telling tales of a diet of hamburgers, cigarettes and pesticides ... (Aaronovitch, *The Independent*, 11 August 2000)

> (Lawler, 2004, p. 115)

In contrast, for the Balham protestors:

> ... identification was invited, so that they became part of a fictive 'we' who are right to be worried about 'our' children. ... There were no references to these women's appearances, their homes or their incomes. The only personal details reported were about their jobs (solidly professional), the ages of their children and in one case, their title (Lady Cosima Somerset). [As reported in *The Times*] [t]hese protestors are 'not rioters, but QCs, bank managers and City traders' (Lawler, 2004, p. 114)

As Reicher would argue, identification is indeed the key term here. Social identity, he suggests, is the clue to the limits of affective communication in crowds and to understanding the forms and directions crowd action takes. Shared identification makes actions and affect intelligible and forms the basis for the construction of the discursive territory of 'reasonable' versus 'unreasonable', 'rational' versus 'irrational', 'mad' versus 'sensible'. We conclude that the affect of those we disagree with spreads by contagion, we decide that our own affect, on the other hand, when we protest, is simply caused by events and is a justifiable reaction. Shared identification and the social practices associated with that identity not only determine how mass affect is seen, it also guides the crowd's affective action, the way it flows, the objects it takes, the kind of affect displayed, and so on.

Reicher defines social identity as 'a model of the self in social relations, along with the actions that are proper and possible given such a social position' (2001, p. 200). In other words, identity, affect, legitimacy and social practice are closely woven together. What can look from the outside like chaotic and indiscriminate rioting, as an example of a mob running wild, makes a lot more sense from this perspective. Reicher, Stott and Drury have conducted a number of empirical investigations of a diverse range of crowds now and provide plausible accounts of the process of affective change within the crowd as the intergroup contexts for salient identities shift. Reicher (1984), in an analysis of the St Paul's riots in Bristol in the early 1980s, for instance, showed how crowd violence, which can look so random, is choreographed. The targets for attack were selective not indiscriminate, tightly linked to the political meaning of the mobilisation.

Above all, this work begins to pull together again the affect, meaning-making and cognition so often split apart in studies of uncanny affective transmission. As Jessica Evans (2003) argues, for instance, for the Paulsgrove protestors, 'the vigilante state of mind' was deeply linked to the 'mind of the state'. That is, the protestors (who were often coming to terms with their own histories of being sexually abused) based the meaning of their actions around government discourse that local communities should act as responsible citizens and were responsible for crime management in their area. They fabricated a list of suspected paedophiles, thus mimicking official actions and registers. The list turned out to be imagined, but it is interesting that this was the meaning-making through which their affective practice was framed.

The Development of Affective Inter-Subjectivity

In Chapter 4 I noted Daniel Stern's (2004, p. 76) claim that our nervous systems are designed to be 'captured by the nervous systems of others' as we observe their gestures, facial expressions, their rising and dampening affect and then model, intuit and re-run their intentions and psychological states. In recent years, a much clearer sense has emerged of the design features involved, how affective inter-subjectivity becomes established in infancy, and then shaped and 'personalised' within the relational patterns and interactional routines of childhood (Fonagy et al., 2004).

Developmental psychologist Colwyn Trevarthen (e.g. 1979, 1993, 1998; see Bråten and Trevarthen, 2007 for a review) has traced out in several decades of research what he sees as the layering of inter-subjective attunement and the patterned emergence of these human capacities. He argues that rudimentary forms of mapping of others' actions and coordination skills evident at birth provide a kind of basic infrastructure for interactions with parents and caretakers which in turn scaffold more sophisticated skills. By the time children are 3–6 years old they are capable of almost the full gamut of understanding of others' emotions and mental states. They can work out what emotion other people are feeling, take other people's perspective on events, accurately finish their sentences, complete their unfinished thoughts, and simulate what is going on for them. They are ready to engage in the ongoing and engrossing business of what Bråten (2007) calls 'alterocentric participation'.

Studies of neonates (Kugiumutzakis, 1988; Meltzoff and Moore, 1988), from a few hours to a few days old, show that they can imitate the facial expressions of others. As Meltzoff and Brooks (2007) report, if an infant focuses on the mother's face, for instance, and watches her deliberately poke out her tongue in play, the infant is able to quieten other body parts, identify his or her own tongue, and move it in response. In other words, what seems to be present at birth is an embryonic capacity to represent one's own body and the other's body and coordinate the two together. Meltzoff and Brooks conclude that 'exteroception (perception of others) and proprioception (perception of self) speak the same language; there is no need for associating the two through prolonged learning because they are bound together at birth' (2007, p. 153). The stage is set for what Meltzoff (2007) calls the 'Like Me Bridge' and much more complex forms of attunement. Babies rapidly move on, for instance, from this 'primary inter-subjectivity' in Trevarthen's terms to be able to follow someone's gaze to look at what they are looking at, to a capacity to maintain a shared focus of attention, and to coordinating actions together with others such as reciprocating the caregivers' spoon feeding.

In recent years the neural basis possibly underlying this self–other connectedness has come into view with the discovery of the 'mirror neurons' discussed in Chapter 2 (see Rizzolatti and Sinigaglia, 2008, for a review and see Hickok, 2009, 2010 for a critique). I say 'possibly' because this research field is relatively new and work is still being done to establish, for example, whether this kind of system might underpin a neonate's abilities (Meltzoff and Brooks, 2007). Daniel Stern provides a useful summary of the main claims and conveys his own conclusions about the phenomenological consequences:

> Mirror neurons sit adjacent to motor neurons. They fire in an observer who is doing nothing but watching another person behave (e.g. reaching for a glass). And the pattern of firing in the observer mimics the pattern that the observer would use if he were reaching for that glass, himself. In brief, the visual information received when watching another act gets mapped on to the equivalent motor representation in our own brain by the activity of these

mirror neurons. It permits us to directly participate in another's actions, without having to imitate them. We experience the other as if we were executing the same action, or feeling the same emotion. This 'participation' in another's mental life creates a sense of feeling/sharing with/understanding them, and in particular their feelings and intentions. (Stern, 2007, pp. 36–7)

As Stern emphasises, this could be a particularly central discovery for studies of affect. Rizzolatti and Sinigaglia (2008) detail the evidence of affective attunement they see emerging and the connected patterns of neural firing evident across observer and the person experiencing the emotion. What is interesting about these lines of investigation from a social researcher's perspective is that they sit so well with social science theories and knowledge. The brain seems to be both plastic, intensely responsive to the patterning of personal history, and designed to be social, intensively responsive, possibly from the very beginning, to the actions of others. Our brains, in other words, are made for social practice.

These lines of research, only roughly sketched here, provide a potentially more robust and elaborated basis for thinking about the social psychological processes behind the circulation of affect than notions of chemical entrainment. They don't address, however, the concerns about the limits of affective contagion, and the boundaries of inter-subjectivity, which I raised earlier. Clearly, a complete analysis of the 'confluence of affect' (to use Bråten and Trevarthen's, 2007, term) would need to consider the larger social organisation of 'we' and 'them' as Reicher argues. Affective attunement combines with social processes that carve out who we pay attention to, whose affect we are open to, and whose experience becomes our experience.

Social Psychoanalysis and Affective Transmission

Social psychoanalysis has a major interest, too, in the movement of affect. This interest is more frequently in interpersonal transmission from one person to another, and transmission in small groups, rather than in crowds or in cases of mass action. I want to argue, however, that such work also misrecognises relatively ordinary affective practice, placing it outside the mundane social, and thus creating unnecessary mystery.

Social psychoanalytic explanations of affective transmission focus on the operation of psychological processes such as 'transference', 'projection' and 'projective identification'. Psychoanalytic notions of transference describe one way in which affect might circulate so that strong feelings emerge mysteriously and unexpectedly, apparently uncaused. Classic transference is thought to occur when an emotion linked to a past situation or past relationship is unconsciously displaced or diverted onto a new object or relationship. A young man, for instance, may discover that he becomes inexplicably anxious when dealing with middle-aged men in the workplace, and finds himself placating them unnecessarily. After several puzzling repetitions his analyst might decide that he is doing so not because of the inherently frightening nature of middle-aged men (he doesn't behave like this with middle-aged women) but because of an unresolved traumatic relationship with his father persisting from childhood. Fear which the analyst concludes properly belonged to his relationship with his father is being *transferred* to these new situations with a different cast of characters but with the same age gap.

As Frosh (2003) points out, classic accounts of transference assumed that it would be relatively easy to make a distinction between transferred affect and ordinary affect. The former would rest on a distorted perception of the other person whereas the latter would reflect their actual reality. But, as psychoanalysis has become more constructionist, however, it has become less confident about the differences between 'reality' and 'distortion' (cf. Chodorow, 1999; Mitchell, 1993, 2000; Mitchell and Aron, 1999, for examples of constructionist trends in relational psychoanalysis). According to Frosh, transference is now seen as a more pervasive phenomenon and as a more usual feature of affective life. Indeed, in practice terms, perhaps we could simply say that past affective routines spill over into present and future affect?

Transference, as described by psychoanalysis, is an example of the potential circulation of affect from one object and context to another but it is not necessarily an example of successful affective transmission. The target of the emotion might not play out their part in the affective relation being re-constructed and re-run. Psychoanalysts, following Melanie Klein, describe transference where there is also successful transmission of affect as *projective identification* (Frosh, 2003). Here, it is claimed, an entire emotion, part of the self or affective relation, is transferred from one person to another. A therapist, for instance, ends up unconsciously experiencing an emotion that has been 'put inside' them by their patient.

Ian Craib (2001, p. 74) gives an example of the ways in which patients might act so as to 'call out' a particular feeling in their therapist. He tells an anecdote about a patient insisting that therapy is worthless and the analyst is incompetent. The patient's complaint is repeated until the analyst begins to experience a feeling of desperation or uselessness and a sense of falling apart and persecution. Craib argues that the patient's communications were unconsciously designed to have this effect – the attacks were not actually about evaluating the therapy and coming to some thoughtful conclusion about its worth – but were an attempt to make the therapist feel awful in just the same way as the patient was feeling, passing on the bad affect. Projective identification thus forms the basis for psychoanalytic therapeutic technique as the therapist tracks their own emerging feelings during the course of a therapeutic session (their own counter-transference) to learn more about the patient's mental states. And, this has been developed, too, as tool for social research (Hollway and Jefferson, 2000; Walkerdine et al., 2001).

The Drama of Projective Identification

I want to look more closely now at one example of projective identification to get some handle on the kind of explanations and assumptions involved in social psychoanalytic accounts of affective transmission. In a fascinating paper, Peter Redman (2009) goes through one clinical example from the psychoanalyst Thomas Ogden (1994) in revealing detail.

Ogden describes a projective identification he maintains had been going on for some time. He sets the scene by describing how he had been starting to feel ill and anxious in sessions with a certain patient. The following episode then clarified why this might be so:

> [During one of our sessions] I felt thirsty and leaned over in my chair to take a sip from a glass of water that I keep on the floor next to my chair (I had on many occasions done the same during Mrs B's hours, as well as with other patients). Just as I was reaching for the glass, Mrs B startled me by abruptly (and for the first time in analysis) turning around on the couch to look at me. She had a look of panic on her face and said, 'I'm sorry I didn't know what was happening to you.'

> It was only in the intensity of this moment, in which there was a feeling of terror that something catastrophic was happening to me, that I was able to name for myself the terror that I had been carrying for some time. I became aware of the anxiety I had been feeling and the ... dread of the meetings with Mrs B (as reflected in my procrastinating behaviour) had been directly connected with an unconscious sensation/fantasy that my somatic symptoms of malaise, nausea and vertigo were caused by Mrs B, and that she was killing me.' (Ogden, 1994, pp. 14–15, cited in Redman, 2009, p. 57–8)

Mrs B went on to say that she thought Ogden was having a heart attack. Ogden reports that he and the patient work out together that as a child Mrs B's parents made her feel like a greedy monster, destructively taking up space. It was this scenario that she was projecting into Ogden making him feel that he was being killed by an intrusive and destructive other. Mrs B was reproducing the affective situation and affective pattern of her childhood. Redman notes that Ogden was also implicated in this scene. Ogden concludes that he was particularly susceptible to Mrs B's projection because of patterns arising in his own personal life. He unconsciously believed that 'achieving his full potential as an analyst would result in the death of a part of himself strongly identified with his own analyst father' (Ogden, 1994, p. 16, cited in Redman, 2009, p. 61). In other words, he was open to the idea he might be killed. This possible double projective identification, then, involves a complicated relational meshing between the analyst and the patient.

Redman argues that this kind of affective circulation suggests there is something more going on in affective episodes than 'the overt social and discursive dimensions of the interaction alone' (p. 58). Redman wants to add an unconscious dimension to Ian Burkitt's multi-dimensional model (1997, 2002) of emotional life. As noted in Chapter 1, Burkitt proposes that an emotion is a complex of mutually constitutive discursive and non-discursive (or bodily) elements. Relational psychoanalysis, Redman suggests, offers a view of the unconscious commensurate with this.

In Redman's terms, this is an approach to the unconscious that is beginning to lose some of its usual topographical connotations, no longer so clearly an object in itself, a secret place, a layer, location, or site in the mind. Relational psychoanalysis turns the unconscious into what he calls 'a register in process – a flow … [which is] elaborated and changed as it comes into contact with other people and things, even as these (particularly in the case of other people) are changed by it' (Redman, 2009, p. 63). In this view, people are assumed to be highly active and agentic in the ways in which they construct personal meaning (Chodorow, 1999). Affective meaning-making in the present will be a mix of past personal and cultural meanings carried forward and meshed with the present relational circumstances. The past, in other words, is available as a kind of unconscious storehouse of possible personal associations and patterns colouring new experience, and constructing perception. It is open to revision and will be constantly re-made in light of the present.

In this line of thinking, the unconscious is also becoming less individualistic and more truly relational. Relational psychoanalysts are moving away from the guiding meta-image found in Freud's work of the solitary individual expressing dammed up unconscious affects through direct and indirect routes. Affective episodes, like Mrs B's panic, are seen as relational patterns shaped by the unconscious of both parties. This is behind Redman's emphasis on Ogden's own mental state and what Ogden tells us he may have been projecting into Mrs B. The scene, then, is understood as a joint product of two intersecting unconscious organisations.

In fact, some (including Ogden himself) argue for a specifically relational unconscious (in addition to the personal unconscious) present in any interpersonal relationship as a kind of 'third'.

> The relational unconscious, as a jointly constructed process maintained by each individual in the relation, is not simply a projection of one person's unconscious self and object representations and interactional schema onto the other, nor is it constituted by a series of such reciprocal projections and introjections between two people. Rather, as used here, the relational unconscious is the unrecognised bond that wraps each relationship, infusing the expression and constriction of each partner's subjectivity and individual unconscious within that particular relation. (Gerson, 2004, p. 72)

Unconscious Communication or Affective Practice?

In many respects, the kind of unconscious being proposed here is simply the more minimal unconscious, or the less psychologised unconscious, I was advocating in the last chapter. I suggested that affective practice is based on a semiotic hinterland organised by personal biography. This hinterland often operates like Christopher Bollas' (1989) 'unthought known' or like Donnel Stern's (1997) notion of 'unformulated experience'. Or, to add another characterisation, it could be seen as what Stolorow and Atwood (1992) describe as the 'unvalidated unconscious' – unvalidated because aspects of experience have not yet found the context to be articulated and recognised. Gerson himself develops a more static but similar conception. He (2004, p. 69) describes the unconscious as 'a holding area whose contents await birth at a receptive moment in the contingencies of evolving experience'. The very best formulation of all, though, is perhaps Gramsci's: the unconscious of affective practice is simply an aspect of what he described as the 'infinity of traces deposited in us without an inventory' (1971).

Redman and social psychoanalysis, however, add other dimensions to this minimal unconscious that tip it back into the territory of the 'dynamic'. As Redman goes on to say (see also Hollway, 2006, 2010; Hollway and Jefferson, 2000), he wants to retain a sense of the unconscious as something more than just unarticulated social practice. Experience and action can be generated by a part of oneself that is literally 'unthinkable'. Redman also wants to retain the notion of one unconscious 'talking' directly to another unconscious with no mediation. In this way he retains aspects of the original notion of the dynamic unconscious with its connotations of the active repression of disturbing meanings. As a consequence, these accounts of affective transmission, 'thirdness' and notions of projective identification run into the same kinds of problems I was trying to highlight in the last chapter.

We have come back full circle again to the uncanny. We are left once more with all the unanswered questions I discussed in the last chapter following Michael Billig's (1999a) investigations of repression. Redman offers a rare and highly lucid attempt to try to clarify the relational unconscious. In most relational psychoanalytic writing, the appeal to a dynamic unconscious is extremely vague. It is hard to determine quite what is meant. But, to repeat again the questions asked in the last chapter. How does the dynamic unconscious work psychologically? What kind of process is repression? What is the status of this 'unthinkable' that can also, it seems, be thought in therapy?

Redman argues that the unconscious exceeds the more usual processes of affective meaning-making. But it is quite hard to tell, in fact, how the social and discursive dimensions of communication and affective meaning-making might have been operating because first Ogden's, and then Redman's, text edits out, glosses and black-boxes most of the social and discursive context. We are given very little information about the preceding interactions, about the 'he said, she said' detail of what followed, or concerning the intensive interpretative work required to retrieve a projective identification from an interactional pattern in the moment. The only live interactional element left is the uncanny affective exchange between Mrs B and Ogden packaged as a stand-alone, enigmatic vignette, part of the curiosity cabinet of psychoanalysis. Case reports and anecdotes about patients in psychoanalytic writing are genre stories *par excellence*, as rigidly structured in their own way as children's fairy-tales. A shared practice, and what is perhaps better seen as negotiable and ongoing joint affective activity, is frequently plotted out in ways designed to make the hair on the back of one's neck stand on end.

According to Bollas (1995, p. 33), Freud understood the uncanny as the unhomely (*unheimlich*). The uncanny, in other words, is an event that is unfamiliar and undomesticated. But this is often to do simply with the angle of view. Take the uncanny attributed to transference, for example. In most habitual responses the context of the application of the practice is usually carried forward with the practice. Fear of public speaking, for instance, may continue as a thread through-out life but we are unlikely to describe a new fear of giving after dinner speeches required by a job promotion in mid-life as transference. The continuity of prac-tice, personal history and context is clear. When we are puzzled by transference perhaps it is because the affective practice has continued but without key ele-ments of the familiar contexts of application? The context is perhaps too embed-ded in pre-history, has to do with a past life, and with relationships that have entirely disappeared from view, or are culturally troubling, and so on.

I am questioning, then, whether the best direction of explanation is from odd and apparently inexplicable moments of affective communication to a general theory of transpersonal affect. Like social psychoanalysis, affective practice also places relationality at the heart of its explanations but understands this in more ordinary terms. The focus is on the ways in which affective habits and associa-tions are acquired. These are inevitably carried forward into new relational fields in all the ways in which past practice sets the contexts for present practice. To go back to an earlier example of classic transference – a pattern of placation and intimidation/contempt learnt early is likely to encourage 'deep' familiarity with both positions in this normative relational pair and to the acting out and re-making of these positions and the old relational routines in new relationships.

Practical knowledge about conventional, normative and paired relational posi-tions, and expertise in performing and inhabiting these patterns, is the unac-knowledged centre of phenomena glossed in social psychoanalysis as unconscious communication. Craib's (2001) patient who rubbishes the therapist, for instance, evokes feelings in the therapist of being attacked and feeling worthless. We could say that the patient has 'put these feelings inside' the therapist and this is an example of unconscious communication. Or, we could say that the patient has embarked on a particular kind of affective practice where the therapist will need to negotiate the possible range of available second 'turns' that are relevant – such as, accept the accusation and feel guilty, retaliate and fight back, contain it, offer a meta-interpretation of the situation, etc.

In a similar vein, I wonder, too, whether the affective–discursive is 'closer in' to moments of unconscious communication than social psychoanalysis suggests. It is impossible to retrieve and understand what went on between Mrs B and Ogden. But perhaps we don't need to formulate it in such dramatic terms. A relatively ordinary, if intense, affective communication between two people turned out to have some useful consequences in developing a new narrative. Much of the effort involved in discovering those consequences seems to have taken place, however, in the probably quite large amount of discursive work and affective meaning-making entailed by the event.

Mrs B experiences intense anxiety for a moment in one session and perhaps more pervasively across many analytic sessions. Her panicked feeling in this particular moment seems to spread to a concern that the therapist in the room with her, sitting behind her, out of her view, is still alive. Intense anxiety can be like that – formulating an entire scene as dangerous and everybody in it as endangered. Once the practice of panic starts it is easy, too, for others to take on an anxious position within it. Ogden sees Mrs B's terror and begins to worry about himself, indeed as one would. Is something awful happening? Together, however, because there is a long history of interaction between them, emerging knowledge of each other, and further conversations to come, they manage to link this moment to a potentially healing investigation of Mrs B's affective history.

The Cultural Politics of Emotion and the Affective Economy

Finally, in this chapter, I want to discuss one further perspective on the circulation of affect from Sara Ahmed (2004a, 2004b). Ahmed (2004b) presents a cultural politics of emotion. That is, she is interested in the cultural constitution of affected subjects and collective bodies, attempting to understand textual representations of affect in newspapers, narratives, political speeches, etc. Her aim is to describe how affect circulates across large-scale cultural domains and to theorise affect and social value. It is this kind of circulation which is at the heart of waves of public feeling. It is evident whenever a campaign, for instance, mounts in the newspapers concerning a celebrity or a politician, enticing millions into amused disgust or sympathetic adulation. These kinds of phenomena are affective–discursive for sure – the power of words to evoke affective re-runs in readers and observers is crucial – but they also build on the kinds of practical social coordinations I have been trying to emphasise in this chapter.

Ahmed's key claim is that as emotion circulates, it brings into being psychic life and social objects. Emotions 'surface' and materialise characters, textual figures and social relations. Ahmed describes, for instance, the construction of the hate figure of the 'asylum seeker' found in British politicians' speeches, tabloid newspapers, in white Aryan websites, and in British National Party propaganda (cf. also Tyler, 2006). She argues perceptively that hate (or any affect) is a relation constituting both its objects and its subjects. As I move into hate, for instance, I become shaped in various ways. I could become subjectified as an accuser, or take on the subject position of a moral agent stuffed full of righteous indignation, or write myself as sadistic. All of these subject positions are possible. I become twisted, in other words, into particular configurations. I acquire a psychic life and a particular kind of surface as a body for other bodies. The same thing happens to the object of my hate. No object, Ahmed argues, is inherently or intrinsically hateful or detestable. I may think so, but rather it is the presence of my hate that materialises someone or something as hateful. If my hate (as hate is reputed to do) turns into love in an instant, the appearance and surface of the object will be transformed by this new affect.

Following this logic, Ahmed decides that emotion has no residence. It is not a property of a pre-existing or fixed individual and it is not an intrinsic feature of an object. As emotions circulate, however, surfacing individual and collective bodies, tracing and forming their shape, they sometimes 'stick'. She suggests that the figure of the 'asylum-seeker' has become just such a 'sticky surface'. Affects such as fear, denigration and feelings of invasion nestle on this figure. Densely clustered, they adhere to form the hated object. This 'stickiness' binds the participating signs and bodies together into a social relationship. The figure of the asylum-seeker in British political discourse, Ahmed (2004a) suggests, is an object of fantasy (it is fantastic, she says). Circulating emotion that has stuck in this way has erased other histories of the production of the asylum-seeker, white citizen-subjects and migrants in outlets such as the tabloid press. Interestingly, Ahmed points out that emotions need not just stick, they can also 'slide'. We could investigate, then, the range of constructed cultural figures which tabloid hates slide over and the figures where hate dwells and proliferate.

For Ahmed, the notion of 'affective economy' is a shorthand that sums up this circulation process and explains the creation of affective value. Her argument about affect and value is complex:

> [E]motions work as a form of capital: affect does not reside positively in the sign or commodity, but is produced only as an effect of its circulation. I am using 'the economic' to suggest that emotions circulate and are distributed across a social as well as psychic field. I am borrowing from the Marxian critique of the logic of capital. In Capital, Marx discusses how the movement of commodities and money, in the formula M-C-M (money to commodity to money), creates surplus value. That is, through circulation and exchange M acquires more value. Or as he puts it, 'The value originally advanced, therefore, not only remains intact while in circulation, but increases its magnitude, adds to itself a surplus-value or is valorised. And this movement converts it into capital.' I am identifying a similar logic: the movement between signs converts into affect. ... What I am offering is a theory of passion not as the drive to accumulate (whether it be value, power, or meaning), but as that which is accumulated over time. Affect does not reside in an object or sign, but is an affect of the circulation between objects and signs (= the accumulation of affective value over time). Some signs, that is, increase in affective value as an effect of the movement between signs: the more they circulate, the more affective they become, and the more they appear to 'contain' affect. (2004a, p. 120)

A sign like 'the asylum seeker', then, accrues more and more 'value' and 'capital' over time. This is not value or capital in any positive sense, as a 'good thing' that can be exchanged for other 'goods', but value as a kind of 'collected together affect' in itself – affect is accumulating around the figure of the asylum-seeker just as money accumulates when a house is bought and then sold in a rising market even though the fabric of the house has not changed at all.

With these theoretical moves, Ahmed sets the scene for analyses of the current circuits of value in cultural production. She provides some brilliant readings of how affect flows through contemporary cultural politics (see Skeggs and Wood, 2009, for similar explorations around reality television). If we go back, for example, to Lawler's (2004) work on the representations of the Paulsgrove women discussed above, we can see exactly how these women have become signs and figures and placed in a circuit of value. Condemnation of the women increases and intensifies as comment succeeds comment, and a particular set of significations and emotions come to 'stick' even more strongly to the figure of the white working-class woman.

Landing and Surfacing or Negotiation and Practice?

Ahmed's work is helpful for understanding waves of public feeling that often seem to diffuse with no apparent originating point (although in the UK a tabloid newspaper often turns out to be at the heart). In many respects, her approach can be seen as mobilising some classic post-structuralist and performativity knowledge strategies to find ways of analysing cultural affect. But, again, it seems to me that more mystery is created here than there need be, and Ahmed's work reproduces many of the problems with post-structuralist theory discussed in Chapter 3. Sticking, surfacing, landing and sliding are in danger of becoming the uncanny of cultural studies. The more I try to grasp Ahmed's theoretical argument about the circulation of affect the more elusive it becomes.

Is affect actually like capital? As signs move and relations are made is the result always the accumulation of affect understood as value, whether positive or negative? Can affect sometimes fail to accumulate, or stop accumulating and lose intensity? Does affect necessarily increase, as it accumulates? Is it actually like money in that respect? Is it not the case that, as hate or love is repeated, the affect can sometimes become less and less intense, until strong emotion is replaced with banality and over-familiarity? Would this be equivalent to buying and selling a house in a falling market? Is the loss of value and capital equivalent to loss of intensity and stickiness, or is it the loss of something defined as a good that could be exchanged for other goods? How, in Ahmed's scheme, do we evaluate the 'value' any particular combination of signs and bodies accumulates?

Perhaps a more crucial problem, though, lies in Ahmed's definition of emotion and affect. Her formulations are hard to decipher. On the one hand, in her writings, emotion looks pretty specific, defined in terms of its content and associated practices, taking conventional psychological forms like 'hate'. I discussed above Ahmed's example of the figure of the asylum-seeker, and how hate might circulate, shaping subjects and objects. In line with this specificity, the list of emotions Ahmed explores in her book pretty much reproduces the basic emotions of traditional psychobiology (love, hate, fear, disgust and shame). But Ahmed also argues, however, that emotion is not specific in her scheme, and is not defined by its content, or its psychology. She wants to take up 'emotion' in one of its oldest definitional senses 'from the Latin, *emovere*, referring to "to move, to move out"' (2004b, p. 11). Emotion is thus not located in social actors or individuals and is peculiarly disembodied – just a force.

Like the models of affect without a subject discussed in the previous chapter, Ahmed understands emotion, then, simply as movement with no particular content. The linking of one sign to another, such as asylum seekers with invasion, or Paulsgrove women with fecklessness, is the driver that leads to the accumulation of affect. But, with this claim, any specificity a focus on emotion or affect might offer is gone. Affect could be any movement of signs. What has happened to affect as the domain of the social that is embodied? I want to dwell on these issues a bit further as they are so important for future research directions. Is it 'emotion' (as a circulating force) which is driving value, or is it people's affective practice? I want to suggest that our focus should be on affective practice, not affect defined abstractly as the movement of signs. What's the difference?

To recapitulate my earlier arguments, I see affective practice as a moment of recruitment and often synchronous assembling of multimodal resources, including, most crucially, body states. It is the participation of the emoting body that makes an assemblage an example of affect rather than an example of some other kind of social practice. I agree with Ahmed that this assembling and recruiting is onto-formative, meaning that it constitutes subjects and objects. In Ahmed's terms, affective practice materialises social and psychic life, creating particular surfaces and kinds of subjects and objects, individual and collective bodies. Affective practice in this way sets up relations between subjects and objects through their intertwined formations and constitutions. But we also need to locate affect, not in the ether, or in endless and mysterious circulations, but in actual bodies and social actors, negotiating, making decisions, evaluating, communicating, inferring and relating. What creates value and/or capital is the direction and history of affective practice over time, and the history of its entanglements with other onto-formative social practices and social formations. The concept of affective practice, then, encompasses the movement of signs but it also tries to explain how affect is embodied, is situated and operates psychologically.

What is missing from Ahmed's account is the particularity of embodiment, the ways in which affective practice mobilises, recruits and stabilises brain/body states, and the kinds of translation processes involved as a particular form of emoting emerges. One could argue that these aspects of affective practice are not relevant in studies of textual representations of affect. But, I think this is a major limit on the explanatory power of Ahmed's scheme. It makes her open to what could be called transposition errors when she ignores the quite narrow applicability of her account and presents it as a general theory of affect and value. Work of this kind in cultural studies sometimes moves too seamlessly across a number of affective–discursive domains. Examples of political rhetoric such as speeches and newspaper articles evoking affect are combined with fragments of personal autobiography, relational records and accounts of personal moments of emotion. But the affective–discursive practices involved in constructing categories of hate-filled objects in a political speech, or in the rant of an extreme right wing group, can follow a very different compositional logic from the affective practices of hate in everyday life. In the first case, it almost makes sense to say the affect is the movement of signs and that 'emotion circulates'. As we move from text to talk-in-interaction, these ideas completely lose their purchase.

In interactions, like the interactions between therapists and patients I have discussed in this chapter, or the interactions between groups of girls in the playground discussed in Chapter 4, it is not actually emotion that circulates. Affect instead is embedded in situated practice. Think back, for example, to Marjorie Goodwin's (2006) example of the 'tag-along girl' discussed in Chapter 4: the two girls involved in that episode, Angela and Sarah, were actively constructing the world for each other through the routines and resources they were drawing upon as a basis for their actions. It was not signs *per se* that were excluding Angela – first and foremost these were the routine actions of the girls in her social group. This was not a mysterious process of signs sliding over each other and sticking at certain points – this was certainly a sticky situation for Angela but it was Sarah who was doing the sticking. To focus just on the circulation of signs is to risk over-idealising affect and, paradoxically, as we have seen, bodies completely disappear from the study of affect. What emerges is an almost completely disembodied account, poised uncomfortably between the cultural and the phenomenological, completely missing the situated domain of daily life.

In this chapter, and indeed in this book as a whole, I have tried to flesh out some of the characteristics of communal affective practice. My main argument has been that it doesn't help to see these as uncanny or *unheimlich*. My commitment, therefore, has been to try to understand the odd, the eerie and the genuinely weird examples of pulses of affect in concrete terms. The continuing task for social research will be to try to find the various 'homes' for waves of feeling in practice and its contexts.

References

Abu-Lughod, L. and Lutz, C. (eds) (1990) *Language and the Politics of Emotion*. Cambridge: Cambridge University Press.

Adkins, L. and Lury, C. (eds) (2009) Special Issue: The Empirical. *European Journal of Social Theory*, 12 (1).

Adolphs, R. and Damasio, A.R. (2001) The Interaction of Affect and Cognition: A Neurobiological Perspective. In J.P. Forgas (ed.), *Handbook of Affect and Cognition*. Mahwah, NJ: Lawrence Erlbaum.

Ahmed, S. (2004a) Affective Economies. *Social Text*, 22 (2), 117–39.

Ahmed, S. (2004b) *The Cultural Politics of Emotion*. New York: Routledge.

Ahmed, S. (ed.) (2007/2008) Special Issue: Happiness. *New Formations*, 63 (Winter).

Alcoff, L. (1996) *Real Knowing: New Versions of Coherence Theory*. Ithaca, NY: Cornell University Press.

Anderson, B. (2003) Time-Stilled Space-Slowed: How Boredom Matters. *Geoforum*, 35, 739–54.

Anderson, B. (2006) Becoming and Being Hopeful: Towards a Theory of Affect. *Environment and Planning D: Society and Space*, 24, 733–52.

Anderson, B. (2009) Affective Atmospheres. *Emotion, Space and Society*, 2, 77–81.

Antaki, C., Finlay, W.M.L. and Walton, C. (2007a) Conversational Shaping: Staff Members' Solicitation of Talk from People with an Intellectual Impairment. *Qualitative Health Research*, 17, 1403–14.

Antaki, C., Finlay, W.M.L. and Walton, C. (2007b) How Proposing an Activity to a Person with an Intellectual Disability can Imply a Limited Identity. *Discourse and Society*, 18, 393–410.

Antaki, C., Finlay, W.M.L. and Walton, C. (2009) Identity at Home: Offering Everyday Choices to People with Intellectual Impairments. In M. Wetherell (ed.), *Theorizing Identities and Social Action*. Basingstoke: Palgrave.

Archer, M. (2003) *Structure, Agency and the Internal Conversation*. Cambridge: Cambridge University Press.

Arnold, M. (1960) *Emotion and Personality*. New York: Columbia University Press.

Arnold, M. and Glasson, J. (1954) Feelings and Emotions as Dynamic Factors in Personality Integration. In M. Arnold and J. Glasson (eds), *The Human Person*. New York: Ronald.

Atkinson, A.P. and Adolphs, R. (2005) Visual Emotion Perception: Mechanisms and Processes. In L.F. Barrett, P.M. Niedenthal and P. Winkielman (eds), *Emotions: Conscious and Unconscious*. New York: Guilford Press.

Averill, J.R. (1982) *Anger and Aggression: An Essay on Emotion*. New York: Springer-Verlag.

Bakhtin, M. (1986) *Speech Genres and Other Late Essays*. Austin, TX: University of Texas Press.

Baldwin, M.W., Carrell, S.E. and Lopez, D.F. (1990) Priming Relationship Schemas: My Advisor and the Pope are Watching Me from the Back of my Mind. *Journal of Experimental Social Psychology*, 26, 435–54.

Baldwin, M.W., Fehr, B., Keedian, E., Seidel, M. and Thompson, D.W. (1993) An Exploration of the Relational Schemata Underlying Attachment Styles: Self Report and Lexical Decision Approaches. *Personality and Social Psychology Bulletin*, 19, 746–54.

Barad, K. (2007) *Meeting the Universe Halfway: Quantum Physics and the Entanglement of Matter and Meaning.* Durham, NC: Duke University Press.

Baraitser, L. and Frosh, S. (2007) Affect and Encounter in Psychoanalysis. *Critical Psychology,* 21, 76–93.

Bargh, J.A. (ed.) (2007a) *Social Psychology and the Unconscious: The Automaticity of Higher Mental Processes.* New York: Psychology Press.

Bargh, J.A. (2007b) Introduction. In J.A. Bargh (ed.), *Social Psychology and the Unconscious: The Automaticity of Higher Mental Processes.* New York: Psychology Press.

Bargh, J., Chen, M. and Burrows, L. (1996) Automaticity of Social Behaviour: Direct Effects of Trait Construct and Stereotype Activation on Action. *Journal of Personality and Social Psychology,* 71, 230–44.

Barrett, L.F. (2005) Feeling is Perceiving: Core Affect and Conceptualization in the Experience of Emotion. In L.F. Barrett, P.M. Niedenthal and P. Winkielman (eds), *Emotions: Conscious and Unconscious.* New York: Guilford Press.

Barrett, L.F. (2006a) Solving the Emotion Paradox: Categorization and the Experience of Emotion. *Personality and Social Psychology Review,* 10, 20–46.

Barrett, L.F. (2006b) Are Emotions Natural Kinds? *Perspectives on Psychological Science,* 1, 28–58.

Barrett, L.F. (2009) Variety Is the Spice of Life: A Psychological Construction Approach to Understanding Variability in Emotion. *Cognition and Emotion,* 23 (7), 1284–306.

Barrett, L.F., Mesquita, B., Ochsner, K.N. and Gross, J.J. (2007) The Experience of Emotion. *Annual Review of Psychology,* 58, 373–403.

Barrett, L.F. and Wager, T.R. (2006) The Structure of Emotion: Evidence from NeuroImaging Studies. *Current Directions in Psychological Science,* 15, 79–83.

Barrett, L., Niedenthal, P.M. and Winkielman, P. (eds) (2005) *Emotion and Consciousness.* New York: Guilford Press.

Barthes, R. (1979) *A Lover's Discourse: Fragments.* London: Cape.

Baugh, B. (2005) Body. In A. Parr (ed.), *The Deleuze Dictionary.* Edinburgh: Edinburgh University Press.

Bennett, C.M., Baird, A.A., Miller, M.B. and Wolford, G.L. (2010) Neural Correlates of Interspecies Perspective Taking in the Post-Mortem Atlantic Salmon: An Argument for Multiple Comparisons Correction. *Journal of Serendipitous and Unexpected Results,* 1 (1), 1–5.

Bennett, T., Savage, M., Silva, E., Warde, A., Gayo-Cal, M. and Wright, D. (2009) *Culture, Class, Distinction.* London: Routledge.

Berlant, L. (1997) *The Queen of America Goes to Washington City: Essays on Sex and Citizenship.* Durham, NC: Duke University Press.

Berlant, L. (2000) Intimacy: A Special Issue. In L. Berlant (ed.), *Intimacy.* Chicago: University of Chicago Press.

Berlant, L. (2005) Unfeeling Kerry. *Theory and Event,* 8 (2). http://proquest.umi.com/pqdweb?did =0000001561024761&Fmt=3&cl ientId=43168&RQT=309&VName=PQD

Berlant, L. (2008a) *The Female Complaint: The Unfinished Business of Sentimentality in American Culture.* Durham, NC: Duke University Press.

Berlant, L. (2008b) Thinking about Feeling Historical. *Emotion, Space and Society,* 1, 4–9.

Billig, M. (1997a) The Dialogic Unconscious: Psychoanalysis, Discursive Psychology and the Nature of Repression. *British Journal of Social Psychology,* 36, 139–59.

Billig, M. (1997b) Discursive, Rhetorical and Ideological Messages. In C. McGarty and S.A. Haslam (eds), *The Message of Social Psychology.* Oxford: Blackwell.

Billig, M. (1999a) *Freudian Repression: Conversation Creating the Unconscious.* Cambridge: Cambridge University Press.

Billig, M. (1999b) Whose Terms? Whose Ordinariness? Rhetoric and Ideology in Conversation Analysis. *Discourse and Society,* 10, 543–58.

Billig, M. (1999c) Conversation Analysis and Claims of Naiveté. *Discourse and Society,* 10, 572–7.

Billig, M., Condor, S., Edwards, D., Gane, M., Middleton, D. and Radley, A. (1988) *Ideological Dilemmas*. London: Sage.

Blackman, L. (2007a) Reinventing Psychological Matters: The Importance of the Suggestive Realm of Tarde's Ontology. *Economy and Society*, 36 (4), 574–96.

Blackman, L. (2007b) Feeling F.I.N.E.: Social Psychology, Suggestion and the Problem of Social Influence. *International Journal of Critical Psychology*, 21, 23–49.

Blackman, L. (2007/2008) Is Happiness Contagious? *New Formations*, 63, 15–31.

Blackman, L. (2008) Affect, Relationality and the 'Problem of Personality'. *Theory, Culture and Society*, 25 (1), 23–47.

Blackman, L. (2010) Embodying Affect: Voice-Hearing, Telepathy, Suggestion and Modelling the Non-Conscious. *Body and Society*, 16 (1), 163–92.

Blackman, L. and Cromby, J. (eds) (2007) Special Issue: Affect and Feeling. *International Journal of Critical Psychology*, 21.

Blackman, L. and Venn, C. (eds) (2010) Special Issue: Affect. *Body and Society*, 16 (1).

Blackman, L. and Walkerdine, V. (2001) *Mass Hysteria: Critical Psychology and Media Studies*. Basingstoke: Palgrave.

Blackman, L., Cromby, J., Hook, D., Papadopoulos, D. and Walkerdine, V. (2008) Editorial: Creating Subjectivities. *Subjectivity*, 22, 1–27.

Blair, T. (2006) A Duty to Integrate. The text of Blair's speech can be found at: http://www.number10.gov.uk/output/Page10563.asp

Bollas, C. (1989) *Forces of Destiny: Psychoanalysis and the Human Idiom*. London: Free Association Books.

Bollas, C. (1995) *Cracking Up: The Work of Unconscious Experience*. New York: Hill and Wang.

Bondi, L., Davidson, J. and Smith, M. (2005) Introduction: Geography's 'Emotional Turn'. In J. Davidson, L. Bondi and M. Smith (eds), *Emotional Geographies*. Aldershot: Ashgate.

Boston Change Process Study Group (2003) Explicating the Implicit: The Interactive Microprocess in the Analytic Situation. *International Journal of Psychoanalysis*, 83, 1051–62.

Bourdieu, P. (1984) *Distinction: A Social Critique of the Judgement of Taste*. Trans. Richard Nice. Cambridge, MA: Harvard University Press.

Bourdieu, P. (1990) *The Logic of Practice*. Trans. Richard Nice. Cambridge: Polity.

Bourdieu, P. (1998) *Practical Reason*. Cambridge: Polity.

Bråten, S. (ed.) (2007) *On Being Moved: From Mirror Neurons to Empathy*. Amsterdam: John Benjamins.

Bråten, S. and Trevarthen, C. (2007) Prologue: From Infant Subjectivity and Participant Movements to Simulation and Conversation in Cultural Common Sense. In S. Bråten (ed.), *On Being Moved: From Mirror Neurons to Empathy*. Amsterdam: John Benjamins.

Brennan, T. (2004) *The Transmission of Affect*. Ithaca, NY: Cornell University Press.

Brown, S., Reavey, P., Cromby, J., Harper, D. and Johnson, K. (2009) On Psychology and Embodiment: Some Methodological Experiments. *Sociological Review*, 56 (S2), 197–215.

Brown, S.D. and Stenner, P. (2001) Being Affected: Spinoza and the Psychology of Emotion. *International Journal of Group Tensions*, 30 (1), 81–105.

Brown, S.D. and Stenner, P. (2009) *Psychology Without Foundations*. London: Sage.

Bruner, J. (1990) *Acts of Meaning*. Cambridge, MA: Harvard University Press.

Burkitt, I. (1997) Social Relationships and Emotions. *Sociology*, 31 (1), 37–55.

Burkitt, I. (1999) *Bodies of Thought: Embodiment, Identity and Modernity*. London: Sage.

Burkitt, I. (2002) Complex Emotions: Relations, Feelings and Images in Emotional Experience. In J. Barbalet (ed.), *Emotions and Sociology*. Oxford: Blackwell.

Burkitt, I. (2005) Powerful Emotions: Power, Government and Opposition in the 'War on Terror'. *Sociology*, 39 (4), 679–95.

Butler, J. (1990) *Gender Trouble*. New York: Routledge.

Butler, J. (2005) *Giving an Account of Oneself*. New York: Fordham University Press.

Byatt, A.S. (2001) *The Biographer's Tale*. London: Vintage.

Cacioppo, J.T., Berntson, G.G., Larsen, J.T., Poehlman, K.M. and Ito, T.A. (2000) The Psychophysiology of Emotion. In M. Lewis and J.M. Haviland-Jones (eds), *Handbook of Emotions*, 2nd edn. New York: Guilford Press.

Cameron, D. (2007) *The Myth of Mars and Venus: Do Men and Women Really Speak Different Languages?* Oxford: Oxford University Press.

Campbell, J. (2007) Transference Streams of Affects and Representations. *International Journal of Critical Psychology*, 21, 50–75.

Campos, G.P., Ramos, C.S. and Bernal, J.J.Y. (1999) Emotion Discourse 'Speaks' of Involvement: Commentary on Edwards. *Culture and Psychology*, 5 (3), 293–304.

Capps, L. and Ochs, E. (1995) *Constructing Panic: The Discourse of Agoraphobia*. Cambridge, MA: Harvard University Press.

Castree, M. and Macmillan, T. (2004) Old News: Representation and Academic Novelty. *Environment and Planning A*, 36, 469–80.

Charlesworth, S.J. (2000) *A Phenomenology of Working Class Experience*. Cambridge: Cambridge University Press.

Chen, S., Fitzsimmons, G.M. and Andersen, S.M. (2007) Automaticity in Closer Relationships. In J. Bargh (ed.), *Social Psychology and the Unconscious: The Automaticity of Higher Mental Processes*. New York: Psychology Press.

Chodorow, N. (1999) *The Power of Feelings*. New Haven, CT: Yale University Press.

Clarke, S. (2009) Thinking Psycho-Socially about Difference: Ethnicity, Community and Emotion. In S. Day-Sclater, D. Jones, H. Price and C. Yates (eds), *Emotion: New Psychosocial Perspectives*. Basingstoke: Palgrave.

Clarke, S. and Garner, S. (2009) *White Identities: A Critical Sociological Approach*. London: Pluto.

Clarke, S., Garner, S. and Gilmour, R. (2009) Imagining the 'Other'/Figuring Encounter: White English Middle-Class and Working Class Identifications. In M. Wetherell (ed.), *Identity in the 21st Century: New Trends in Changing Times*. Basingstoke: Palgrave.

Clay-Warner, J. and Robinson, D. (eds) (2008) *Social Structure and Emotion*. Amsterdam: Academic Press.

Clore, G.L. and Ortony, A. (2000) Cognition in Emotion: Always, Sometimes, or Never? In R.D. Lane and L. Nadel (eds), *Cognitive Neuroscience of Emotion*. Oxford: Oxford University Press.

Clore, G.L., Storbeck, J., Robinson, M.D. and Centerbar, D. (2005) Seven Sins in the Study of Unconscious Affect. In L. Feldman Barrett, P.M. Niedenthal and P. Winkielman (eds), *Emotion and Consciousness*. New York: Guilford Press.

Clough, P.T. (2000) *Autoaffection: Unconscious Thought in the Age of Teletechnology*. Minneapolis, MN: University of Minnesota Press.

Clough, P.T. (2007) Introduction. In P.T. Clough with J. Halley (eds), *The Affective Turn*. Durham, NC: Duke University Press.

Clough, P.T. (2008a) The Affective Turn: Political Economy, Biomedia and Bodies. *Theory, Culture and Society*, 25 (1), 1–22.

Clough, P.T. (2008b) (De)Coding the Subject-in-Affect. *Subjectivity*, 23, 140–55.

Clough, P.T. (2009) The New Empiricism: Affect and Sociological Method. *European Journal of Social Theory*, 12 (1), 22–62.

Clough, P.T., Goldberg, G., Shiff, R., Weeks, A. and Willse, C. (2007) Toward a Theory of Affect-Itself. *Ephemera*, 7 (1), 60–77.

Clough, P.T. with Halley, J. (eds) (2007) *The Affective Turn*. Durham, NC: Duke University Press.

Colebrook, C. (2006) *Deleuze: A Guide for the Perplexed*. London: Continuum.

Coleman, F. (2005) Affect. In A. Parr (ed.), *The Deleuze Dictionary*. Edinburgh: Edinburgh University Press.

Collins English Dictionary (2003) Complete and Unabridged Sixth Edition. London: HarperCollins.

Connell, R.W. (1987) *Gender and Power*. Cambridge: Polity.

Connolly, W.E. (2002) *Neuropolitics: Thinking, Culture, Speed*. Minneapolis, MN: University of Minnesota Press.

Coulter, J. and Sharrock, W. (2007) *Brain, Mind, and Human Behaviour in Contemporary Cognitive Science: Critical Assessments of the Philosophy of Psychology*. Lewiston, NY: The Edwin Mellen Press.

Coupland, N. and Jaworski, A. (eds) (2008) *Sociolinguistics: Critical Concepts*. London: Routledge.

Craib, I. (1994) *The Importance of Disappointment*. London: Routledge.

Craib, I. (2001) *Psychoanalysis: A Critical Introduction*. Cambridge: Polity.

Cromby, J. (2007a) Toward a Psychology of Feeling. *International Journal of Critical Psychology*, 21, 94–118.

Cromby, J. (2007b) Integrating Social Science with Neuroscience: Potentials and Problems. *Biosocieties*, 2, 149–69.

Crossley, N. (2001) *The Social Body: Habit, Identity and Desire*. London: Sage.

Crossley, N. (2006) *Reflexive Embodiment in Contemporary Society*. Maidenhead: Open University Press.

Damasio, A.R. (1995) *Descartes' Error: Emotion, Reason and the Human Brain*. London: Papermac.

Damasio, A.R. (1999) *The Feeling of What Happens: Body and Emotion in the Making of Consciousness*. New York: Harcourt Brace and Company.

Damasio, A.R. (2004) *Looking for Spinoza: Joy, Sorrow and the Feeling Brain*. London: Vintage.

Daum, I., Markowitsch, H.J. and Vandekerckhove, M. (2009) Neurobiological Basis of Emotions. In B. Röttger-Rössler and H.J. Markowitsch (eds), *Emotions as Bio-Cultural Processes*. New York: Springer.

Davidson, J., Smith, M., Bondi, L. and Probyn, E. (2008) Editorial Introduction. *Emotion, Space and Society*, 1 (1), 1–3.

Davidson, R.J. (1994) Complexities in the Search for Emotion-Specific Physiology. In P. Ekman and R.J. Davidson (eds), *The Nature of Emotions: Fundamental Questions*. Oxford: Oxford University Press.

Davidson, R.J. (2003) Commentary – Seven Sins in the Study of Emotion: Correctives from Affective Neuroscience. *Brain and Cognition*, 52, 129–32.

Davidson, R.J., Jackson, D.C. and Kalin, N.H. (2000) Emotion, Plasticity, Context, and Regulation: Perspectives from Affective Neuroscience. *Psychological Bulletin*, 126 (6), 890–909.

Davidson, R.J., Pizzagalli, D., Nitschke, J.B. and Kalin, N.H. (2003) Parsing the Subcomponents of Emotion and Disorders of Emotion: Perspectives from Affective Neuroscience. In R.J. Davidson, K.R. Scherer and H.H. Goldsmith (eds), *Handbook of Affective Sciences*. Oxford: Oxford University Press.

Davidson, R.J., Scherer, K.R. and Goldsmith, H.H. (eds) (2003a) *Handbook of Affective Sciences*. Oxford: Oxford University Press.

Davidson, R.J., Scherer, K.R. and Goldsmith, H.H. (2003b) Introduction: Neuroscience. In R.J. Davidson, K.R. Scherer and H.H. Goldsmith (eds), *Handbook of Affective Sciences*. Oxford: Oxford University Press.

Dawson, G. (1994) *Soldier Heroes: British Adventure, Empire and the Imagining of Masculinities*. London: Routledge.

Deleuze, G. (1988) *Spinoza: Practical Philosophy*. Trans. R. Hurley. San Francisco, CA: City Lights Books.

Deleuze, G. (1992) Ethology: Spinoza and Us. In J. Crary and S. Kwinter (eds), *Incorporations*. New York: Zone Books.

Deleuze, G. (1994) *Difference and Repetition*. Trans. P. Patton. New York: Columbia University Press.

Deleuze, G. (2007) Desire and Pleasure. In G. Deleuze, *Two Regimes of Madness*, rev. edn. Ed. by D. Lapoujade, Trans. by A. Hodges and M. Taormina. Los Angeles: Semiotext(e).

Deleuze, G. and Guattari, F. (1977) *Anti-Oedipus: Capitalism and Schizophrenia*. Trans. R. Hurley, M. Seem and H. R. Lowe. New York: Viking Press.

Despret, V. (2004a) *Our Emotional Makeup: Ethnopsychology and Selfhood.* Trans. M. De Jager. New York: Other Press.

Despret, V. (2004b) The Body We Care for: Figures of Anthropo-Genesis. *Body and Society,* 10 (2/3), 111–34.

Dewsbury, J.D. (2003) Witnessing Space: 'Knowledge Without Contemplation'. *Environment and Planning A,* 35 (11), 1907–32.

Dijksterhuis, A., Aarts, H. and Smith, P.K. (2005) The Power of the Subliminal: On Subliminal Persuasion and Other Potential Applications. In R.R. Hassin, J.S. Uleman and J. Bargh (eds), *The New Unconscious.* Oxford: Oxford University Press.

Dijksterhuis, A., Chartrand, T. and Aarts, H. (2007) Effects of Priming and Perception on Social Behaviour and Goal Pursuit. In J. Bargh (ed.), *Social Psychology and the Unconscious: The Automaticity of Higher Mental Processes.* New York: Psychology Press.

Dixon, T.M. (2003) *From Passions to Emotions: The Creation of a Secular Psychological Category.* Cambridge: Cambridge University Press.

Doidge, N. (2007) *The Brain that Changes Itself.* New York: Viking Penguin.

Drury, J. and Reicher, S. (1999) The Intergroup Dynamics of Collective Empowerment: Substantiating the Social Identity Model of Crowd Behaviour. *Group Processes and Intergroup Relations,* 2, 382–402.

Duncan, S. and Barrett, L.F. (2007) Affect Is a Form of Cognition: A Neurobiological Analysis. *Cognition and Emotion,* 21 (6), 1184–211.

Edley, N. (2001) Analysing Masculinity: Interpretative Repertoires, Subject Positions and Ideological Dilemmas. In M. Wetherell, S. Taylor and S.J. Yates (eds), *Discourse as Data: A Guide to Analysis.* London : Sage.

Edley, N. and Wetherell, M. (1997) Jockeying for Position: The Construction of Masculine Identities. *Discourse and Society,* 8, 203–17.

Edwards, D. (1995) Two to Tango: Script Formulations, Dispositions and Rhetorical Symmetry in Relationship Troubles Talk. *Research on Language and Social Interaction,* 28 (4), 319–50.

Edwards, D. (1997) *Discourse and Cognition.* London: Sage.

Edwards, D. (1999) Emotion Discourse. *Culture and Psychology,* 5, 271–91.

Edwards, D. (2005) Moaning, Whinging and Laughing: The Subjective Side of a Complaint. *Discourse Studies,* 7 (1), 5–29.

Edwards, D. and Potter, J. (1992) *Discursive Psychology.* London: Sage.

Edwards, D. and Potter, J. (2005) Discursive Psychology, Mental States and Descriptions. In H. te Molder and J. Potter (eds), *Conversation and Cognition.* Cambridge: Cambridge University Press.

Ekman, P. (1972) Universals and Cultural Differences in Facial Expressions of Emotions. In J. Cole (ed.), *Nebraska Symposium on Motivation.* Lincoln, NB: University of Nebraska Press.

Ekman, P. (1994) All Emotions are Basic. In P. Ekman and R.J. Davidson (eds), *The Nature of Emotion: Fundamental Questions.* New York: Oxford University Press.

Ekman, P. (2003) *Emotions Revealed: Understanding Thoughts and Feelings.* London: Weidenfeld and Nicolson.

Ekman, P. and Davidson, R.J. (eds) (1994) *The Nature of Emotion: Fundamental Questions.* New York: Oxford University Press.

Ekman, P. and Friesen, W.V. (1971) Constants across Cultures in the Face and Emotion. *Journal of Personality and Social Psychology,* 17, 124–9.

Elias, N. (2000) *The Civilising Process,* rev. edn. Trans. E. Jephcott. Oxford: Blackwell.

Engelen, E-M., Markowitsch, H.J., von Scheve, C., Röttger-Rössler, B., Stephan, A., Holodynski, M. and Vandekerckhove, M. (2009) Emotions as Bio-Cultural Processes: Disciplinary Debates and an Interdisciplinary Outlook. In Röttger-Rössler, B. and Markowitsch, H.J. (eds), *Emotions as Bio-Cultural Processes.* New York: Springer.

Evans, J. (2003) Vigilance and Vigilantes: Thinking Psychoanalytically about Anti-Paedophile Action. *Theoretical Criminology*, 7, 163–89.

Flax, J. (1993) *Disputed Subjects: Essays on Psychoanalysis, Politics and Philosophy*. New York: Routledge.

Fonagy, P., Gergely, G., Jurist, E.L. and Target, M. (2004) *Affect Regulation, Mentalization and the Development of Self*. London: Karnac.

Forgas, J.P. (2001) Introduction: Affect and Social Cognition. In J.P. Forgas (ed.), *Handbook of Affect and Cognition*. Mahwah, NJ: Lawrence Erlbaum.

Foucault, M. (2000) *Power (The Essential Works of Foucault, 1954–1984, Volume 3)*. Edited by J. Faubion. Trans. R. Hurley. New York: New Press.

Frank, A. (2007) Phantoms Limn: Silvan Tomkins and Affective Prosthetics. *Theory and Psychology*, 17 (4), 515–28.

Fraser, M., Kember, S. and Lury, C. (eds) (2005) Special Issue: Inventive Life: Approaches to the New Vitalism. *Theory, Culture and Society*, 22 (1).

Frosh, S. (1987) *The Politics of Psychoanalysis: An Introduction to Freudian and Post-Freudian Theory*. London: Macmillan.

Frosh, S. (2003) *Key Concepts in Psychoanalysis*. New York: New York University Press.

Frosh, S. (2004) A.S. Byatt in Conversation with Stephen Frosh. *Psychology and Psychotherapy*, 77, 145–59.

Frosh, S. (2006) Melancholy without the Other. *Studies in Gender and Sexuality*, 7, 363–78.

Frosh, S. (2008) Elementals and Affects or On Making Contact with Others. *Subjectivity*, 24, 314–24.

Frosh, S. (2010) *Psychoanalysis Outside the Clinic*. Basingstoke: Palgrave.

Frosh, S. and Emerson, P. (2009) *Critical Narrative Analysis in Psychology: A Guide to Practice*. Basingstoke: Palgrave Macmillan.

Frosh, S., Phoenix, A. and Pattman, R. (2003) Taking a Stand: Using Psychoanalysis to Explore the Positioning of Subjects in Discourse. *British Journal of Social Psychology*, 42, 39–53.

Frijda, N. (1986) *The Emotions*. Cambridge: Cambridge University Press.

Garfinkel, H. (1967) *Studies in Ethnomethodology*. Englewood Cliffs, NJ: Prentice-Hall.

Garfinkel, H. (1991) Respecification: Evidence for Locally Produced, Naturally Accountable Phenomena of Order, Logic, Reason, Meaning, Method etc. in and as of the Essential Haeccity of Immortal Ordinary Society I – an Announcement of Studies. In G. Button (ed.), *Ethnomethodology and the Human Sciences*. Cambridge: Cambridge University Press.

Garner, S. (2007) *Whiteness: An Introduction*. London: Routledge.

Gergen, K.J. (1994) *Realities and Relationships: Soundings in Social Construction*. Cambridge, MA: Harvard University Press.

Gerson, S. (2004) A Relational Unconscious: A Core Element of Intersubjectivity, Thirdness and Clinical Process. *Psychoanalytic Quarterly*, LXXIII, 63–97.

Giddens, A. (1991) *Modernity and Self-Identity*. Cambridge: Polity.

Gill, R. and Pratt, A. (2008) In the Social Factory? Immaterial Labour, Precariousness and Cultural Work. *Theory, Culture and Society*, 25 (7–8), 1–30.

Gilroy, P. (2004) *Postcolonial Melancholia*. New York: Columbia University Press.

Goffman, E. (1961) *Encounters*. Indianapolis, IN: Bobbs–Merrill.

Goffman, E. (1981) *Forms of Talk*. Philadelphia, PA: University of Pennsylvania Press.

Goodwin, C. (2000) Action and Embodiment within Situated Human Interaction. *Journal of Pragmatics*, 32, 1489–522.

Goodwin, M.H. (2006) *The Hidden Life of Girls: Games of Stance, Status and Exclusion*. Malden, MA: Blackwell.

Gramsci, A. (1971) *Selections from the Prison Notebooks*. London: Lawrence and Wishart.

Green, A. (1977) Conceptions of Affect. *International Journal of Psychoanalysis*, 58, 129–56.

Grosz, E. (2004) *The Nick of Time: Politics, Evolution, and the Untimely*. Durham, NC: Duke University Press.

Gumbrecht, H. (2004) *Production of Presence: What Meaning Cannot Convey*. Stanford, CA: Stanford University Press.

Hanks, W.F. (1990) *Referential Practice: Language and Lived Space among the Maya*. Chicago, IL: University of Chicago Press.

Haraway, D. (2004) *The Haraway Reader*. New York: Routledge.

Hardt, M. (1999) Affective Labour. *boundary 2*, 26 (2), 89–100.

Harré, R. (1986) An Outline of the Social Constructionist Viewpoint. In R. Harré (ed.), *The Social Construction of Emotions*. Oxford: Blackwell.

Hassin, R.R., Uleman, J.S. and Bargh, J. (eds) (2005) *The New Unconscious*. Oxford: Oxford University Press.

Hemmings, C. (2005) Invoking Affect: Cultural Theory and the Ontological Turn. *Cultural Studies*, 19, 548–67.

Heritage, J. (1984) *Garfinkel and Ethnomethodology*. Cambridge: Polity.

Hickok, G. (2009) Eight Problems for the Mirror Neuron Theory of Action Understanding in Monkeys and Humans. *Journal of Cognitive Neuroscience*, 21 (7), 1229–43.

Hickok, G. (ed.) (2010) Special Issue: Mirror Neurons: Prospects and Problems for the Neurobiology of Language. *Brain and Language*, 112 (1), 1–84.

Hochschild, A.R. (1983) *The Managed Heart: Commercialization of Human Feeling*. Berkeley, CA: University of California Press.

Hollway, W. (1984) Gender Difference and the Production of Subjectivity. In J. Henriques, W. Hollway, C. Urwin, C. Venn and V. Walkerdine (eds), *Changing the Subject*. London: Methuen.

Hollway, W. (2006) *The Capacity to Care*. London: Routledge.

Hollway, W. (2010) Relationality: The Intersubjective Foundations of Identity. In M. Wetherell and C. Talpade Mohanty (eds), *The Sage Handbook of Identities*. London: Sage.

Hollway, W. and Jefferson, T. (2000) *Doing Qualitative Research Differently: Free Association, Narrative and the Interview Method*. London: Sage.

Hollway, W. and Jefferson, T. (2005) Panic and Perjury: A Psychosocial Exploration of Agency. *British Journal of Social Psychology*, 44 (2), 147–63.

Horgan, J. (1994) Can Science Explain Consciousness? *Scientific American*, July, 76–7.

Hsieh, L. (2008) Interpellated by Affect: The Move to the Political in Brian Massumi's *Parables for the Virtual* and Eve Sedgwick's *Touching Feeling*. *Subjectivity*, 23, 219–35.

Hutchby, I. and Wooffitt, R. (2008) *Conversation Analysis*, 2nd edn. Cambridge: Polity.

Illouz, E. (1997) Who Will Care for the Caretaker's Daughter? Towards a Sociology of Happiness in the Era of Reflexive Modernity. *Theory, Culture and Society*, 14 (4), 31–66.

Isen, A.M. and Diamond, G.A. (1989) Affect and Automaticity. In J.S. Uleman and J.A. Bargh (eds), *Unintended Thought: Limits of Awareness, Intention and Control*. New York: Guilford Press.

Izard, C.E. (1977) *Human Emotions*. New York: Plenum.

Janig, W. (2003) The Autonomic Nervous System and Its Coordination by the Brain. In R.J. Davidson, K.R. Scherer and H. Hill Goldsmith (eds), *Handbook of Affective Sciences*. Oxford: Oxford University Press.

Jenkins, R. (1992) *Pierre Bourdieu*. London: Routledge.

Johnson-Laird, P.N. and Oatley, K. (1992) Basic Emotions, Rationality and Folk Theory. *Cognition and Emotion*, 6, 201–23.

Kappas, A. (2008) Psst! Dr Jekyll and Mr. Hyde are Actually the Same Person! A Tale of Regulation and Emotion. In M. Vandekerckhove, C. von Scheve, S. Ismer, S. Jung and S. Kronast (eds), *Regulating Emotions: Culture, Social Necessity and Biological Inheritance*. Malden, MA: Blackwell.

Katz, J. (1999) *How Emotions Work*. Chicago, IL: University of Chicago Press.

Kemper, T.D. (ed.) (1990) *Research Agendas in the Sociology of Emotions*. Albany, NY: State University of New York Press.

Kendon, A. (1990) *Conducting Interaction: Patterns of Behaviour in Focused Encounters*. Cambridge: Cambridge University Press.

Kirk, J. (2007) *Class, Culture and Social Change: On the Trail of the Working Class*. Basingstoke: Palgrave.

Kitzinger, C. and Frith, H. (1999) Just Say No? The Use of Conversation Analysis in Developing a Feminist Perspective on Sexual Refusal. *Discourse and Society*, 10 (3), 293–316.

Kornhuber, H.H. and Deecke, L. (1965) Hirnpotentialanderungen bei Wilkurbewegungen und passiv Bewegungen des Menschen: Berietschaftpotential und Reafferente Potentiale. *Pflugers Archiv fur Gesamte Psychologie*, 284, 1–17.

Kugiumutzakis, G. (1988) Neonatal Imitation in the Intersubjective Companion Space. In S. Bråten (ed.) *Intersubjective Communication and Emotion in Early Ontogeny*. Cambridge: Cambridge University Press.

Lacan, J. (1988) *Freud's Papers on Technique 1953–1954*. Trans. S. Tomasseli and J. Forrester. Ed. J.A. Miller. New York: W.W. Norton.

Laclau, E. (1993) Politics and the Limits of Modernity. In T. Docherty (ed.), *Postmodernism: A Reader*. London: Harvester Wheatsheaf.

Latour, B. (2004) How to Talk about the Body? The Normative Dimensions of Science Studies. *Body and Society*, 10 (2/3), 205–30.

Latour, B. (2005) *Reassembling the Social: An Introduction to Actor-Network-Theory*. Oxford: Oxford University Press.

Laurier, E. and Philo, C. (2006) Possible Geographies: A Passing Encounter in a Café. *Area*, 38 (1), 353–63.

Law, J. (1994) *Organizing Modernity*. Oxford: Blackwell.

Law, J. and Hassard, J. (eds) (1999) *Actor Network Theory and After*. Oxford: Blackwell.

Law, J. and Mol, A. (eds) (2006) *Complexities: Social Studies of Knowledge*. Durham, NC: Duke University Press.

Lawler, S. (1999) Getting Out and Getting Away: Women's Narratives of Class Mobility. *Feminist Review*, 63, 3–24.

Lawler, S. (2000) *Mothering the Self: Mothers, Daughters, Subjects*. London: Routledge.

Lawler, S. (2004) Rules of Engagement: Habitus, Power and Resistance. In L. Adkins and B. Skeggs (eds), *Feminism After Bourdieu*. Oxford: Blackwell.

Lawler, S. (2005) Disgusted Subjects: The Making of Middle-Class Identities. *The Sociological Review*, 3 (3), 429–46.

Layton, L. (2002) Psychoanalysis and the 'Free' Individual. *Journal of Psycho-Social Studies*, 1 (1), http://www.btInternet.com/~psycho_social/vol 1/JPSS-LL1.htm

Layton, L. (2004) A Fork in the Royal Road: On 'Defining' the Unconscious and Its Stakes for Social Theory. *Psychoanalysis, Culture and Society*, 9, 33–51.

Layton, L. (2006) That Place Gives Me the Heebie Jeebies. In L. Layton, N.C. Hollander and S. Gutwill (eds), *Psychoanalysis, Class and Politics: Encounters in the Clinical Setting*. London: Routledge.

Layton, L. (2007) What Psychoanalysis, Culture and Society Mean to Me. *Mens Sana Monographs*, 5, 146–57.

LeDoux, J. (1996) *The Emotional Brain*. New York: Touchstone.

Levenson, R.W. (2003) Autonomic Specificity and Emotion. In R.J. Davidson, K.R. Scherer, and H.H. Goldsmith (eds), *Handbook of Affective Sciences*. Oxford: Oxford University Press.

Levenson, R.W., Ekman, P. and Friesen, W.V. (1990) Voluntary Facial Action Generates Emotion-Specific Autonomic Nervous System Activity. *Psychophysiology*, 27, 363–84.

Lewis, G. (2009) Birthing Racial Difference: Conversations with My Mother. *Studies in the Maternal*, 1 (1), www.mamsie.bbk.ac.uk

Libet, B., Gleason, C.A., Wright, E.W. and Pearl, D.K. (1983) Time of Conscious Intention to Act in Relation to Onset of Cerebral Activity (Readiness Potential): The Unconscious Initiation of a Freely Voluntary Act. *Brain*, 106, 623–42.

Lingis, A. (1991) We Mortals. *Philosophy Today*, 35 (2), 119–26.

Lingis, A. (2000) *Dangerous Emotions*. Berkeley, CA: University of California Press.

Lorimer, H. (2005) Cultural Geography: The Busyness of Being 'More–Than-Representational'. *Progress in Human Geography*, 29 (1), 83–94.

Lorimer, H. (2008) Cultural Geography: Non-Representational Conditions and Concerns. *Progress in Human Geography*, 32 (4), 551–9.

Lucey, H. and Reay, D. (2000) Social Class and the Psyche. *Soundings*, 15, 139–54.

Lucey, H., Melody, J. and Walkerdine, V. (2003) Uneasy Hybrids: Psychosocial Aspects of Becoming Educationally Successful for Working-Class Young Women. *Gender and Education*, 15 (3), 285–9.

Lupton, D. (1998) *The Emotional Self*. London: Sage.

Lutz, C. (1988) *Unnatural Emotions: Everyday Sentiments on a Micronesian Atoll and Their Challenge to Western Theory*. Chicago, IL: University of Chicago Press.

MacLean, P.D. (1990) *The Triune Brain in Evolution*. New York: Plenum.

MacLean, P.D. (1993) Cerebral Evolution of Emotion. In M. Lewis and J.M. Haviland (eds), *Handbook of Emotions*. New York: Guilford Press.

Massey, D. (2005) *For Space*. London: Sage.

Massumi, B. (1996) The Autonomy of Affect. In P. Patton (ed.), *Deleuze: A Critical Reader*. Oxford: Blackwell.

Massumi, B. (2002) *Parables for the Virtual: Movements, Affect, Sensation*. Durham, NC: Duke University Press.

Massumi, B. (2005) Fear (The Spectrum Said). *positions*, 13, 31–48.

Mauss, M. (1979) *Sociology and Psychology*. Trans. B. Brewster. London: Routledge and Kegan Paul.

Maybin, J. (2001) Language, Struggle and Voice: The Bakhtin/Volosinov Writings. In M. Wetherell, S. Taylor and S.J. Yates (eds), *Discourse Theory and Practice: A Reader*. London: Sage.

McAvoy, J. (2009) Negotiating Constructions of Success and Failure: Women in Mid-Life and Formations of Subject, Subjectivity and Identity. Unpublished PhD, Open University.

McCormack, D. (2003) An Event of Geographical Ethics in Spaces of Affect. *Transactions of the Institute of British Geographers*, 28 (4), 488–507.

McCormack, D. (2006) For the Love of Pipes and Cables: A Response to Deborah Thien. *Area*, 38 (3), 330–2.

McCormack, D. (2007) Molecular Affects in Human Geographies. *Environment and Planning A*, 39, 359–77.

McGinn, C. (2003) Fear Factor. *New York Times Book Review*, 23 February, p. 11.

McHoul, A. and Rapley, M. (2005) Representing Culture and the Self: (Dis) agreeing in Theory and Practice. *Theory and Psychology*, 15 (4), 431–47.

McIlwain, D. (2007) Pleasure in Mind: Silvan Tomkins and Affect in Aesthetics, Personality Theory and Culture. *Theory and Psychology*, 17 (4), 499–504.

Meltzoff, A.N. and Brooks, R. (2007) Intersubjectivity Before Language: Three Windows on Preverbal Sharing. In S. Bråten (ed.), *On Being Moved: From Mirror Neurons to Empathy*. Amsterdam: John Benjamins.

Meltzoff, A.N. and Moore, M.K. (1988) Infant Intersubjectivity: Broadening the Dialogue to Include Imitation, Identity and Intention. In S. Bråten (ed.), *Intersubjective Communication and Emotion in Early Ontogeny*. Cambridge: Cambridge University Press.

Meltzoff, A.N. (2007) The 'Like Me' Framework for Recognizing and Becoming an Intentional Agent. *Acta Psychologia*, 124 (1), 26–43.

Middleton, D. and Brown, S. (2005) *The Social Psychology of Experience: Studies in Remembering and Forgetting*. London: Sage.

Mitchell, J. (2002) Response to Lynne Segal. *Studies in Gender and Sexuality*, 3 (2), 217–28.

Mitchell, S.A. (1993) *Hope and Dread in Psychoanalysis*. New York: Basic Books.

Mitchell, S.A. (2000) *Relationality: From Attachment to Intersubjectivity*. Hillsdale, NJ: The Analytic Press.

Mitchell, S.A. and Aron, L. (eds) (1999) *Relational Psychoanalysis: The Emergence of a Tradition*. Hillsdale, NJ: The Analytic Press.

Motzkau, J.F. (2007) Cross-examining Suggestibility: Memory, Childhood, Expertise. Unpublished doctoral thesis, Loughborough University.

Motzkau, J. (2009) Exploring the Transdisciplinary Trajectory of Suggestibility. *Subjectivity*, 27, 172–94.

Murdoch, I. (1967 [1964]) *The Italian Girl*. London: Penguin.

Negri, A. (1999) Value and Affect. *boundary 2*, 26 (2), 77–88.

Ngai, S. (2005) *Ugly Feelings*. Cambridge, MA: Harvard University Press.

Nielsen, H.B. (2003) Historical, Cultural, and Emotional Meanings: Interviews with Young Girls in Three Generations. *NORA*, 11 (1), 14–26.

Nielsen, H.B. and Rudberg, M. (2000) Gender, Love and Education in Three Generations. *European Journal of Women's Studies*, 7 (4), 423–53.

Nowotny, H. (1981) Women in Public Life in Austria. In C. Fuchs Epstein and R. Laub Coser (eds), *Access to Power: Cross-National Studies of Women and Elites*. London: George Allen & Unwin.

Nussbaum, M. (2001) *Upheavals of Thought: The Intelligence of Emotions*. Cambridge: Cambridge University Press.

Oatley, K., Keltner, D. and Jenkins, J.M. (2006) *Understanding Emotions*, 2nd edn. Oxford: Blackwell.

Ogden, T.H. (1994) The Analytic Third: Working with Intersubjective Clinical Facts. *International Journal of Psychoanalysis*, 75 (1), 3–19.

Ortner, S.B. (2006) *Anthropology and Social Theory: Culture, Power and the Acting Subject*. Durham, NC: Duke University Press.

Ortony, A. and Turner, T.J. (1990) What's Basic about Basic Emotions? *Psychological Review*, 97, 315–31.

Panksepp, J. (1994a) The Basics of Basic Emotion. In P. Ekman and R.J. Davidson (eds), *The Nature of Emotion: Fundamental Questions*. New York: Oxford University Press.

Panksepp, J. (1994b) Basic Emotions Ramify Widely in the Brain, Yielding Many Concepts That Cannot Be Distinguished Unambiguously … Yet. In P. Ekman and R.J. Davidson (eds), *The Nature of Emotions: Fundamental Questions*. Oxford: Oxford University Press.

Panksepp, J. (1998) *Affective Neuroscience: The Foundations of Animal and Human Emotion*. New York: Oxford University Press.

Panksepp, J. (2000) Emotions as Natural Kinds within the Mammalian Brain. In M. Lewis and J.M. Haviland-Jones (eds), *Handbook of Emotions*, 2nd edn. New York: Guilford Press.

Panksepp, J. (2003) Damasio's Error? Review of 'Looking for Spinoza: Joy, Sorrow and the Feeling Brain' by A. Damasio. *Consciousness and Emotion*, 4 (1), 111–34.

Papoulias, C. and Callard, F. (2010) Biology's Gift: Interrogating the Turn to Affect. *Body and Society*, 16 (1), 29–56.

Patton, P. (2000) *Deleuze and the Political*. Abingdon: Routledge.

Phoenix, A. (2008) Claiming Liveable Lives: Adult Subjectification and Narratives of 'Non-Normative' Childhood Experiences. In J. Kofoed and D. Staunaes (eds), *Magtballader (Adjusting Reality)*. Copenhagen: Danmarks Paedagogiske Universitetsforlag.

Phoenix, A., Frosh, S. and Pattman, R. (2002) *Young Masculinities: Understanding Boys in Contemporary Society*. Basingstoke: Palgrave.

Phoenix, A. and Pattynama, P. (eds) (2006) Special Issue on Intersectionality. *European Journal of Women's Studies*, 13 (3).

Pile, S.J. (2010) Emotions and Affect in Recent Human Geography. *Transactions of the Institute of British Geographers*, 35 (1), 5–20.

Plutchik, R. (1980) *Emotion: A Psychoevolutionary Synthesis*. New York: Harper and Row.

Potter, J. (1996) *Representing Reality*. London: Sage.

Potter, J. (2004) Discourse Analysis as a Way of Analysing Naturally Occurring Talk. In D. Silverman (ed.), *Qualitative Analysis: Issues of Theory and Method*, 2nd edn. London: Sage.

Potter, J. (ed.) (2007) *Discourse and Psychology*. Vols 1–3. London: Sage.

Potter, J. and Edwards, D. (2001) Discursive Social Psychology. In W.P. Robinson and H. Giles (eds), *The New Handbook of Language and Social Psychology*. London: John Wiley and Sons.

Potter, J. and Wetherell, M. (1987) *Discourse and Social Psychology: Beyond Attitudes and Behaviour*. London: Sage.

Potter, J., Wetherell, M., Gill, R. and Edwards, D. (1990) Discourse – Noun, Verb or Social Practice?' *Philosophical Psychology*, 3, 205–17.

Prigogine, I. (1997) *The End of Certainty*. New York: Free Press.

Prigogine, I. and Stengers, I. (1984) *Order Out of Chaos: Man's New Dialogue with Nature*. New York: Bantam.

Probyn, E. (2004a) Everyday Shame. *Cultural Studies*, 18 (2/3), 328–49.

Probyn, E. (2004b) Shame in the Habitus. In L. Adkins and B. Skeggs (eds), *Feminism after Bourdieu*. Oxford: Blackwell.

Probyn, E. (2005) *Blush: Faces of Shame*. Minneapolis, MN: University of Minnesota Press.

Protevi, J. (2009) *Political Affect: Connecting the Social and the Somatic*. Minneapolis, MN: University of Minnesota Press.

Reay, D. (2004) Gendering Bourdieu's Concept of Capitals? Emotional Capital, Women and Social Class. In L. Adkins and B. Skeggs (eds), *Feminism After Bourdieu*. Oxford: Blackwell.

Reay, D. (2005) Beyond Consciousness?: The Psychic Landscape of Social Class. *Sociology*, 39, 911–28.

Reay, D. (2008) Psychosocial Aspects of White Middle-Class Identities: Desiring and Defending Against the Class and Ethnic 'Other' in Urban Multi-Ethnic Schooling. *Sociology*, 42 (6), 1072–88.

Reay, D., Crozier, G. and James, D. (2011) *White Middle-Class Identities and Urban Schooling*. Basingstoke: Palgrave.

Reay, D. and Lucey, H. (2003) The Limits of 'Choice': Children and Inner City Schooling. *Sociology*, 37 (1), 121–42.

Reddy, W. (2001) *The Navigation of Feelings: A Framework for the History of Emotions*. Cambridge: Cambridge University Press.

Reddy, W.M. (2009) Saying Something New: Practice Theory and Cognitive Neuroscience. *Arcadia: International Journal for Literary Studies*, 44, 8–23.

Redman, P. (2009) Affect Revisited: Transference-Countertransference and the Unconscious Dimensions of Affective, Felt and Emotional Experience. *Subjectivity*, 26, 51–68.

Reed-Danahay, D. (2005) *Locating Bourdieu*. Bloomington, IN: Indiana University Press.

Reicher, S. (1984) The St Paul's 'Riot': An Explanation of the Limits of Crowd Action in Terms of a Social Identity Model. *European Journal of Social Psychology*, 14, 1–21.

Reicher, S. (1987) Crowd Behaviour as Social Action. In J. Turner, M. Hogg, P. Oakes, S. Reicher and M. Wetherell, *Rediscovering the Social Group: A Self-Categorisation Theory*. Oxford: Blackwell.

Reicher, S. (1996) The Battle of Westminster: Developing the Social Identity Model of Crowd Behaviour in Order to Deal with the Initiation and Development of Collective Conflict. *European Journal of Social Psychology*, 26, 115–34.

Reicher, S. (2001) The Psychology of Crowd Dynamics. In M.A. Hogg and S. Tindale (eds), *Blackwell Handbook of Social Psychology: Group Processes*. Oxford: Blackwell.

Reynolds, J. and Wetherell, M. (2003) The Discursive Climate of Singleness: The Consequences for Women's Negotiation of a Single Identity. *Feminism and Psychology*, 13, 489–510.

Riley, D. (2005) *Impersonal Passion*. Durham, NC: Duke University Press.

Rizzolatti, G. and Sinigaglia, C. (2008) *Mirrors in the Brain: How Our Minds Share Actions and Emotions*. Trans. Frances Anderson. Oxford: Oxford University Press.

Rogaly, B. and Taylor, B. (2009) *Moving Histories of Class and Community*. Basingstoke: Palgrave.

Rosaldo, M.Z. (1980) *Knowledge and Passion: Ilongot Notions of Self and Social Life*. Cambridge: Cambridge University Press.

Rosaldo, M.Z. (1984) Toward an Anthropology of Self and Feeling. In R.A. Shweder and R. LeVine (eds), *Culture Theory: Essays on Mind, Self and Emotion.* Cambridge: Cambridge University Press.

Rose, J. (1986) *Sexuality in the Field of Vision.* London: Verso.

Rose, N. (1998) *Inventing Ourselves: Psychology, Power and Personhood.* Cambridge: Cambridge University Press.

Rose, S. (1997) *Lifelines: Biology Beyond Determinism.* Oxford: Oxford University Press.

Rose, S. (2005) *The 21st-Century Brain: Explaining, Mending and Manipulating the Mind.* London: Jonathan Cape.

Roseneil, S. (2006) The Ambivalences of Angel's 'Arrangement': A Psychosocial Lens on the Contemporary Condition of Personal Life. *Sociological Review,* 54 (4), 846–68.

Rosenwein, B.H. (2006) *Emotional Communities in the Early Middle Ages.* Ithaca, NY: Cornell University Press.

Russell, J.A. (2003) Core Affect and the Psychological Construction of Emotion. *Psychological Review,* 110(1), 145–72.

Russell, J.A. (2009) Emotion, Core Affect and Psychological Construction. *Cognition and Emotion,* 23 (7), 1259–83.

Russell, J.A. and Barrett, L.F. (1999) Core Affect, Prototypical Emotional Episodes, and Other Things Called Emotion: Dissecting the Elephant. *Journal of Personality and Social Psychology,* 76, 805–19.

Russell, J.A. and Fernández-Dols, J.M. (1997) What Does a Facial Expression Mean? In J.A. Russell and J.M. Fernández-Dols (eds), *The Psychology of Facial Expression.* New York: Cambridge University Press.

Sayer, A. (2005) *The Moral Significance of Class.* Cambridge: Cambridge University Press.

Schacter, S. and Singer, J. (1962) Cognitive, Social and Physiological Determinants of Emotional State. *Psychological Review,* 69, 379–99.

Schatzki, T. (2001) Introduction: Practice Theory. In T.R. Schatzki, K. Knorr-Cetina and E. von Savigny (eds), *The Practice Turn in Contemporary Theory.* London: Routledge.

Schegloff, E. (1997) Whose Text? Whose Context? *Discourse and Society,* 8, 165–87.

Schegloff, E. (1998) Reply to Wetherell. *Discourse and Society,* 9, 413–16.

Schegloff, E. (1999a) Schegloff's Texts as Billig's Data: A Critical Reply. *Discourse and Society,* 10, 558–72.

Schegloff, E. (1999b) Naiveté Versus Sophistication or Discipline Versus Self-Indulgence: A Rejoinder to Billig. *Discourse and Society,* 10, 577–83.

Scherer, K.R. (1994) Toward a Concept of 'Modal Emotions'. In P. Ekman and R.J. Davidson (eds), *The Nature of Emotion: Fundamental Questions.* New York: Oxford University Press.

Scherer, K.R. (2005) Unconscious Processes in Emotion: The Bulk of the Iceberg. In L. Barrett, P.M. Niedenthal and P. Winkielman (eds), *Emotion and Consciousness.* New York: Guilford Press.

Scherer, K.R. (2009) The Dynamic Architecture of Emotion: Evidence for the Component Process Model. *Cognition and Emotion,* 23 (7), 1307–51.

Sedgwick, E.K. (2003) *Touching Feeling: Affect, Pedagogy, Performativity.* Durham, NC: Duke University Press.

Sedgwick, E.K. and Frank, A. (eds) (1995) *Shame and Its Sisters: A Silvan Tomkins Reader.* Durham, NC: Duke University Press.

Seigworth, G.J. (2005) From Affection to Soul. In C.J. Stivale (ed.), *Gilles Deleuze: Key Concepts.* Chesham: Acumen.

Seymour-Smith, S. and Wetherell, M. (2006) 'What He Hasn't Told You ...': Investigating the Micro Politics of Gendered Support in Couples' Co-Constructed Accounts of Illness. *Feminism and Psychology,* 16 (1), 105–27.

Shapiro, M. (1992) *Reading the Postmodern Polity.* Minneapolis, MN: University of Minnesota Press.

Shotter, J. (1993) *Conversational Realities: Constructing Life through Language.* London: Sage.

Shweder, R.A. (1994) 'You're not sick, you're just in love': Emotion as an Interpretive System. In P. Ekman and R.J. Davidson (eds), *The Nature of Emotion: Fundamental Questions*. New York: Oxford University Press.

Shweder, R.A. and LeVine, R.A. (1984) *Culture Theory: Essays on Mind, Self and Society*. Cambridge: Cambridge University Press.

Skeggs, B. (2004a) *Class, Self and Culture*. London: Routledge.

Skeggs, B. (2004b) Exchange, Value and Affect: Bourdieu and 'the Self'. In L. Adkins and B. Skeggs (eds), *Feminism After Bourdieu*. Oxford: Blackwell.

Skeggs, B. (2005) The Making of Class and Gender Through Visualizing Moral Subject Formation. *Sociology*, 39 (5), 965–82.

Skeggs, B. (2010) Class, Culture and Morality: Legacies and Logics in the Space for Identification. In M. Wetherell and C. Talpade Mohanty (eds), *The Sage Handbook of Identities*. London: Sage.

Skeggs, B. and Wood, H. (2009) The Transformation of Intimacy: Classed Identities in the Moral Economy of Reality Television. In M. Wetherell (ed.), *Identity in the 21st Century: New Trends in Changing Times*. Basingstoke: Palgrave.

Squire, C. (2001) The Public Life of Emotions. *International Journal of Critical Psychology*, 1, 16–27.

Stearns, P.N. with Stearns, C.Z. (1985) Emotionology: Clarifying the History of Emotions and Emotional Standards. *American Historical Review*, 90 (4), 813–36.

Stengers, I. (1997) *Power and Invention*. Minneapolis, MN: University of Minnesota Press.

Stenner, P. (2008) A.N. Whitehead and Subjectivity. *Subjectivity*, 22, 90–109.

Stern, D.B. (1997) *Unformulated Experience*. Hillsdale, NJ: Analytic Press.

Stern, D.N. (2004) *The Present Moment in Psychotherapy and Everyday Life*. New York: W.W. Norton.

Stern, D.N. (2007) Applying Developmental and Neuroscience Findings on Other-Centred Participation to the Process of Change in Psychotherapy. In S. Bråten (ed.), *On Being Moved: From Mirror Neurons to Empathy*. Amsterdam: John Benjamins.

Stewart, K. (2007) *Ordinary Affects*. Durham, NC: Duke University Press.

Stokoe, E. (2009) Doing Actions with Identity Categories: Complaints and Denials in Neighbour Disputes. *Text and Talk*, 29 (1), 75–97.

Stokoe, E. and Edwards, D. (2009) Accomplishing Social Action with Identity Categories: Mediating and Policing Neighbour Disputes. In M. Wetherell (ed.), *Theorizing Identities and Social Action*. Basingstoke: Palgrave.

Stolorow, R.D. and Atwood, G.E. (1992) *Contexts of Being: The Intersubjective Foundations of Psychological Life*. Hillsdale, NJ: Analytic Press.

Stott, C. and Reicher, S. (1998) Crowd Action as Intergroup Process: Introducing the Police Perspective. *European Journal of Social Psychology*, 26, 509–29.

Swartz, D. (1997) *Culture and Power: The Sociology of Pierre Bourdieu*. Chicago, IL: University of Chicago Press.

Tamboukou, M. (2003) Interrogating the 'Emotional Turn': Making Connections with Foucault and Deleuze. *European Journal of Psychotherapy, Counselling and Health*, 6 (3), 209–23.

Tamboukou, M. (2008a) Machinic Assemblages: Women, Art, Education, Space. *Discourse: Studies in the Cultural Politics of Education*, 29 (3), 359–75.

Tamboukou, M. (2008b) Re-Imagining the Narratable Subject. *Qualitative Research*, 8, 283–92.

Taylor, S. (2010) *Narratives of Identity and Place*. Basingstoke: Palgrave Macmillan.

Ten Have, P. (2007) *Doing Conversation Analysis*, 2nd edn. London: Sage.

Terada, R. (2001) *Feeling in Theory: Emotions after the 'Death of the Subject'*. Cambridge, MA: Harvard University Press.

Thien, D. (2005) After or Beyond Feeling? A Consideration of Affect and Emotion in Geography. *Area*, 37 (3), 450–6.

Thrift, N. (2000) Still Life in Nearly Present Time: The Object of Nature. *Body and Society*, 6 (3/4), 34–57.

Thrift, N. (2004) Intensities of Feeling: Towards a Spatial Politics of Affect. *Geografiska Annaler*, 86 B (1), 57–78.

Thrift, N. (2008a) *Non-Representational Theory: Space, Politics and Affect*. London: Routledge.

Thrift, N. (2008b) I Just Don't Know What Got Into Me: Where Is the Subject? *Subjectivity*, 22, 82–9.

Tooby, J. and Cosmides, L. (1990) The Past Explains the Present: Emotional Adaptations and the Structure of Ancestral Environments. *Ethological Sociobiology*, 11, 375–424.

Tolia-Kelly, D. (2006) Affect – An Ethnocentric Encounter? Exploring the 'Universalist' Imperative of Emotional/Affectual Geographies. *Area*, 38, 213–17.

Tomkins, S.S. (1962) *Affect, Imagery, Consciousness. Vol. 1: The Positive Affects*. New York: Springer.

Tomkins, S.S. (1963) *Affect, Imagery, Consciousness. Vol 2: The Negative Affects*. New York: Springer.

Trevarthen, C. (1979) Communication and Cooperation in Early Infancy: A Description of Primary Intersubjectivity. In M. Bullowa (ed.), *Before Speech*. Cambridge: Cambridge University Press.

Trevarthen, C. (1993) The Self Born in Intersubjectivity: An Infant Communicating. In U. Neisser (ed.), *The Perceived Self*. New York: Cambridge University Press.

Trevarthen, C. (1998) The Concept and Foundations of Infant Intersubjectivity. In S. Bråten (ed.), *Intersubjective Communication and Emotion in Early Ontogeny*. Cambridge: Cambridge University Press.

Turner, J.C. (1991) *Social Influence*. Milton Keynes: Open University Press.

Turner, J.C., Hogg, M., Oakes, P., Reicher, S. and Wetherell, M. (1987) *Rediscovering the Social Group: A Self-Categorisation Theory*. Oxford: Blackwell.

Turner, J.H. (2000) *On the Origins of Human Emotions: A Sociological Inquiry into the Evolution of Human Affect*. Stanford, CA: Stanford University Press.

Turp, M. (2001) *Psychosomatic Health: The Body and the Word*. Basingstoke: Palgrave.

Tyler, I. (2006) 'Welcome to Britain': The Cultural Politics of Asylum. *European Journal of Cultural Studies*, 9 (2), 185–202.

Tyler, I. (2008) 'Chav Mum, Chav Scum': Class Disgust in Contemporary Britain. *Feminist Media Studies*, 8 (1), 17–34.

Van Dijk, T. (ed.) (2007) *Discourse Studies*. London: Sage.

Venn, C. (2010) Individuation, Relationality, Affect: Rethinking the Human in Relation to Living. *Body and Society*, 16 (1), 129–61.

Vygotsky, L. (1962) *Thought and Language*. Cambridge, MA: MIT Press.

Walkerdine, V. (1991) Film: *Didn't She Do Well*. Working Pictures.

Walkerdine, V. (2007) *Children, Gender, Video Games*. Basingstoke: Palgrave.

Walkerdine, V. (2009) Steel, Identity, Community: Regenerating Identities in a South Wales Town. In M. Wetherell (ed.), *Identity in the 21st Century: New Trends in Changing Times*. Basingstoke: Palgrave.

Walkerdine, V. (2010) Communal Belongingness and Affect: An Exploration of Trauma in an Ex-Industrial Community. *Body and Society*, 16 (1), 91–116.

Walkerdine, V. and Bansel, P. (2010) Neoliberalism, Work and Subjectivity: Towards a More Complex Account. In M. Wetherell and C. Talpade Mohanty (eds), *The Sage Handbook of Identities*. London: Sage.

Walkerdine, V. and Lucey, H. (1989) *Democracy in the Kitchen: Regulating Mothers and Socialising Daughters*. London: Virago.

Walkerdine, V., Lucey, H. and Melody, J. (2001) *Growing Up Girl: Psychosocial Explorations of Gender and Class*. Basingstoke: Palgrave.

Waller, J. (2008) *A Time to Dance, A Time to Die*. London: Icon Books.

Walton, C., Coyle, A. and Lyons, E. (2004) Death and Football: An Analysis of Men's Talk about Emotion. *British Journal of Social Psychology*, 43, 1–16.

Wark, P. (2009) Suitable Endings by the Queen of Crime Fiction. *Times2*, 22 September, pp. 4–5.

Weatherall, A. (2000) Gender Relevance in Talk-in-Interaction and Discourse. *Discourse and Society*, 11, 286–8.

Wegner, D. (2002) *The Illusion of Conscious Will*. Cambridge, MA: MIT Press.

West, C. and Zimmerman, D. (1987) Doing Gender. *Gender and Society*, 1 (2), 125–51.

Wetherell, M. (1998) Positioning and Interpretative Repertoires: Conversation Analysis and Post-Structuralism in Dialogue. *Discourse and Society*, 9, 431–56.

Wetherell, M. (2001) Debates in Discourse Research. In M. Wetherell, S. Taylor and S. Yates (eds), *Discourse Theory and Practice: A Reader*. London: Sage.

Wetherell, M. (2003) Paranoia, Ambivalence and Discursive Practices: Concepts of Position and Positioning in Psychoanalysis and Discursive Psychology. In R. Harré and F. Moghaddam (eds), *The Self and Others: Positioning Individuals and Groups in Personal, Political and Cultural Contexts*. New York: Praeger/Greenwood Publishers.

Wetherell, M. (2007) A Step Too Far: Discursive Psychology, Linguistic Ethnography and Questions of Identity. *Journal of Sociolinguistics*, 11 (5), 661–82.

Wetherell, M. (2005) Unconscious Conflict or Everyday Accountability? *British Journal of Social Psychology*, 44 (2), 169–75.

Wetherell, M. (2010) The Field of Identity Studies. In M. Wetherell and C. Talpade Mohanty (eds), *The Sage Handbook of Identities*. London: Sage.

Wetherell, M. and Edley, N. (1999) Negotiating Hegemonic Masculinity: Imaginary Positions and Psycho-Discursive Practices. *Feminism and Psychology*, 9, 335–56.

Wetherell, M. and Potter, J. (1988) Discourse Analysis and the Identification of Interpretative Repertoires. In C. Antaki (ed.), *Analysing Lay Explanations: A Case-Book*. London: Sage.

Wetherell, M. and C. Talpade Mohanty (eds) (2010) *The Sage Handbook of Identities*. London: Sage.

Wetherell, M., Taylor, S. and Yates, S.J. (2001a) *Discourse Theory and Practice: A Reader*. London: Sage.

Wetherell, M., Taylor, S. and Yates, S.J. (2001b) *Discourse as Data: A Guide to Analysis*. London: Sage.

Whitehead, A.N. (1933/1935) *Adventures in Ideas*. Cambridge: Cambridge University Press.

Wierzbicka, A. (1992) Defining Emotion Concepts. *Cognitive Science*, 16, 539–81.

Wierzbicka, A. (1999) *Emotions across Languages and Cultures*. New York: Cambridge University Press.

Williams, C. (2010) Affective Processes without a Subject: Rethinking the Relation Between Subjectivity and Affect with Spinoza. *Subjectivity*, 3, 245–62.

Williams, R. (1958) *Culture and Society 1780–1950*. London: Chatto and Windus.

Williams, R. (1977) *Marxism and Literature*. Oxford: Oxford University Press.

Wilson, E.A. (2004) *Psychosomatic: Feminism and the Neurological Body*. Durham, NC: Duke University Press.

Wise, J.M. (2005) Assemblage. In C.J. Stivale (ed.), *Gilles Deleuze: Key Concepts*. Chesham: Acumen.

Wood, H. (2009) *Talking with Television: Women, Talk Shows and Modern Reflexivity*. Urbana, IL: University of Illinois Press.

Zajonc, R.B. (1968) Attitudinal Effects of Mere Exposure. *Journal of Personality and Social Psychology*, 9, 1–27.

Index

Redman, P. 152–3, 154
Reed-Danahay, D. 107
Reicher, S. 145, 147–8, 150
relational histories 120–39
relational moves 86–8
relational psychoanalysis 142
relational subjectivities 138–9
relationality 24
representation 58, 66–7, 76
  negotiating affect 51–76
repression 131–2, 136
Riley, D. 125
Rizzolatti, G. 34, 35, 149, 150
Rose, J. 131
Rose, N. 23, 128
Rose, S. 35, 44, 46, 66
Roseneil, S. 127
Rosenwein, B. 7, 71
Rudberg, M. 13
'running polyphony' 35–6, 46
Russell, J. 47–8, 50, 52

St Vitus cults 5, 14, 21
Sayer, A. 105, 111, 116, 117
Schatzki, T. 23
Scherer, K. 40, 45, 46, 48–50,
  52, 62
secondary emotions 31
Sedgwick, E. 10–11
self-composing 122
semiotic modes 89
Shapiro, M. 78
Sharrock, W. 63, 64
Shweder, R. A. 41, 42, 46
Sinigaglia, C. 34, 35, 149, 150
situating affect 77–101
Skeggs, B. 105, 110, 111–12, 113–14,
  157
'small worlds' 81–4
social class 16–17, 109, 110–12, 115,
  117
social construction 17–19, 41
social distinction 108–9
social emotions see secondary
  emotions
social psychoanalysis 150–1
social psychology 115–16, 119, 142

social value 109–10
solidifying affect 102–19
speech act theory 69
Spinoza, B. 34, 48, 67, 75, 124
'state of emotion' 32–3, 35
'state of feeling' 32, 33–4, 35
'state of knowing the feeling' 32,
  33–4, 35, 41, 98
status/power effects 87
Stearns, C. 18
Stearns, P. 18
Stengers, I. 86
Stenner, P. 15, 66, 126–7
Stern, D. B. 130–1, 153
Stern, D. N. 77, 78, 85–6, 87–8,
  148, 149–50
Stewart, K. 2, 54–5
Stokoe, E. 90–2
Stolorow, R. D. 153
Stott, C. 147, 148
Strasbourg's dancing plague 5–6, 14,
  18, 20, 89
'structures of feeling' 14, 104
subjectivity 66, 120–39

Thien, D. 60–1
Thrift, N. 19, 53–67, 74–5, 81, 123–4,
  125, 126, 127
Tomkins, S. 10–11, 37, 41, 50
Tooby, J. 38
transference 150–1
translation 69, 73
transmission of emotion 21,
  140–60
Trevarthen, C. 149, 150
Turner, T. J. 42
Turp, M. 8–9, 13
Tyler, I. 110
type-type identity theories 37

unconscious of affective practice
  129–31, 153–6
universal emotions 17–18, 37–8,
  39–40, 41

Vandekerckhove, M. 40
Vygotsky, L. 24, 74

Indexed by Caroline Eley